The True
Size of
Government

PAUL C. LIGHT

The True Size of Government

BROOKINGS INSTITUTION PRESS
Washington, D.C.

Copyright © 1999
THE BROOKINGS INSTITUTION
1775 Massachusetts Avenue, N.W., Washington, D.C. 20036
www.brookings.edu

Library of Congress Cataloging-in-Publication data

Light, Paul Charles.
The true size of government / Paul C. Light.
p.   cm.
Includes index.

ISBN 0-8157-5266-0 (alk. paper)
ISBN 0-8157-5265-2 (pbk. : alk. paper)
1. Civil service—United States. 2. United States—Officials and
employees. 3. Government consultants—United States. I. Title.
JK692 .L54   1999   98-58143
352.6'3'0973—dc21   CIP

9 8 7 6 5 4 3 2 1

The paper used in this publication meets minimum requirements of the American
National Standard for Information Sciences—Permanence of Paper for Printed
Library Materials: ANSI Z39.48-1984.

Typeset in Minion

Composition by Cynthia Stock
Silver Spring, Maryland

Printed by R. R. Donnelley and Sons
Harrisonburg, Virginia

Foreword

THE PAST THIRTY YEARS have witnessed
the most significant change in the federal public service since the modern
civil service system was created in 1883. So Paul C. Light argues in *The True
Size of Government*. Under nearly constant pressure to do more with less,
the federal government has created a blended public work force composed
of federal employees and their private, nonprofit, and state and local partners. Although the federal government has been contracting out for goods
and services since the Revolutionary War, Light argues that it has never been
more dependent on a shadow work force to accomplish its mission.

The True Size of Government provides the first rigorous estimates of just
how large this blended work force is and asks both why it evolved and how it
has changed. In doing so, Light seeks to reframe the contemporary debate
about how government performs its tasks, arguing that Congress and the
president spend too much time focusing on the number of civil servants
and too little asking what kind of work force the government needs to hold
the core competency to assure merit, capacity, accountability, and performance. Although the book clearly challenges recent conclusions regarding
the end of the era of big government as measured by total civil service employment, its primary concern is with the evolving nature of public service
in an era when it is difficult to tell where the federal mission ends and contract, grant, and state and local mandates begin.

As Light suggests, this new public service was created by both accident and intent. But whatever the cause, he argues persuasively that the new public service is here to stay. Americans will never tolerate a civil service work force as large as the federal mission. The question for Light is not whether a blended work force is good or bad per se, but how the federal government can manage that work force to assure basic public values such as merit. Future research by Light will examine how America's top public policy and administration graduate schools have adjusted to these changes, how America's most talented citizens view careers in this changing service, and what Congress and the president can do to make traditional public service jobs more competitive in attracting talented Americans to serve.

This book marks Light's first publication as the Douglas Dillon Senior Fellow at Brookings, but not his first book supported by the Dillon Fund. His award-winning Brookings book, *Thickening Government: Federal Hierarchy and the Diffusion of Accountability,* was also supported by the Fund. Both Light and the Brookings Institution thank the Dillon Fund for providing the resources to make Light's continuing research possible. Of particular note is the Dillon Fund's readiness to join with Light and Brookings in staking out an entirely new research program in building an agenda for public service reform.

Light would also like to thank his many colleagues at the Pew Charitable Trusts in Philadelphia for their continued friendship and support as he made the transition from grantmaker to chairholder. The Trust's president, Rebecca W. Rimel, was unwavering in her support for his intellectual explorations and has his enduring gratitude for giving him the room to continue as a scholar and grantmaker. Light also thanks his staff in the Public Policy Program, most notably Jennifer Bolton and Elaine Casey, for tolerating his occasional absences, both literal and figurative, as he worked through the pieces of this project. In addition, Light would like to thank his colleagues at *Government Executive,* including the publisher, Tim Clark, reporters Ann Laurent and Tom Shoop, and editor Susan Forney, for their suggested improvements, as well as the faculties and students at Harvard University's John F. Kennedy School of Government, whose feedback at various stages of the writing process improved the manuscript immeasurably. In particular, Light wishes to acknowledge the helpful criticisms of Alan Altshuler, Joseph Kalt, Elaine Kamarck, Steve Kelman, Rosalyn Kleeman, Mark Moore, and Peter Zimmerman. He also thanks Kathleen Hall Jamieson of the University of Pennsylvania's Annenberg School of Communications for her enduring friendship and colleagueship, and the three anonymous reviewers who contributed their suggested improvements. Thanks also go to Carol Neves, who read the first draft of the manuscript and offered a variety of suggestions for tightening the argument and strengthening the data analysis.

The project would have been impossible without the help of a formidable team of researchers and assistants, all of whom are acknowledged throughout the manuscript. Of particular note here is the readiness of Paul Murphy, president of EagleEye Publishers, for his persistence and rigor in developing the model for estimating the total number of jobs created through federal contracts and grants.

Light also thanks his colleagues at Brookings, including the director of Governmental Studies, Tom Mann, and his staff, most notably Susan Stewart and Judy Light, each of whom smoothed his transition from Philadelphia to Washington in their own way. He also thanks Kristen Lippert-Martin, who provided essential assistance at the later stages of the project, and Carole Plowfield, who verified the book's contents assiduously. Light would not be at Brookings but for the unrelenting enthusiasm of Robert Katzmann, who has been so instrumental over the past decade in shaping Light's thinking on government reform. Finally, Light thanks his editorial team at the Brookings Institution Press, including Robert Faherty, Janet Walker, and Susan Woollen. Gary Kessler edited the manuscript, and Mary Mortensen provided the index.

Despite all the acknowledgments, Light notes that he alone is responsible for this book. He invites readers to accept the book as the opening of a long overdue reframing of the debate on who should do what in the new public service.

MICHAEL H. ARMACOST
President

Washington, D.C.
June 1999

Contents

The True
Size of
Government

CHAPTER ONE

The Illusion
of Smallness

THIS BOOK ASKS a simple question: How many people produce goods and services for the federal government? Narrow the question to federal full-time civilian employees, which is the number that led President Clinton to declare that the era of big government was over in 1996, and the answer is simple: as of Clinton's announcement, the true size of government was roughly 1.9 million civil servants, down almost 400,000 jobs since the height of the Vietnam War in 1968.

Broaden the question to include people who produced goods and services of any kind for the federal government under contracts, grants, and mandates, however, and this illusion of smallness disappears. As of 1996, this "shadow of government," as it will be called in this book, consisted of 12.7 million full-time-equivalent jobs, including 5.6 million generated under federal contracts, 2.4 million created under federal grants, and 4.6 million encumbered under mandates to state and local government.

Add the 12.7 million to the 1.9 million, then broaden the question still further to include 1.5 million uniformed military personnel and 850,000 postal service workers, and nearly 17 million people produced goods and services for the federal government in 1996, a number nine times larger than the one people used to declare the era of big government over. Although that one total has been shrinking, government is clearly bigger than advertised. It takes a very big government to deliver what Americans want.

1

Counting Heads

Whether the true size of government has expanded or contracted depends almost entirely on how one sorts the dates and the data. Start with the number of people who receive their paychecks directly from the U.S. Treasury. At first glance, which is the glance that Congress and the president usually take, total federal employment, civilian plus military, declined by nearly 900,000 jobs between 1984 and 1996, the two years that anchor the estimates of the shadow work force discussed below and in chapter two.

At second glance, however, the Department of Defense accounted for more than 100 percent of the decline. Subtract its contributions from the totals, and the civilian work force actually grew by 60,000 over the twelve years. Add in 145,000 new Postal Service jobs, and the non-Defense civilian work force grew by 200,000.

This is not to question the real downsizing that has occurred over the past five years as part of Vice President Al Gore's reinventing government campaign. Non-Defense civilian employment fell by nearly 100,000 full-time-equivalent jobs between 1993 and 1996, with particularly deep cuts coming at the General Services Administration, Departments of Housing and Urban Development and Interior, and the Office of Personnel Management (OPM).

Nevertheless, absent the Defense downsizing, federal employment would have remained well above the 1960 mark that allowed President Bill Clinton to make his claim about big government. Expressed in the aggregate, total federal full-time-equivalent employment declined steadily since reaching a post–World War II high of 5.9 million employees and military personnel in 1968, and was much smaller in 1996 than it was in 1960. But remove Defense from the totals, and the non–Defense Department civilian work force grew by nearly half from Kennedy's first inauguration to Clinton's second, increasing from 760,000 employees to 1.1 million.

Turn next to the number of people who receive their paychecks under federal contracts and grants. Again at first glance, the shadow of government fell 950,000 jobs between 1984 and 1996. But subtract the Defense Department cuts once again, and the shadow actually grew by more than 610,000 jobs, most of which were created through service contracts. Once again, absent the steep cuts created by five years of military base closures, the shadow of government grew almost 16 percent between 1984 and 1996. As the Defense shadow declined, so did the purchase of products. In 1984 one out of two contract-created jobs involved products; by 1996 the number was down to just one out of five.

Unfortunately, it is much more difficult to establish a trend line back to the 1960s on the shadow work force. There is little reliable data on federal contracts before 1984, when the General Services Administration finally smoothed out the problems in its new Federal Procurement Data System (FPDS), and there is almost no effective method for estimating either the number of jobs created under federal noncontingent grants or mandates to state and local government. The best available surrogate for the contract and grant data comes from the U.S. Bureau of Economic Analysis, which produces annual estimates of federal "consumption expenditures" as part of its National Income and Product Accounts. By definition, consumption expenditures include all purchases of goods and services. Calculated in constant 1990 dollars, these expenditures increased from $240 billion in 1960 to $357 billion in 1968, $393 billion in 1984, and $452 billion in 1988 and stood at $449 billion in 1992 and $409 billion in 1996. Although these consumption expenditures include military and civilian civil service compensation, those costs have either declined (military) or remained relatively constant (civilian) over the period, suggesting that the federal government's contract work force increased steadily during the 1960s and 1970s, only leveling off in the late 1980s and early 1990s with the Defense downsizing.

Turn last to the number of people who spend their time fulfilling federal mandates to state and local government. The problem here is that one cannot go back in time to ask state and local employees how much of their time was devoted to federal mandates. Suffice it to note that the number of mandates increased dramatically since the 1960s, as Congress and the president figured out how to encumber state and local governments at no cost to the U.S. Treasury.

Ultimately, the message from the trend lines is simple. The federal government may be turning back the clock on the number of civil servants, but it continues to need a sizable shadow to accomplish its mission. These employees may not show up in the civil service head counts that allow presidents to claim that the era of big government is over, but they are essential nonetheless. They are part of the vast shadow that is created when the federal government decides to produce goods and services through private, nonprofit, or state and local means. Given the head count constraints that have existed for the better part of a half century, the federal government simply could not do its job without the shadow.

This shadow is already well recognized as a source of employment among students at America's top schools of public policy and administration, who know that many of the nation's most challenging public service jobs are now to be found outside the federal government, not inside. At Harvard University's John F. Kennedy School of Government, for example, fewer than half the members of the class of 1997 took jobs in government, with nearly a quarter going to the nonprofit sector. "Training for the nonprofit sector is one area in which public policy schools need to redirect their focus," writes Kennedy School dean Joseph Nye. "And those who enter the private sector will profit from an understanding of public policy, environmental issues, the global economy, the impact of the new technologies, and the development of public-private partnerships—many of which require a reformulation of the skills and knowledge we have offered students in the past."[1]

A 1998 survey of 1,000 public administration graduate students confirms the movement away from government. Asked about their preferred employers, 53 percent of the students ranked government first, with the federal government preferred by 27 percent and state and local government by 26 percent. The rest of these future public servants chose the shadow of government, with the private sector preferred by 27 percent and nonprofits by 22 percent.[2]

Some readers will object to including private contractors in the public service. After all, contractors deliver their products for a price, while civil servants provide their labor for a wage. "Pure types are rare," John D. Donahue counters in his prescient 1989 book, *The Privatization Decision.* "In practice, *publicness* and *privateness* are contingent, even slightly artificial categories."[3] If head counts are to be used in measuring the true size of government, it only seems reasonable to count every head in the total. "'The government' is a shorthand term for a collection of people acting within some particular network of rules and expectations," writes Donahue. "To examine any instance of 'government production' is invariably to discover *people*, variously organized and variously motivated, doing the producing."[4]

Instead of engaging in an endless effort to keep the civil service looking small, Congress and the president would be better off asking just how many of the 16.9 million federal "producers" should be kept in-house. One can easily argue that the answer would be a larger, not smaller, civil service, or at least a civil service very differently configured. There are many good reasons to cast a shadow, whether to improve government performance, to protect taxpayer interests, or to preserve civil society. But maintaining the illusion of smallness is not one of them.

Moreover, many of the shadow jobs discussed in this book have significant elements of publicness. More than a third (4.6 million) of the federal government's 1996 shadow worked for state and local government, which makes them public employees, not private; a sixth (2.3 million) worked for grantees of one kind or another, including public and private universities, producing everything from knowledge to smoother highways; a quarter (4 million) worked for private contractors producing services of one kind or another, and a twentieth (850,000) worked for the Postal Service. Only an eighth (1.6 million) actually worked delivering products to government in the prototypical contractor relationship.

It is particularly difficult to draw lines between public and private categories when contractors and civil servants do the same jobs often in the same office at the same time.[5] Besides the size of the paycheck and the level of job security, there may be little discernible difference between the management analyst who works for the Commerce Department and one who works for Arthur Andersen, the computer programmer who works for the Treasury Department and one who works for Unisys, the faculty member who teaches for the Agriculture Department Graduate School and one who teaches for Georgetown University, or the cancer researcher who works for the National Institutes of Health and the one who works for Upjohn. Again, there may be good reason for casting shadows, not the least of which may be the federal government's inability to pay a competitive wage for key jobs. But civil servants and shadow workers can still share a common sense of service. Like identical twins raised apart, they may find themselves working in different sectors at different pay, but for very similar reasons.

Even if they have no commitment to public service, shadow employees do still have public obligations. Just because they receive their paychecks and identification cards from private firms or nonprofit agencies does not mean they can be ignored as parts of the federal service. They may be motivated by profit, and may serve multiple customers, but they accept a public service obligation whenever they act on behalf of the federal government. The Rockwell employees who bolt the space shuttle hatches are no less obligated to do the job properly than the NASA employees who work at their side; the Lockheed Martin employees who administer state welfare programs are no less obligated to be fair and accurate than the employees they replace; the ICF-Kaiser employees who meet with concerned citizens at Superfund sites are no less obligated to be responsive than the Environmental Protection Agency employees they represent; the Westinghouse employees who clean up nuclear waste sites are no less obligated to protect public safety than the Department of Energy employees who guide their contracts. The more the federal government relies on third parties to deliver public services once delivered in-house, the more those third parties must recognize the public obligations of their private or nonprofit service.

Estimating the True Size of Government

This book is less about how the shadow of government grew so large, and much more about how the federal civil service stayed so small. The answer can be found in the political incentives created by the illusion of smallness. Republicans can advertise their success in protecting private business from government encroachment; Democrats their creation of a leaner, meaner, and, therefore, more capably activist government; presidents their leadership of a more responsive, customer friendly bureaucracy; and members of Congress their victories in the war on waste.

Everyone, including the civil service and federal employee unions, appears to win from a government that looks smaller and delivers at least as much. "We cut staff, cut perks, even trimmed the fleet of federal limousines," President Clinton announced to bipartisan applause in his 1994 State of the Union address. "After years of leaders whose rhetoric attacked bureaucracy but whose actions expanded it, we will actually reduce it by 252,000 people over the next 5 years. By the time we have finished, the federal bureaucracy will be at its lowest point in 30 years." Two years later, he made his era-of-big government declaration.

Clinton was right, of course, only if the federal government is defined as composed solely of full-time-equivalent civil servants, and if the Defense and non–Defense work forces are added together. But he was quite wrong if the federal government is defined as composed of anyone who produces goods or services on the federal government's behalf, and if the Defense Department is excluded from the trends. Similarly, Republicans were right in attacking Clinton's claim only if the steep cut in contract-created jobs under Clinton is ignored, and if the millions of state and local government jobs encumbered under federal mandates are included. But they were quite wrong if they defined the federal government to include the jobs they helped push downward and outward to the private sector, and if they acknowledged the consequences of mandates on state and local government.

The challenge in tracking the true size of government is not in measuring the full-time-equivalent civil service, however. The government keeps scrupulous records on every member of its full-time work force. Rather, the challenge comes in estimating the shadow of government. "Shadow" is a metaphor well chosen, for no federal agency keeps exact data on just how many Americans earn their living or spend their time producing goods and services through federal contracts, grants, or mandates. It is not the kind of data that government likes to keep, especially not in an era of public anger and frustration toward big government.

Lacking official data, one must estimate the shadow through other means. The federal government clearly knows how much it spends for contracts and grants, making that information accessible through the General Service Administration's FPDS, which tracks all contracts over $25,000, and the Department of Commerce's Federal Assistance Awards Data System (FAADS), which tracks grants of any kind. Both systems also track what the contracts and grants purchase. The FPDS tracks all contract transactions with a standard industrial classification (SIC) code, which identifies exactly what the dollars in each transaction were used to purchase in specific goods and service, while the FAADS provides a textual description of every grant program, which can be converted into an SIC code through a careful reading.

The federal government also knows what each sector of the economy spends on labor costs and makes that information available through the Commerce Department's input-output model of the U.S. economy, which is maintained by the Bureau of Economic Analysis. The input-output model divides the economy by SIC code, meaning that it is possible to generate rough estimates of what an inflation-adjusted dollar in revenue will generate in actual jobs, no matter where that dollar comes from. By multiplying each federal contract dollar and each noncontingency grant dollar through the input-output model, a rough estimate can be generated of just how many jobs, direct and indirect, the federal government generated through its grant and contract expenditures. In 1984 the federal government spent over $280 billion in inflation-adjusted dollars on contracts and grants, generating 8.8 million direct and indirect jobs. In 1996 the federal government spent over $225 billion on contracts and grants, generating 8 million jobs. As already noted, the decline in jobs created by contracts and grants resulted almost entirely from the downsizing of the defense budget.

The contract and grant estimates used in this book were generated by EagleEye Publishers, Inc., a northern Virginia research firm specializing in use of the FPDS and FAADS data. EagleEye made a number of judgments in cleaning the contract and grant data, all of which were designed to include only those dollars that were clearly spent on the purchase of goods and services. These judgments were particularly important in sorting through the grant data, which include everything from job training grants (excluded) to highway construction grants (included) and agricultural subsidies that are contingent on specific crop prices (excluded). All questionable dollars were removed even when they may have included actual purchases of labor. Moreover, because the FPDS does not track roughly $20 billion a year in purchases of under $25,000, and because the input-output model used for this analysis did not contain multipliers for roughly $10 billion a year in foreign purchases, the final estimates likely understated the true size of the contract work force by 15 percent in 1996.

Would that the estimates of the federal mandate work force conveyed such precision. Past estimates of the mandate work force have suffered from a range of threats to their validity, not the least of which is the tendency of states and localities to overestimate the degree to which mandates drain their time and energy. Constrained by budget, the best available option is to ask a random sample of state and local employees to estimate how much time they spend complying with federal mandates of one kind or another.

The answers, while clearly subject to self-reporting bias, are inexpensive to collect and produce a surprisingly large number of hours. Multiplying time estimates from a 1997 survey by The Pew Research Center for The People & The Press against the total state and local work force of 16.7 million that year produced the 4.7 million mandate-equivalent work force positions discussed above. Much more so than with the contract and grant estimates, which involve carefully validated data, it is best to use this mandate estimate as a device for sharpening the discussion about the true size of government.

None of these estimates would be necessary, of course, if the federal government actually kept records of its own. It was only in 1995 that Congress and the president finally agreed to start tracking the costs of mandates through the Unfunded Mandates Reform Act. Even then, the Congressional Budget Office was only required to provide estimates for all federal mandates costing more than $50 million. By defining a mandate as any provision in legislation, statute, or regulation that would impose an "enforceable duty" on state and local government, the act exempted "implied" responsibilities as well as conditions attached to contracts and grants. Congress and the president have responded to the Unfunded Mandates Reform Act by pushing increased responsibilities into the implied and conditional categories, further reducing the tracking obligation on specific legislation.

As for tracking the impacts of federal contracts and grants on federal employment, neither Congress nor the president has ever seemed interested. Despite a decade of badgering by Senator David Pryor (D-Ark.) and his colleagues on the Senate Governmental Affairs Committee, the executive branch has never been pushed hard to generate the needed data, even though this book demonstrates that the data are hardly either expensive or difficult to produce.

The fact is that the illusion of smallness benefits both branches and both parties. The reason Bill Clinton could win such bipartisan applause in declaring the end of big government is that Democrats and Republicans alike understand the conceit. They know the true size of government is not to be found in head counts, but they also appear to believe that the American public just cannot be trusted with the truth. As we shall see, most members of Congress, presidential appointees, and senior career executives believe that the media exaggerates the amount of waste in the federal government, and most do not believe the American public knows enough about the issues to form wise opinions about what should be done. It is hardly surprising, therefore, that Congress and the president might focus on head counts as the simplest way to explain government. It is hard enough to hold national conversations on race and Social Security, let alone broach the topic of outsourcing. Having convinced the American public that head counts are a reasonable metric for tracking the size of government, Congress and the president seem to have accepted the illusion, too.

Overview of the Book

Given the current state of research on the true size of government, this book raises far more questions than it could possibly answer. If there is one conclusion worth noting early, it is that government should be as deliberate as possible whenever it creates a shadow. Too much of the federal government's current shadow appears to be an accident of political pressure, cowardly leadership, and tepid analysis.

This is not to argue, however, that the shadow of government should be smaller. It is entirely possible that careful analysis might lead to the need for an even larger contract, grant, and mandate work force. Unfortunately, no one knows just how big or small the assorted parts of the federal work force should be, in large part because the definition of what constitutes an "inherently governmental" function is a moving target. Two hundred years ago, inherently governmental meant almost everything that government did, down to baking bread and making rifles. Government even made shoes for its soldiers and sailors. As the political pendulum has swung over the decades, inherently governmental has become a much narrower term. But for a handful of functions dealing with national security and criminal justice, it is not clear that there is a pure and inherently governmental function left today.

What is clear is that the true size of government appears to be much larger than advertised, particularly when the effects of the Defense downsizing are removed. It is also clear that policymakers prefer a government that looks smaller, that federal head count policy has reshaped the civil service work force, and that shadows can both hide weakness and acquire strengths.

Nevertheless, the number of unanswered questions is staggering. There is little information, for example, about who works in the shadow of government. Beyond a general description of what kinds of goods are being produced (products or services), what kind of organization is doing the producing (small business, large business, minority firm, nonprofit, state and local government), and which agency is doing the buying, the federal government knows almost nothing about who is out there, what kinds of benefits they receive, how long they stay on the job, whether the government is sacrificing short-term savings for long-term costs, or even if there are savings at all over what the goods would have cost to produce inside government, and, perhaps most important, where the public service ends and the private service begins.

Thus this book is best viewed as a first cut at a topic that deserves much closer empirical scrutiny. It is hardly the first book to raise questions about what public administration scholars such as Donald Kettl and Brent Milward call "government by proxy" and "hollow government," respectively, but it is the first book that attempts to establish firm estimates on the size of the proxy and degree of the hollowing, while identifying head counts as the ultimate culprit in the hollowing out. Long before outsourcing became fashionable in the private sector, the federal government had honed the tools of keeping head counts down.

These estimates form the basis for the second chapter of the book. Readers are forewarned that the estimates of the true size of government are just that, estimates. Even the contract estimates, which are reasonably firm, are constantly evolving as the federal government updates its procurement database. Thus the estimates should be taken only as illustrations of likely trends. It must be up to future Congresses and presidents to mandate much tighter estimates of the total federal work force.

The third chapter deals with the incentives that make the illusion of smallness so attractive. Congress, presidents, interest groups, political parties, even civil servants have ample reason to prefer a government that looks smaller. The shadow of government allows presidents to reclaim a role in controlling administrative behavior, a role that was mostly eclipsed by Congress in the post-Watergate era. In turn, the shadow gives Congress new opportunities to claim credit for jobs created back home, while assuring a steady source of campaign financing. It also allows Democrats to reposition themselves as the party of bureaucratic reform, thereby weakening traditional Republican attacks. Finally, it may even create higher job satisfaction and pay for the senior- and middle-level executives left behind by the downsizings.

The fourth chapter of the book examines the primary tools of staying small: head count ceilings, freezes, and limits to restrain total federal full-time permanent employment. The first modern head count constraint was created just after World War II, when Congress demanded a radical downsizing of the federal work force, a downsizing, incidentally, that was ten times larger than the cut mandated by the 1994 Workforce Restructuring Act. Even as the federal government changed its informal work force policy in response, driving more and more jobs into the shadow, Congress and the president maintained the head count pressure. Much of the credit goes to Representative Jamie Whitten (D-Miss.), whose record-setting longevity in Congress assured that federal departments and agencies would worry about head count to the present. The result is what appears to be a lengthening shadow, one driven more by accident than by deliberation.

The fifth chapter examines the primary tools for sorting out what should stay in government and what should move to the shadow, tools that are imprecise, confusing, and, ultimately, not very effective. As already noted, shadows can strengthen government, allowing departments and agencies to acquire scarce capacity, to surge and decline with mission, and to reap the benefits of competition, while protecting the private sector from government encroachment. There are also equally inappropriate reasons for casting shadows. Shadows can also hide government weakness, permitting departments and agencies to avoid the tough decisions involved in downsizing, to evade legitimate pay limits established in law, to excuse the poor performance of their own employees, and otherwise to insulate themselves from accountability for their actions. The chapter concludes by suggesting an alternative method for deciding what should stay inside government and what should be outsourced. Instead of continuing to use ambiguous prohibitions against government involvement in any commercial activities or contracting out any inherently governmental functions, the chapter suggests a new model based on the core competencies needed to perform the government's mission.

The sixth and final chapter of the book asks how the illusion of small-ness affects the management of the government by creating at least four other illusions: an illusion of merit as the government enforces strict rules for its own work force, but not for its shadow; an illusion of accountability as the government manages an ever-larger inventory of shadow relation-ships with an ever-shrinking acquisitions and human resources work force; an illusion of capacity as the government becomes dependent on private and nonprofit agencies for everything from janitorial services to policy analy-sis; and an illusion of a unified public service as many of the government's high-impact programs migrate to the private and nonprofit sectors. The fi-nal chapter concludes with a discussion of how the federal government can better manage the new public service it has built over the past half century.

CHAPTER TWO

The True Size
of Government

Aʟᴛʜᴏᴜɢʜ ʜɪs ᴄᴏʟʟᴇᴀɢᴜᴇs in Congress and the White House have been pretending for a half-century that the true size of government is smaller than it is, Senator David Pryor never embraced the illusion of smallness. From almost his first day on the Senate Governmental Affairs Committee in 1979 to his last in 1996, Pryor pressed for answers about what the true size of government was. Using his Civil Service Subcommittee as a platform, he chaired nearly four dozen hearings over the years on the role of contractors and consultants in government.

Pryor's 1989 investigation of the Environmental Protection Agency (EPA) is just one example. "We have just undergone a transition from the Reagan Administration to the Bush Administration," Pryor said at the first of three consecutive hearings on EPA that year. "There are new faces all over town and throughout the Cabinet. . . . This hearing will look into the part of Government that remains the same, no matter who wins or who loses an election. You may think of the civil service, and while they do provide a very great measure of continuity, I am talking about a group that often remains with the agency and with the Government even longer. I am referring to a very large, invisible, unelected bureaucracy of consultants who perform an enormous portion of the basic work of and set the policy for the Government."[1]

The investigation revealed the all-too-familiar conflicts of interest, hidden costs, and poor performance associated with contracting out. Some contractors were working for EPA and were representing regulated parties at the same time; others were using subcontractors to evaluate their own work; still others were doing menial tasks at anything but menial costs. The investigation also suggested that EPA was using consultants to perform what appeared to be inherently governmental functions. "If EPA contracts are to be believed," Pryor's investigative report concluded, "it is almost impossible to identify important EPA functions not being performed by consultants."[2] Consultants were analyzing proposed legislation, drafting EPA's budget documents, overseeing the agency's field investigation teams, preparing work statements for other EPA contracts, writing draft preambles to formal rules, responding to public comments on those rules as part of the formal rule-making process, developing guidelines for monitoring other contractors, organizing and conducting public hearings, and advising senior officials on legislative reauthorizations, even though federal regulations explicitly prohibited consultants from engaging in exactly that kind of policymaking function.

Awash in a sea of anecdotes, Pryor became increasingly frustrated by the lack of even the slightest information on the size of the contractor and consultant work force. Lacking hard numbers, how could he make the case that contractors were becoming the backbone of government? In October 1989, for example, Pryor wrote EPA to ask exactly how many contract employees were engaged in rule making, enforcement, preparation of congressional reports, and communication with the public. The agency's response was typical of the dozens he received over the years: "EPA does not track the information requested. The Agency has the ability to compile it, but it would require a substantial amount of time and effort to do so. The activities in question may be performed under any of several hundred contracts. Each contract would include hundreds, if not thousands, of individual work assignments."[3]

Having spent so many years in a futile quest for data, Pryor must have hoped that his Arkansas friend, Bill Clinton, would provide the needed executive leverage for finally defining the true size of government. "Dear Leon," Pryor began his first letter to the new budget director, Leon Panetta, in February 1993, "I am writing to express my concerns about the government's extensive reliance on contractors and consultants. . . . I believe that the Office of Management and Budget should establish a Contract Review Board to take a hard, close look agency-by-agency of every contract awarded. The agencies should have to justify each contract, explain why it is necessary in these tough budgetary times to continue to rely on a private sector work force, and consider more cost effective ways of getting the job done."[4]

The letter produced a victory of sorts. Panetta warned departments and agencies about the misuse of contracts, reminding them that contracting out was to be used only when warranted by cost or need. But Pryor wanted more than a simple warning and fired a fusillade of letters asking for tighter oversight. He wrote Panetta a month later, on March 16, calling for an agency-by-agency review, and followed with letters to Panetta's new deputy director for management, Philip Lader, on March 24, Vice President Gore on April 2, and Panetta again on May 4. He could not have made his position clearer. By late summer he had finally decided that the only way to get action was to make the Clinton administration count the contractor work force. "If we cannot count the Federal government's contractor work force," he wrote Panetta on August 30, "we are left without complete information when it comes time to make decisions regarding the appropriate size of our Federal work force. In this regard, I request that you consider developing a more complete system to measure the government's total work force."[5] The OMB's response was classic bureaucratic evasion:

> As you are aware, there are a number of issues associated with trying to collect private sector employment figures. It is not clear, for example, what the definition of the "Federal work force" should include. A definition might include employees in the States, local governments, and universities that work under contracts funded through Federal grants, Federal prime contract and subcontract employees, and private sector employees involved in the manufacture, sale and delivery of both military and non-military products purchased by the Federal Government. Collecting the information would require developing standard agency reports; providing guidance on how to accommodate such things as seasonal or temporary requirements; overhead resource allocations, benefit packages; and adjusting existing contracts and grants to provide the information required. It is not at all clear, however, that the benefits of such an effort would exceed its costs.[6]

Undaunted, Pryor continued what was becoming a mythic quest for information. He persuaded his colleagues to prohibit agencies from using contractor employees to fill in for federal employees lost to downsizing created under the Federal Workforce Restructuring Act of 1994, then he pestered OMB to measure any such shifts. Once again, OMB pleaded the difficulties inherent in counting contractor heads. "Some contractors and their service and material subcontractors, for example, may be reluctant to provide such detailed employment data because the number of persons fluctuates over the life of the contract," new OMB director Alice Rivlin wrote Pryor in response to yet another letter. "Under fixed price contracts, which the Administration is encouraging, the number of persons required for contract performance may not be available. Thus, we suspect that even if we imposed an employment data collection requirement on the agencies, it would not provide the true number of persons working on Federal contracts."[7]

It is actually quite easy to generate reasonable estimates of the shadow work force. All it takes is valid multipliers of the end demand created by federal contracts and grants and some way to identify the time commitments of federal mandates on state and local employees. Before turning to such estimates in some detail and asking how the true size of government varies over time, however, it is useful to ask why Pryor never got an answer from OMB. It is obviously not because he was willing to take no for an answer.

Comparing Apples to Apples

The obvious reason Pryor never got an answer is that the data simply did not exist. The procurement and grant offices that purchase shadow capacity deal in dollars, not head counts. They see workers as another commodity to be acquired, rather like computers, water bottles, or furniture. They measure their economic impacts not by the number of jobs each dollar creates, but by the services or products produced.

But the reason the data did not exist is not because they are so difficult to collect. The General Services Administration already collects a portfolio of information on each contract let by the executive branch of the federal government. Its Federal Procurement Data System (FPDS) contains fifty data elements on every contract issued since 1978, including the kind of contract action, amount of money involved, type of contract instrument (which is different from kind of action), a product or service code (which reveals what is being purchased), a standard industrial classification (SIC) code (which reveals the nature of the industry involved), estimated completion date, contractor name and entity code, parent company, contractor owner (if there is one), place where the work is being performed, solicitation procedures used to make the contract, type of contractor (small, large, nonprofit, and so on), minority preference program (if the contract involved one), subcontracting plan (if there was one), emerging small business indicator (if the contractor was one), size of small business (including a specific number of employees), labor statutes applicable to the contract, and whether the contractor was minority or woman owned.[8]

At a minimum, the General Service Administration could easily develop an estimator of labor impacts for each contract modeled on the one used in this book.[9] Indeed, that is precisely what OMB suggested in 1998 under pressure from Representative Dennis Kucinich (D-Ohio). After once again noting that such estimates would not be either "useful or important," Deputy Director G. Edward DeSeve admitted that the FPDS data could be used to develop reasonable estimates of the number of federal contract employees, based on a range of economic and performance assumptions and using reported contract dollar values.[10]

At a maximum, GSA could require departments and agencies to collect work force estimates as part of the ordinary tracking process involved in contract transactions. Although such tracking would create a new paperwork burden on contractors, it is the only way to generate information on pay and benefits of the contract work force, which is what Kucinich and his colleague, Representative Stephen Horn (R-Calif.) also requested in 1998.[11]

The Advantage of Ignorance

The reason the data do not exist, therefore, is that no one wants them to exist. Hard numbers can only do damage to the head count conceit. Having lived by one head count that shows a leaner, meaner government, Congress and the president would rather not die by another head count that shows a shadow work force of surprising proportions. Far better to deny the shadow than sharpen it through careful measurement.

That was certainly the case in the wake of a March 1996 *New York Times* story entitled "As Payroll Shrinks, Government's Costs for Contracts Rise." After first telling readers that federal payroll and contract costs were unrelated, reporter Jeff Gerth proceeded to suggest that the two trends were actually tightly linked. "Even as President Clinton and Congressional Republicans race to take credit for shrinking the Federal payroll," his lead sentence began, "the Government's cost for outside, or contract, employees keep rising."[12]

Central to Gerth's hypothesis was a chart comparing federal payroll costs, which had fallen slightly since 1993, to service contract costs, which had increased by 3.5 percent a year. Although the chart was hardly dramatic, the trends were clearly moving in opposite directions. Service contracts had increased from just over $100 billion in 1993 to $114 billion in 1995, while federal payroll costs had fallen from $104 billion to $103 billion in the same period. After quoting Pryor, who argued that using private contractors to cover what were once federal jobs "is not an honest portrayal of what's going on with tax dollars," Gerth criticized the Clinton administration for claiming paper job cuts when "many of the responsibilities are now being fulfilled by outside contractors." Gerth also quoted OMB Deputy Director John Koskinen, who acknowledged that the federal government does not know how many private workers it employs. "You can use any number you want," Koskinen admitted. "But whatever it is it is a lot of people."

Despite his earlier cautions to the contrary, Gerth concluded his story with a sweeping indictment of the administration's personnel policy. "Eliminating Federal jobs and giving them to private contractors is a trend not only at rapidly shrinking agencies, like the Pentagon, but at departments that are still growing, like the Justice Department. There, the Administration plans to cede broad new law-enforcement responsibilities to private contractors, who will run most new Federal prisons but will not be subject to Federal rules."

With the vice president's political future riding in part on the reinventing government campaign, the Gore team reacted quickly. Reading the article as an attack on reinventing, Gore's staff released a study just four weeks later, which argued that replacing downsized federal workers with more expensive private sector contractors "is not and never has been, the intent of the Clinton/Gore Administration."[13] The fact sheet noted the controlling legal authorities prohibiting such a shift, paying homage to the Workforce Restructuring Act, which specifically states, "The President shall take appropriate action to ensure that there is no increase in the procurement of service contracts by reason of the enactment of this Act, except in cases in which a cost comparison demonstrates such contracts would be to the financial advantage of the Federal Government." It then presented an apples-and-oranges analysis comparing agency-by-agency reductions in full-time federal personnel to changes in federal spending on an ambiguous subset of service contracts. While the chart clearly showed that twelve out of nineteen "major" agencies had shown cuts in both civil service head count and service contract dollars from 1993 to 1995, the chart did not, could not, compare head count to head count.

Gerth and Gore were both stretching their data beyond reasonable limits, however. Although Gerth did a better job comparing apples (service contract costs) to apples (payroll costs), he reached beyond his data in concluding that downsized federal jobs were being contracted out. There is simply no way to know whether the jobs lost to attrition or voluntary buyouts made their way to contractors or simply disappeared altogether. Gore was well beyond the data envelope, too, particularly in allowing his staff to entitle the fact sheet "Downsized Workers Are Not Being Replaced by Contractors." The staff charts told two essentially unrelated stories on head count and contract costs, comparing apples and oranges.

The challenge in tracking the true size of government, of course, is to compare apples to apples. Since federal employee head counts have become the coin of the realm for measuring the size of government, apples-to-apples analysis means creating reasonable estimates of how many people work for the federal government under contracts, grants, and mandates. Although the numbers presented below look precise, they are only rough approximations of the shadow work force and should be treated with caution.

The Contract Work Force

The methodology used for estimating the contract work force involves simple multiplication, albeit using a model of the U.S. economy that has taken decades to perfect. The methodology starts with the five hundred thousand contract transactions recorded annually in the FPDS, each one of which carries a dollar amount, agency source, and the location, size, and status of the contractor, and concludes with the job multipliers supplied by the Bureau of Economic Analysis input-output model of the economy.[14]

The bridge between the contract dollars, which were adjusted for inflation, and the input-output model, which provided multipliers for 471 categories of the economy, is the SIC code attached to each transaction. That code reveals the type of work purchased by each contract, differentiating between specific products and services produced. Once each SIC code is matched to its appropriate input-output identifier, the dollars involved can be multiplied to determine the estimated end demand in jobs. Simply stated, contract dollars in, estimates out.[15] Table 2-1 shows the top job-producing product and service contracts in 1984 and 1996.

As noted in chapter one, this estimate methodology tends to undercount the total number of jobs created through contracts and grants, not because of some fatal flaw in the underlying assumptions, but because the federal procurement database does not count roughly $20 billion a year in small purchases and $10 billion in foreign contracts.[16] Nevertheless, the input-output model does produce a single head count against which to illustrate shifts in the contract-created work force over time. Table 2-2 shows the estimated contract work force for four years: 1984, 1990, 1993, and 1996.

The table reveals a number of patterns underpinning the true size of

Table 2-1. *The Top Five Job Producers, 1984 and 1996*

Estimated number of FTE jobs created

1984		1996	
Products		*Products*	
Fixed wing aircraft	517,000	Fixed wing aircraft	332,000
Aircraft engines	155,000	Aircraft engines	53,000
Electronic countermeasures	136,000	Guided missile systems	47,000
Guided missile systems	108,000	Data processing systems	46,000
Airframe components	86,000	Miscellaneous communication equipment	39,000
Services		*Services*	
Operation of government facilities	528,000	Operation of government facilities	519,000
R & D missile/space engines	233,000	Technical engineering	190,000
R & D communications	92,000	Data processing/telecommunications	111,000
R & D aircraft engines	68,000	R & D aircraft engines	78,000
Systems engineering	58,000	R & D missile/space operating systems	60,000

Source: Estimates provided by EagleEye Publishers.

government. Democrats and Republicans alike can take some pride in noting the sharp decline in the estimated contract work force. Starting at nearly 6.8 million in 1984, the work force falls by well over 1 million by 1996, with roughly two-thirds of the drop coming under Reagan and Bush. Whether measured in deflated dollars or head counts, the total contract work force has been shrinking.

There are important variations lower in table 2-2, however. First, the decrease in the contract work force is due entirely to reductions in contracts for products. The federal government just did not buy as many tanks, missiles, ships, and fighter planes in 1996 as it did in 1984. And though it did buy more computers than ever before, competition in the industry reduced unit costs, thereby reducing the job per contract dollar accordingly.

The biggest decline in estimated jobs occurred in the defense industry, resulting almost entirely from shrinking demand for weapons systems. Declining purchases of fixed-wing aircraft, for example, accounted for the loss of nearly 200,000 estimated jobs, electronic countermeasures for another 120,000, aircraft engines for 100,000, nuclear reactors for 40,000, and liquid propellants for 50,000. Although some product categories showed an increase in estimated jobs, particularly in personal and mainframe computers, those gains were not enough to offset the declining Defense budget.

As we shall see later in this chapter, this downsizing is a key explanation in the illusion of smallness that allows Congress and the president to claim victory in shrinking government. For now, the Defense downsizing is confirmed in the head counts presented in table 2-2. The Defense Department declined from 5.24 million contract-created jobs in 1984 to just 3.63 million in 1996, accounting for all but 100,000 of the overall reduction in contract-created jobs during the period.

Many observers credit the 1988 military base closing commission with the Defense Department employment decline. Convinced of the need to close hundreds of obsolete military bases but unwilling to inflict the political pain, Congress and the president created the commission to provide the targets in a series of all-or-nothing lists. By the time the commission disbanded in 1995, it had closed 243 bases and eliminated over 100,000 civilian jobs. The commission could not have succeeded, however, absent the end of the cold war. Having lost its durable enemy, the Defense Department was bound to have problems convincing the American public of the need for continued investment in a far-flung necklace of bases.

Even as the Defense Department contract work force declined, its shadow grew, in large measure driven by the purchase of services. By 1996 the ser-

Table 2-2. *Estimated Contract Work Force, 1984, 1990, 1993, and 1996*

Estimated number of FTE jobs created, unless otherwise specified

Measure	1984	1990	1993	1996
Total contract work force	6,790,000	6,347,000	6,010,000	5,635,000
Change from prior data point				
Dollars	...	372,000	337,000	375,000
Percent	...	–5.5	–5.3	–6.2
Total in 1994 dollars	235,355,000	204,172,000	188,545,000	173,241,000
Change from prior data point				
Dollars	...	31,183,000	15,627,000	15,304,000
Percent	...	–13.3	–7.7	–8.1
Work performed				
Products	3,298,000	2,435,000	1,939,000	1,637,000
Percentage of work force	49	38	32	29
Services	3,492,000	3,912,000	4,071,000	3,999,000
Percentage of work force	51	62	68	71

Agency				
Defense	5,243,000	4,287,000	3,847,000	3,634,000
Percentage of work force	77	68	64	65
Energy	708,000	779,000	768,000	633,000
Percentage of work force	10	12	13	11
NASA	171,000	433,000	409,000	351,000
Percentage of work force	3	7	7	6
All other agencies	668,000	848,000	986,000	1,017,000
Percentage of work force	10	13	16	18
Organization[a]				
Small minority owned	193,000	291,000	361,000	402,000
Percentage of work force	3	5	6	7
Small business	943,000	825,000	729,000	743,000
Percentage of work force	14	13	12	13
Big business	4,936,000	4,510,000	4,115,000	3,674,000
Percentage of work force	73	71	69	65
All nonprofit	396,000	336,000	372,000	319,000
Percentage of work force	6	5	6	6
State and local government	103,000	173,000	172,000	149,000
Percentage of work force	2	3	3	3

Source: Estimates provided by EagleEye Publishers.
a. Percentages do not total 100 percent because smaller categories were not included.

vice work force accounted for nearly three out of four contract-created jobs, up by half over 1984. Had the service work force followed the same pattern as the product work force followed, the total contract work force would have fallen to roughly 3.4 million. Instead, the service work force grew by 14 percent over the period. Much of the growth results from information technology, which shows up as hardware in product contracts but which shows up as everything from research and development to installation, maintenance, operations, and systems integration in services contracts.

Service contracts are likely to increase over time as government struggles to reap the benefits of new technologies. As of 1998, for example, the Federal Aviation Administration was planning to spend $1.3 billion on modernizing its air traffic control systems, the Internal Revenue Service $500 million on yet another run at rebuilding its antiquated tax systems, the Veterans Affairs Department nearly as much on medical record keeping in its 172 hospital centers, the Defense Department $200 million on a new communications system, and the Education Department $172 million on a new student loan-servicing system. And those are just the acquisition and programming costs. Once up and running, each of the new systems will require ongoing maintenance, operations, and administrative service contracts.

Agencies vary greatly in the mix of products and services purchased, however. Defense purchased roughly two service jobs for every one product job in 1996, while the Department of Energy and NASA purchased roughly twenty service jobs for every one product job. The Department of Energy uses contractors to operate the nation's nuclear weapons plants and to clean up the waste those plants create, while NASA uses contractors to stack the space shuttle and pack the payload before each launch and to recover the reusable solid rocket engines afterwards. NASA even uses a single contractor to oversee the work of the other contractors. Together, the two agencies contract for nearly one million service workers and fewer than fifty thousand product workers. The rest of the federal government, which includes every agency from the American Battle Monuments Commission to EPA, the Social Security Administration, and the Departments of Agriculture, Health and Human Services, and State, purchased roughly three service jobs for every product job.

The analysis of product versus service jobs leads to one simple, inescapable conclusion confirmed later in this chapter: but for a nearly 1.7 million decline in the number of jobs created by Defense purchases, the total federal shadow work force would have grown dramatically. Much as Congress and presidents like to claim credit for creating a leaner federal government, it is the fall of the Soviet Union that provided the essential lever for the shrinking shadow.

Buried even further in the data underpinning table 2-2 (as presented in appendix A at the end of this book) is a partial vindication of Pryor's complaint about the shift of service jobs from federal agencies to private contractors. Although the growth in service jobs among the "other" agencies slowed somewhat with reinventing government, dropping from a 26 percent rate in the 1984–90 period to 6 percent in the 1993–96 period, there is limited evidence that some agencies did replace downsized federal employees with private providers.

Overall, total federal employment fell 10 percent from 1984 to 1996, from 2.1 million to 1.9 million, while contract-purchased jobs dropped 17 percent, from 6.8 million to 5.6 million. Some agencies appeared to compensate for cuts in one work force with gains in another, however. Agriculture took a 7 percent cut in its civil service, but it acquired an 8 percent increase in its contract work force; Labor took a 14 percent cut in its civil service, but it acquired a 15 percent gain in its contract work force; State took a 5 percent cut in its civil service, but it made a 111 percent gain in its contract work force; and Education took a 6 percent cut in its civil service, but it made a 129 percent gain in its contract work force.

In all, twelve of the twenty-two agencies shrank their civil service but expanded their contract work force (Agriculture, Education, Health and Human Services, Housing and Urban Development, Labor, State, the Agency for International Development, the General Services Administration, NASA, the Social Security Administration, the Tennessee Valley Authority, and the United States Information Service); five increased both work forces (Commerce, Justice, Transportation, Treasury, and EPA); three shrank both work forces (Defense, Interior, and OPM); and two expanded their civil service but shrank their contract work force (Energy and Veterans Affairs).

Contrary to the Gore staff analysis, which compared civil service apples to contract oranges, fourteen of the twenty-two agencies show at least some circumstantial link between the surge and decline across the two work forces. This link, coupled with the earlier data on the growing service work force and data presented later on the role of Defense in masking the true size of government, provides enough evidence to suggest that further empirical analysis should be conducted of the possible shift of civil service jobs to the shadow work force in the form of service contractors. It is a problem worth investigating, particularly given the anecdotal evidence suggesting some use of contractors to fill the gaps created by what was an essentially random downsizing.[17]

Table 2-2 also shows several intriguing patterns in the shift of jobs across the private and nonprofit sectors. Big business took the biggest cuts in the Defense downsizing, losing almost 1.3 million estimated jobs. All of the losses came in product jobs, however. Further analysis of the data shows that big business lost 1.5 million product jobs over the twelve years covered in table 2-2 but gained roughly 250,000 service jobs, reaping its fair share of the growing service market. It was small business, not big, that absorbed the disproportionate share of job cuts. Small business product jobs were cut nearly in half from 1984 to 1996, falling from 400,000 to 195,000, while service jobs remained essentially flat. The only category of small businesses to prosper during the period was that of small, minority-owned businesses, which gained ground across the board in large part because of continued federal incentives. Although minority-owned firms never had a significant share of product jobs (only 55,000 in 1996), they almost doubled their service jobs.

All but a handful of the jobs created by state and local government and nonprofit agencies were created through service contracts. State and local governments created most of their jobs for contract-based research and development at public universities, while almost all of the nonprofit jobs were purchased by the Department of Defense, NASA, and the Department of Energy through contracts to nonprofit Federally Funded Research and Development Centers (FFRDCs) such as the National Renewable Energy Laboratory, the Pacific Northwest Laboratory, the Aerospace Corporation, Arroyo Center, the National Defense Research Institute, Mitre's C³I Division, and the Logistics Management Institute.

FFRDCs are a special breed of federal organization established during and after World War II to meet highly specialized research demands on a semipermanent basis. By government charter, they receive 70 percent or more of their financial support from Washington and are available on call for whatever tasks might be needed. By 1995 thirty-nine FFRDCs were in the federal budget, some nonprofit, others university based, and still others private. The technical expertise does not come cheap. According to a 1996 General Accounting Office (GAO) report, Defense Department FFDRC technical staff members each cost approximately $181,000 per year.[18]

The Grant Work Force

Once past the contract work force, the data on the shadow of government become increasingly soft. Grant-created jobs are particularly difficult to estimate, not because there is no data whatsoever, but because it is so difficult to convert for the input-output model. Unlike the Federal Procurement Data System, which contains an SIC code for each and every contract, which in turn links easily to the input-output model, the Federal Assistance Awards Data System uses a standard code from the *Catalog of Federal Domestic Assistance*, which inventories roughly 600 federal assistance programs. Each record may contain up to thirty-four pieces of information, including the type of recipient (state, county, city, special district, Indian tribe, private, nonprofit), the amount of the grant, the type of assistance (block grant, formula grant, project grant, cooperative agreement, direct payment, loan, guaranteed loan, and insurance), and a *Catalog of Federal Domestic Assistance* code that tells the user just what the grant is purchasing.[19]

Unfortunately, the catalog does not provide SIC codes that might be used as a link to the input-output model. The only way to crosswalk the data is to create an implied SIC code for every entry in the *Catalog of Federal Domestic Assistance*. Before doing so, it is important to winnow the list of grants to those that produce goods or services on the federal government's behalf. That means, for example, eliminating grants that involve transfer payments, insurance, and loans. Such grants go directly to individual citizens and do not create a shadow work force for the federal government. That also means eliminating block grants that eventually involve transfer payments, insurance, and loans. Even though such grants contain administrative overhead that finds its way into the state and local head count, it is impossible to separate the shadow administrative jobs from the transfer payments. Finally, that means eliminating what the *Catalog* labels as "contingent liabilities" such as crop insurance. Those liabilities rise and fall with disasters and market forces and do not purchase shadow jobs of any kind.

By definition, the shadow work force must be restricted to the production of public goods, whether through the purchase of products or services. Thus the following analysis of grant-created jobs is restricted to formula grants, project grants, and cooperative agreements, all of which can be used to purchase shadow jobs. In 1996, for example, this winnowing produced $232 billion in eligible expenditures. Once this first pass through the data set is completed, each remaining grant can be attached to an SIC code based on a careful reading of its project title. With these ersatz SIC codes in hand, the grants can be winnowed even further to exclude transfer payments and ambiguities hidden in the eligible expenditures.

Once all the winnowing is completed, the final dollars can be pushed through the input-output model. Because the original Federal Assistance

Table 2-3. *Estimated Grant Work Force, 1984, 1990, and 1996*

Estimated number of FTE jobs created, unless otherwise specified

Measure	1984	1990	1996
Total grant work force	2,207,000	2,416,000	2,413,000
Change from prior data point			
Number	...	209,000	–3,000
Percent	...	+9.5	–0.1
Total 1994 dollars	50,088,000	54,523,000	54,925,000
Change from prior data point			
Dollars	...	4,435,000	402,000
Percent	...	+8.9	+0.7
Agency			
Transportation	645,000	567,000	642,000
Education	518,000	684,000	762,000
Labor	359,000	190,000	166,000
Health and Human Services	336,000	599,000	395,000
Environmental Protection Agency	207,000	157,000	143,000

Source: Estimates provided by EagleEye Publishers.

Awards Data System records do not provide information on what each grant purchases by way of products and services or who is actually delivering the services by way of business, nonprofits, and state and local government, the input-output analysis can only provide a gross estimate of grant-created jobs agency by agency. Table 2-3 shows the results from three years: 1984, 1990, and 1996.

Not all of the estimated jobs were created solely to produce federal goods. Unlike contract-created jobs, where the jobs exist entirely because of the federal dollar, state and local governments are notorious for using federal grants to subsidize jobs that are already on their payrolls. Past research suggests that states use roughly 60 cents out of every federal grant dollar as a substitute for their own spending, meaning that only 40 cents actually is new spending. Studies of highway construction grants, education grants, and sewage system construction grants all suggest that federal grants have very high substitution effects, sometimes reaching 100 percent. Although grants differ greatly in the degree to which they allow substitution of federal dollars for state and local dollars, including dollar-for-dollar matching requirements and more deliberate accounting of spending patterns, the vast majority of grants included in this analysis permit substitution.

The fact is that the federal government exerts little control over the public goods purchased through these grants. After assessing all 633 federal grants available to state and local governments for everything from public assistance to highway construction and education to boating safety, GAO concluded that most grants are simply not designed to maximize federal control. Although 617 were grant programs that were narrow-purpose categorical grants, which theoretically would prevent substitution, GAO concluded that "few federal grants contain the combination of design features that would encourage states to maintain their spending levels and reduce the extent of substitution. About half the 87 largest grants, representing 30 percent of the funds for those programs, did not require state matching. Of the grants containing matching provisions, almost all had federal shares in excess of 50 percent."[20]

The question is how such substitution affects the shadow of government. Simply asked, is it reasonable to count grant-created state and local government jobs as part of the federal shadow? On the one hand, little anecdotal evidence exists to suggest that federal agencies see grants as a way to extend their reach in an era of downsizing. Grants do not so easily lend themselves to intentional shadow casting. If they did, more directive behavior in the grant instruments likely would be seen.

On the other hand, even if state and local governments use federal dollars to displace costs that would have otherwise been used to cover their own employees, the federal dollar makes the substitution possible. In buying a share of the state and local government payroll, the federal government lengthens its own reach, albeit without much direct control. Those jobs, while not as closely linked to federal agencies as contract jobs, are still part of the shadow. Whether a job resides at the murky boundary of the shadow with a library construction grant or at the sharp center with a federal services contract, and whether the worker is laying asphalt on Interstate 80 in Iowa or collecting soil samples from a toxic waste dump in New Jersey, it is still in the shadow and should be counted as such. Much as those highway workers on Interstate 80 might complain about big government and vote for "New Democrats" and "Blue Dogs" who promise to cut government, they are actually more dependent on big government than the civil service workers, who at least have some protection when the downsizings begin.

As table 2-3 suggests, the number of noncontingent grant-created jobs has gone up by 9 percent since 1984. The biggest jump occurred from 1984 to 1990, with a very slight decrease in the six years that followed. The 1996 figures include five especially large job categories:

—640,000 highway and street construction jobs, most of which likely passed through state government directly into the private sector,

— 602,000 research jobs, most which likely passed to public and private universities,

— 555,000 job training jobs, most of which likely passed to state governments on their way down to a mix of local governments and nonprofit organizations,

— 401,000 school and education service jobs, most of which likely passed through state government on the way out to local schools and institutions of higher education, and

— 125,000 engineering services jobs, most of which likely passed through state governments on the way down to city and county environmental projects.

The emphasis here is on the word "likely" because the FAADS does not record the ultimate provider of the grant-purchased good or service, making it impossible to know exactly where the dollars ended up. Created under federal law, the data system is designed to track what Congress deems most important: who receives the dollars first, not who gets them last. Thus the data system records the congressional district in which the grant recipient resides, but not the congressional district in which the final demand was created.

Given the mix of jobs described above, it is hardly surprising that the top five producers of grant-created jobs would be EPA and the Departments of Education, Health and Human Services, Labor, and Transportation. At Education, for example, the big job-producing grants involve Indian education, education for the disadvantaged, special education, rehabilitation services, vocational and adult education, higher education, and library construction. What is more interesting perhaps is that none of these departments was a particularly large producer of contract-created jobs. Education purchased just 16,000 contract jobs in 1996, Labor just 33,000, EPA 43,000, Health and Human Services 102,000, and Transportation 180,000. But putting the contract and grant work forces together, Transportation becomes the second largest shadowmaker in government at 822,000, well behind Defense at 3.7 million, and just ahead of Education at 778,000, Energy at 673,000, Health and Human Services at 490,000, NASA at 376,000, Labor at 190,000, and EPA at 186,000.

The Mandate Work Force

There is little doubt that federal mandates encumber the state and local work force. Some might even argue that such encumbrance is the whole point. Unfortunately, there is no database to mandates, ongoing list of impacts, standard methodology for estimating effects, or summary table of costs against which to calculate the employment effects of mandates to the states, Indeed, but for occasional "top ten" lists of the most oppressive mandates generated by state and local government trade associations, it is impossible to assemble a comprehensive list of mandates against which to measure impacts. The one agency that used to make mandates its business, the U.S. Advisory Commission on Intergovernmental Relations, was summarily abolished in a frenzy of budget cutting in 1995.

Yet mandates may be the most important, even pernicious, of all the shadow-casting instruments. Unlike contracts and grants, where Washington provides all or at least some of the dollars needed to produce the goods, mandates require state and local governments to shift priorities to cover the costs. Much as the Americans with Disabilities Act or Clean Air Act can be admired, such legislation clearly shifts costs from the federal government down to states and localities, while giving Congress and the president tight control over the actual design of public goods. By the 1950s, writes Martha Derthick, "Congress discovered the political advantages of mandates without money—it could order other governments to do worthwhile things like give health care to pregnant women and children or educate handicapped children or treat sewage to a very high standard or guarantee transportation for the disabled while leaving them to figure out how to pay much of the cost. . . . The result often has been domestic policymaking by federal decree, while frustrated governors and their budget officers and department heads devised strategies for shifting the costs right back to Washington through exploiting whatever fiscal loopholes in federal law they could find. And they found a great many."[21]

Efforts to estimate the impact of such mandates have been beset by difficulties, not the least of which involves the definition of just what a mandate is. Congress struggled mightily with the issue in drafting the Unfunded Mandate Reform Act of 1995. A centerpiece of the Republican Contract with America, the act defines mandates as (1) "a condition of Federal assistance," (2) "a duty arising from participation in a voluntary Federal program," unless that duty is offset by other federal support, or (3) any change in an existing entitlement program that would increase "the stringency of conditions of assistance," "place caps upon, or otherwise decrease, the Federal Government's responsibility to provide funding," or demand participation by governments that "lack authority under that program to amend their financial or programmatic responsibilities to continue providing required services that are affected by the legislation." The problem is that the definition does not distinguish between mandates that fit with prior state and local intent and those that create a significant disruption in priorities.

According to the Advisory Commission on Intergovernmental Relations, the most onerous mandates are ones that (1) require state and local governments to expend substantial amounts of their own resources in a manner that significantly distorts their spending priorities, (2) establish terms or conditions for federal assistance in which state and local governments have little discretion over whether or not to participate, (3) abridge historic powers of state and local governments, (4) impose compliance requirements that make implementation difficult or impossible, and (5) create widespread objections and complaints.[22]

Under this more subjective definition, the commission identified fourteen major mandates of concern in 1996. From the commission's perspective, seven of the mandates did not have enough national interest to justify the intrusion on state and local governments: the Fair Labor Standards Act, the Family and Medical Leave Act, the Occupational Safety and Health Act, and federal rules requiring drug and alcohol testing of commercial drivers, metric conversion, medicaid access, and the use of recycled crumb rubber in asphalt pavement. Under the Family and Medical Leave Act, for example, state and local governments are required to give their employees the same weeks of unpaid leave each year to care for newborns and for seriously ill parents, children, or spouses that private employees must provide, which clearly alters state and local personnel policy and requires the hiring of temporary employees or the reallocation of work.

The commission also identified three mandates that, while necessary, were deemed too costly or stringent: the Clean Water Act, the Individuals with Disabilities Education Act, and the Americans with Disabilities Act. Under the last act, state and local governments face what the commission viewed as a double penalty: they must cover their own workers and must also meet accessibility requirements for their building and a wide range of public services, most notably public transportation. The cost is not in the design of new buildings, of course, but in the renovation of existing structures.

Finally, the commission urged changes in the implementation of four mandates that it viewed as acceptable national goals: the Safe Drinking Water Act, the Endangered Species Act, the Clean Air Act, and an assortment of labor relations statutes, most notably the Davis-Bacon Act. Under the Clean Water Act, for example, states are required to develop and implement plans for meeting water quality standards. According to the commission, state and local governments are concerned that federal rules, especially those dealing with storm water drainage, have become increasingly expensive, even as federal funding has dwindled to near zero. It is a complaint at least indirectly supported by table 2-3, which shows a steady decrease in EPA grant-created jobs over the 1984–96 period. As the grant dollars fell, state and local government had to absorb an increasing share of the costs of environmental protection.

The commission is hardly the only source of concern about mandate costs, of course. The National Association of Counties has its own list of twelve burdensome mandates, including seven environmental statutes, while the United States Conference of Mayors has its top ten, including eight environmental statutes. All three organizations agree on Clean Air, Clean Water, Safe Drinking Water, Endangered Species, Americans with Disabilities, and Fair Labor Standards, while the counties and cities add asbestos abatement, leaking underground storage tanks, lead-based paint, and solid waste disposal. Counties throw in Superfund, immigration, and constraints on municipal bonds. Although none of the organizations offers any indication of the general costs involved, let alone the number of workers, it is clear that EPA would be the lead producer of most mandate-created state and local jobs.

Even if consensus existed on a list of top mandates against which to measure actual costs, it is not clear that a reasonable method to count heads could be created. It is easy to discover how difficult such estimating can be, however. Just read through the studies that the National Association of Counties and Conference of Mayors produced in advance of the Unfunded Mandate Reform Act. Both studies were conducted by Price Waterhouse and were released on October 26, 1993. Both also used a simple survey methodology.[23]

The city study was based on a mail questionnaire to over one thousand cities with populations over thirty thousand, meaning all members of the Conference of Mayors. Respondents were asked to estimate the employee hours and dollar costs of complying with ten specific mandates. Having received 314 responses, Price Waterhouse extrapolated its data to all cities that were sent questionnaires, and concluded that the cities had spent 92 million hours and $6.5 billion implementing the ten mandates in fiscal year 1993. Clean Water was by far the most expensive mandate for the cities, accounting for an estimated 57 million hours and $3.6 billion. Assuming that an average employee year consisted of 2,000 hours, the mandates would have encumbered forty-six thousand full-time-equivalent employees, of which roughly forty-three thousand could be tracked to environmental mandates.

The county study used a similar mail questionnaire to a random sample of the nation's three thousand counties. This time, however, respondents were only asked to estimate the dollar costs of complying with twelve mandates. Having received 128 responses, Price Waterhouse extrapolated its data to all counties, and concluded that the counties had spent $3 billion, not including capital costs, implementing the twelve mandates in fiscal year 1993. This time immigration reform was by far the most expensive mandate, accounting for an estimated $1.5 billion of the total. Assuming that county staff costs were roughly the same as city costs, and again assuming a 2,000-hour year, all twelve mandates would have encumbered seventy-five thousand full-time-equivalent employees, of which roughly thirty-eight thousand could be tracked to the immigration mandate, and another twenty-five thousand to an assortment of environmental mandates that again included Clean Water.

Such estimates are highly suspect, of course. Price Waterhouse never gave the respondents instructions on just how to do the estimates and did not have the funds to verify any of the responses. As a result, it is not clear whether cities or counties subtracted offsetting federal grants or state support in making their final cost estimates.

These and other problems eventually prompted a caustic staff report from the Senate Committee on Environment and Public Works. After quoting the famous maxim "garbage in, garbage out," the report concluded that "the Price Waterhouse survey is an ineffective tool for measuring the cost of unfunded mandates. Its estimate of $11.3 billion in unfunded federal mandates lacks credence. It overestimates the problem by billions of dollars and provides inaccurate and misleading cost figures for specific federal programs. It also does not consider the enormous benefits of federal mandates."[24] Better not to know at all, the staff report seemed to conclude, than to not have absolute precision.

If self-assessment by states and localities is fraught with bias, mandate-by-mandate review from Capitol Hill is prohibitively expensive. Under the Unfunded Mandate Reform Act, the Congressional Budget Office (CBO) became responsible for detailed cost estimates for any legislation that imposes a duty exceeding $50 million on state and local government. Having done occasional estimates of state and local impacts since 1982, CBO was the logical place to handle the comprehensive estimating required under the new legislation. The agency only needed to create a new state and local government cost estimates unit and allocate enough staff to cover the twenty-four staff years required annually to do the job. In 1996 calculating the cost of mandates meant reviewing the 718 bills that could have contained state and local mandates and another 673 that could have created private sector mandates. Of the 718 state and local possibilities, 69 actually had mandates, of which 11 had costs exceeding the $50 million threshold and 6 had costs that could not be estimated. After completing their first-year analysis, CBO staffers concluded that most mandates did not impose significant costs and that most significant mandates imposed costs on state and local governments as employers, not as governing bodies. Interestingly, according to the CBO staff, the estimating method is highly idiosyncratic from bill to bill. Staffs use any and all resources at their disposal, including conversations with trade associations. (To date, the Senate Environmental and Public Works Committee has not issued a report on the CBO methodology.)[25]

Lacking a precise mandate-by-mandate method for estimating job impacts, the best that can be done is to estimate the overall impact of federal mandates through subjective means. Doing so for this book involved a secondary analysis of a 1997 Pew Research Center for The People & The Press survey of 1,772 Americans, of whom 358 were state and local government employees. The state and local employees were asked the following question: "How much time do you spend in your work doing things that are required by the federal government in Washington—for example, following certain rules that the federal government, not the state or local government, asks you to follow?" The answers fell into five categories: no time, less than 25 percent, between 25 percent and half, between half and 75 percent, and more than 75 percent. When the five categories are converted using conservative percentages (no time equals zero, less than 25 percent equals 10 percent, between 25 and 50 percent equals 37.5 percent, between 50 and 75 percent equals 62.5 percent, and more than 75 percent equals 75 percent), they can be multiplied against the total 1997 state and local government employees of 16,669,000 to produce an estimated mandate-created work force of 4.6 million. Table 2-4 provides the methodology and the result.

Obviously, 4.6 million is a very large number. By random sample, it would include a very large proportion of school teachers, with smaller but still large numbers of police and fire fighters, and with still smaller concentrations of health workers and corrections guards. Of the 16 million or so state and local, roughly a third work for school districts, another quarter for

Table 2-4. *Estimated Mandate Work Force, 1997*

Percentage of time spent complying with mandates	Percentage of survey respondents selecting category	Estimated number of state and local employees in category	Estimated number of FTE positions encumbered by mandates
Zero	18	3,000,420	0
10	35	5,834,150	583,415
37.5	19	3,167,110	1,187,662
62.5	12	2,000,280	1,250,175
75	13	2,166,970	1,625,228
Don't know	3	500,700	0
Total who estimate mandate time spent	79	13,168,510	4,646,000

Source for survey: The Pew Research Center for The People & The Press, October–November, 1997; total sample was 1,772, of which 358 were state and local government employees.

Source for total state and local government employment: "Government Employment and Population: 1962–1996," *Historical Tables, Budget of the United States Government, Fiscal Year 1998*, table 17.5 (Government Printing Office, 1997), p. 271.

state government, slightly more than an eighth for cities, an eighth for municipalities, and less than 5 percent each for special districts and townships.

The question is whether such an estimate can be taken seriously. There are several reasons to be cautious, not the least of which is that the survey did not ask respondents whether the time spent was purchased under a grant or contract. Since a sizable proportion of grant-created jobs involve state and local employees, there likely is some double counting in the survey. Moreover, like the self-report surveys from cities and counties, the question certainly allowed respondents to take their anger out on Washington.

Nevertheless, for the purposes of this book, the question gives a little greater definition to what has been an acknowledged, if poorly measured, part of the federal shadow. Koskinen was quite right about the shadow of government:, you can use any number you want, but whatever it is it is a lot of people. Unfortunately, the number presented here is much too weak to withstand any further analysis. Where the 4.6 million jobs are, which mandates created them, and whether the number might be increasing or decreasing cannot be discerned. The best that can be done is to muse about the potential size of the mandate-created work force and encourage others with more resources to become much more rigorous in measuring what appears to be "a lot of people," indeed.

Exploring the Shadow of Government

Like any shadow, the shadow of government is sharp in some places, particularly in the contract-created jobs, and quite fuzzy in others, obviously in the mandate estimates. Whether the boundaries are sharp or blurred, however, the data reveal an implied federal work force of surprising reach. The era of big government may be over in civil service head count, but not in the shadow. Like a small figure projected on a distant screen, the federal government casts a very large shadow.

As coming chapters will show, there are good reasons, political, legislative, and managerial, for keeping the civil service small. For now, suffice it to say that almost everyone involved in government, including federal labor unions, wants to keep government looking small. The illusion of smallness allows Congress and the president, Democrats and Republicans, and even civil servants to declare victory against big government even as they satisfy the public's demand for more of virtually everything the federal government delivers. Before turning to this political economy of looking small, however, it is important to ask two questions about the numbers presented earlier in this chapter: what do the combined numbers reveal about the true size of the federal work force, particularly when compared with other sectors of the economy, and how has the true size of government changed over the shorter and longer term?

Is the True Size of Government Big or Small?

When defined as the total work force needed to fulfill its mission, whatever that mission might be and wherever that work force might be employed, the true size of government in 1996 was 16.9 million. As table 2-5 shows, that number includes 1.9 million full-time-equivalent federal civilian employees, 1.5 million uniformed military personnel, 850,000 Postal Service workers, and 12.7 million contract, grant, and mandate employees. Whether 16.9 million is a big or small number depends in part on what it is compared against and which numbers are used. Consider, for example, the relative size of the federal government compared against state and local governments, the private sector, and other nations.

When compared to state and local government, the federal civilian employment has always looked relatively small. *The Budget of the United States Government* has long advertised that fact in its historical tables comparing government employment to population. In 1996, for example, total federal

Table 2-5. *The True Size of Government, 1984, 1990, and 1996*

Estimated number of FTE jobs created, unless otherwise specified

Measure	1984	1990	1996
1. Federal civilian work force	2,083,000	2,174,000	1,892,000
2. Federal contract-created jobs	6,790,000	6,347,000	5,635,000
3. Federal grant-created jobs	2,207,000	2,416,000	2,413,000
4. State and local mandate-created jobs	...	...	4,646,000
5. Total federal shadow work force A (2 + 3)	8,997,000	8,763,000	8,048,000
6. Total federal shadow work force B (2 + 3 + 4)	...	...	12,694,000
7. Total federal work force A (1 + 2 + 3)	11,080,000	10,937,000	9,940,000
8. U.S. postal workers	707,000	817,000	852,000
9. Uniformed military personnel	2,178,000	2,106,000	1,507,000
10. Total federal work force B (1 + 2 + 3 + 8 + 9)	13,965,000	13,860,000	12,299,000
11. Total federal work force C (4 + 10)	...	...	16,945,000

Source for federal civilian work force: "Total Executive Branch Full-Time Equivalent (FTE) Employees: 1981–1999," *Historical Tables, Budget of the United States Government, Fiscal Year 1998,* table 17.3 (Government Printing Office, 1997), p. 269.

Source for postal workers: U.S. Office of Personnel Management, *The Fact Book: Federal Civilian Workforce Statistics, 1998 Edition* (September 1998), p. 8 <www.opm.gov>.

Source for military personnel: "Government Employment and Population: 1962–1996," *Historical Tables, Budget of the United States Government, Fiscal Year 1998,* table 17.5 (Government Printing Office, 1997), p. 271.

civilian employment, including postal workers but excluding uniformed military personnel, represented just 13.3 percent of what OMB estimated to be 21 million federal, state, and local government employees, a number that includes federal civilian, uniformed military, federal judicial and legislative, and all state and local personnel, while federal civilian employment represented roughly 11 federal employees per 1,000 Americans.[26]

When the federal contract and grant work force is added to the civilian, military, and postal service head count presented in table 2-5, and when the 4.6 million mandate jobs are moved from the state and local total to the federal, the relative size of governments changes dramatically. Instead of accounting for just 13 percent of all federal, state, and local employees combined, this true federal work force accounts for nearly three out of every five Americans employed by federal, state, and local government in 1996, making the federal government the largest, not smallest, public employer in the nation. Instead of accounting for 11 employees per 1,000 Americans, the true federal work force accounts for 64 per 1,000, while state and local employment falls by a third to 45 workers per 1,000. Although the federal government's relative size likely is overstated due to of the lack of hard numbers on state and local contracting out, it is clearly much bigger than advertised.

When compared to the private sector using Bureau of Labor Statistics (BLS) data, federal civilian employment looks relatively small a second time. According to BLS, America's service industry accounted for 360 jobs per 1,000 in 1996, the manufacturing sector for 69 jobs per 1,000, and the federal government for 11 per 1,000. When the federal shadow is added to the totals however, the federal work force becomes almost as large as that of the manufacturing sector. Moreover, when the service sector is broken down into its discrete components, the federal work force begins to look very large, indeed. Although it remains smaller than retail trade, which accounted for 81 jobs per 1,000 in 1996, the true size of the federal work force is larger than that of financial trade, which accounted for 26 jobs per 1,000, and wholesale trade, which accounted for 24 jobs per 1,000. Put all the government employees together—federal, state, and local—and government accounted for 115 jobs per 1,000 in 1996, making it the second largest employer in the nation. And this number does not include more than a handful of the 10 million full- and part-time employees who work for America's 1.1 million nonprofit institutions, delivering services on behalf of or in lieu of government.[27] Nor does it include the growing number of state and local shadow employees.

Finally, when compared to other governments using data compiled by the Organization for Economic Cooperation and Development (OECD), federal civilian employment looks small a third time. At less than 2 percent of the nation's total employment, public and private, the U.S. federal work force is among the smallest in the world. By comparison, the central government in Britain accounts for nearly 5 percent of its total employment; France, Italy, and Sweden for roughly 10 percent; and Mexico for nearly 12 percent. When the shadow is added to the U.S. totals, however, the relative size of governments change. At 17.9 million, the federal government rises to just under 14 percent of total employment, larger than any of the central governments studied by OECD.

Because many of those governments hide their work forces in public enterprises of one kind or another, however, the only fair comparison between nations is to total all employees—national, state, and local, general government and public enterprises. Using this expansive definition of the public sector, U.S. government employment sans shadow regains its illusion of smallness, accounting for just 15 percent of the nation's total employment, far behind Denmark at 39 percent, Sweden at 38 percent, Finland and France at 27 percent, and Mexico at 26 percent. But when the federal shadow is added into the totals, total U.S. government employment rises to roughly 22 percent of total employment, placing it right in the middle of the international pack.[28] Although this analysis could grossly understate the amount of private contracting used by other governments, it does illustrate how the traditional measure of federal employment can create an illusion of smallness far out of proportion to a more accurate head count, which, in turn, may lead the public to believe that government employment can and should shrink year after year with no appreciable loss in effectiveness.

Two caveats are in order before examining the true size of the government over time. First, the state and local work force is not likely to remain smaller than the federal work force for long. According to *Governing* magazine's Jonathan Walters, "local and state government both win a place on the BLS top-10 list of growth industries in the 1990s. Local government ranks third behind 'business services,' having added more than 1.2 million jobs. State government ranks eighth, with 200,000 new jobs. All told, between 1990 and 1996, state and local government accounted for more than one-seventh of all the new jobs in the U.S. non-farm economy."[29] Moreover, as Walters also notes, state and local governments are employing increasing numbers of contract employees. "Nationwide, at a minimum, tens of thousands of individuals work full time for state and local government on a contract basis."

Second and more important, the federal government is clearly not alone in using contractors and contingent employees. There is no question, for example, that the private sector has become expert at using what it sometimes labels contingent, or supplemental workers. According to a recent *Business & Legal Reports* survey of 1,100 private firms, nine out of ten firms used temporary employees in 1997, six out of ten used part-time employees, and four out of ten used independent contractors. Forty percent of the supplemental employees were in technical jobs, 35 percent in service jobs, and 28 percent in professional jobs. Earlier surveys by the conference board and the W. E. Upjohn Institute for Employment Research found similar patterns.[30] The supplemental work force is clearly here to stay.

Where the federal government differs from the private sector is its much greater dependency on supplemental workers to fill out its work force. According to the conference board survey cited above, only a fifth of all private firms surveyed used supplemental employees to cover more than 10 percent of their total work force demand. The vast majority used supplemental employees as 5 percent or less of their total work force. Depending upon how the shadow work force in 1996 is counted, the federal government used supplemental employees to cover anywhere from half (service contracts only) to three-quarters (service contracts plus state and local mandates) to nearly 90 percent of its work force.

Is the True Size of Government Getting Bigger or Smaller?

The past decade and a half have produced what appears to be steady slimming of both the body (full-time-equivalent work force) civil service and the shadow (contract- and grant-created work force) of government. As table 2-5 shows, all federal work forces have all shrunk since 1984, with most of the decline occurring since 1990. After growing from 1984 to 1990, the grant-created shadow work force is also down ever so slightly. At this first aggregate glance, Clinton was quite right to declare the era of big government over.

It would be a mistake, however, to interpret the decline as entirely or even significantly the result of the Workforce Restructuring Act of 1994 or of the Gore reinventing government campaign. The heaviest cuts fell exactly where expected after the end of the cold war, in the Department of Defense. Although domestic agencies did absorb significant civil service cuts here and there, most notably in the Departments of Interior (down nearly 6,500 jobs from 1984 to 1996) and Agriculture (down 8,000), the General Services Administration (down almost 10,000), the Tennessee Valley Authority (down 16,000), and the Social Security Administration (down almost 16,000), the federal government never would have met the downsizing targets without the 260,000-position Defense cut. Remove the Defense Department from the tables in this chapter and the federal civil service grew 5 percent from 1984 to 1996 (up from 1.06 million to 1.11 million), the contract work force grew 29 percent (up from 1.54 to 2 million), and the grant work force grew 7 percent (up from 2.2 million to 2.36 million).

Tables 2-6 and 2-7 provide two portraits of the masking effects of the Defense downsizing on the true size of government. When the Defense

Table 2-6. *Masking Effects of Defense Downsizing, 1984, 1990, and 1996*

Number of FTE employees and estimated FTE jobs

Work force	1984	1990	1996
Total federal work force[a]	13,965,000	13,860,000	12,299,000
Total federal work force minus Defense shadow work force	8,717,000	9,571,000	8,612,000
Total federal work force minus Defense civil service and military	5,498,000	6,459,000	6,326,000

a. Includes civil service, uniformed military personnel, postal service, contract- and grant-created jobs, but not mandate-created jobs.

Department's contributions are subtracted from the 1984–96 comparisons, the effects of the recent downsizing are significantly muted. Instead of a dramatic 1.7 million drop in the true size of government, the non-Defense work force (civil service, postal, contract, and grant) grows dramatically over the 1980s, adding almost 1 million jobs from 1984 to 1990, then dropping 133,000 from 1990 to 1996. Assuming that the Defense grant-created work force would have been under 50,000 jobs in 1993, a fair assumption given the trend line revealed in appendix A, and assuming that the Defense downsizing would have occurred with or without Clinton in the White House, the Clinton administration can take credit for shrinking the true size of government by roughly 300,000 full-time-equivalent jobs (civil service plus shadow), or about 3 percent, far from the kind of sweeping downsizing that might support the claim that the era of big government is over, but still a significant achievement given the growth in the 1980s.

The masking effects of the Defense Department on the true size of government are even more obvious in table 2-7. Remove Defense civil servants from the total end-of-year head count, which was the traditional measure of government employment until OMB switched to the full-time-equivalent measure in the 1980s, and there is a mostly steady rise in the non-Defense service from 1960 until 1992, when Clinton and Congress did, in fact, order a serious, often painful downsizing for most domestic agencies. Add in the postal service, which has grown steadily since the 1960s, and the totals would be much higher.

Unfortunately, there is no way to go back to 1960 and survey state and local employees on their mandate burdens, and the procurement database only goes back to 1984. Although it might be possible to track the grant-created work force back to 1960 by coding the *Catalog of Federal Domestic*

Table 2-7. *Defense Department Illusion of Smallness, 1960–96*
Number of end-of-year employees, unless otherwise specified

Year	End-of-year civilian employment	Minus Defense civilian employment	Consumption expenditures (in billions of 1992 dollars)	Minus Defense consumption expenditures (in billions of 1992 dollars)
1960	1,808,000	761,000	239.5	31.0
1964	1,884,000	854,000	277.5	66.0
1968	2,289,000	972,000	357.0	72.2
1972	2,117,000	1,009,000	315.2	84.9
1976	2,157,000	1,147,000	305.0	94.8
1980	2,161,000	1,201,000	341.7	109.0
1984	2,171,000	1,127,000	393.0	96.2
1988	2,222,000	1,172,000	452.0	106.7
1992	2,225,000	1,273,000	448.9	130.0
1996	1,934,000	1,166,000	408.9	138.2

Sources: "Total Executive Branch Civilian Employees: 1940–1996," table 17.1, p. 267; "Federal Transactions in the National Income and Product Accounts," *Historical Tables, Budget of the United States Government, Fiscal Year 1998* (Government Printing Office, 1997), table 14.1.

a. Does not include postal service employees.

Assistance, which records all grants, the cost of doing so would be prohibitive. The best that can be done to illustrate possible long-term trends is to deflate the annual consumption expenditures recorded in the National Income and Product Accounts of the Bureau of Economic Analysis (BEA).[31] Although BEA defines consumption expenditures to include both military and civil service compensation, the data do include every last dollar spent on purchases of durable (aircraft, missiles, ships, electronic equipments, and so forth) and nondurable (fuel, ammunition, food, supplies, water bottles, and so forth) goods, as well as every last dollar spent on services (research and development, weapons support, personnel support, travel) and structures.

Assuming that military compensation has declined over time as the armed services have contracted out work, and that civilian compensation has remained relatively stable, there can be little doubt that the combined Defense and non-Defense shadow work force has grown since 1960, perhaps by doubling over time. When Defense expenditures are removed from the equation, the growth of the shadow seems undeniable, rising nearly fourfold over the thirty-six-year period to 1996. Although Defense consumption expenditures have certainly declined since the end of the cold war, non-Defense consumption expenditures have gone steadily up, showing no parallel decline with the civil service downsizing described above. Instead of taking the true size of government back to 1960, it seems more accurate to argue that the recent downsizing has taken the size of the Defense Department work force (civilian plus shadow jobs) back to the 1970s, and that the downsizing has taken the size of the non-Defense work force back to the mid-1980s. Both may be notable achievements, of course, for the earlier trend lines were all rising. But it is only by the most limited reading of the federal work force data that it could be concluded that the era of big government is over, if, in fact, it ever began.

Conclusion

Some readers will interpret the figures presented above as proof positive that the federal government is, indeed, a giant wolf in the New Democrat's clothing. Others will see troubling evidence that the federal government has cut too deeply, forcing agencies to push inherently governmental functions into the shadow work force, while creating a new class of highly vulnerable, underpaid workers, who shift from job to job in search of security. Still others will see evidence of a new kind of military-industrial complex, involving domestic, not defense, agencies. The problem is that none of these views can be disputed by the evidence presented in this book. The data are so sketchy that just about any specter can be seen in the shadow of government.

The one irrefutable finding is that the true size of government is much larger than federal civil service head counts suggest. Faced with constant pressure to look smaller, most government agencies did what comes naturally: they pushed more and more of their mission out to contractors, grantees, and state and local governments, while protecting the middle and upper tiers of the work force. As Donald Kettl writes,

> The inescapable reality is that the federal government is organized for a world that no longer exists. Government is organized hierarchically and managed through authority, but its fundamental strategies increasingly are neither. The federal government, in particular, does relatively little itself. It mails Social Security checks, manages air-traffic control, inspects meat, and collects taxes, among other functions. But it does most of its work through contracts with the for-profit and not-for-profit sectors, grants to state and local governments, special provisions in the tax code, and regulations on corporate and individual behavior.[32]

David Pryor would not be so sanguine about the new public service, however. He would lecture us, as he did in 1989, about the dangers of abdicating our responsibilities "to a private work force, unseen, unmonitored, and unchecked." He would warn us about the lost accountability, hidden costs, and the potential for mischief in transferring the government's institutional memory to a smaller and smaller number of larger and larger contractors. If there is one lesson in this chapter, it is that Pryor was right about the general trend. "If we looked at Commerce, if we looked at HUD, if we looked at the Department of Defense," he said in 1989, "we would see those same patterns: a reduced official work force where we know how many people are employed and in what function, and what their salaries are in addition to a private contractor work force that has grown dramatically and at alarming rates. Their influence and impact is becoming more and more significant."[33]

The question for the next chapter is how the federal government got into this situation. The answer can be found in the structure of incentives that makes the illusion of smallness so attractive to almost everyone involved: the public, Congress and the president, Democrats and Republicans, civil servants, and even federal employee unions, if only on occasion.

CHAPTER THREE

The Politics
of Illusion

ONLY THREE YEARS after Republicans swept control of Congress in 1994 and barely two after Bill Clinton declared the era of big government over, the conservative press had concluded that the era of big government was still alive and well. The *Economist* and *American Enterprise* both featured cover stories on the death of downsizing, the former under the title "The Visible Hand: Big Government Is Still in Charge," and the latter under the title "What Ever Happened to Downsizing Government?"

Neither magazine questioned the declining number of federal civil servants, but neither used that number in measuring the true size of government, either. The reliably conservative *Economist* used gross domestic product, for example, in arguing that big government was still in charge across the globe. Despite years of promised spending cuts, most government spending, at least as measured in gross domestic product, had gone up. And even where it had gone down, as in Sweden and Britain, even the deepest of cuts produced only modest reductions. Twenty years of unrelenting budget cutting in Britain drove government spending all the way down from 43 percent of gross domestic product to 42 percent. "Sickened in the end by this remorseless brutality," wrote the *Economist*, "the British electorate earlier this year swept Labour back into power with a landslide majority."[1]

In contrast, the *American Enterprise* used the increased dependency of American citizens on federal funding as its measure. "Remember 1994?" asked editor in chief, Karl Zinsmeister, as he introduced the issue. "It seems like another world now. . . . It is somewhere between amusing and nauseating to note that under Republican leadership the House of Representatives Public Works Committee (Pork Barrel Central for highway projects, dams, etc.) has ballooned to a record membership of 73 congressmen. Seventy-three! Ideal for clipped debate and crisp decision-making, I guess."[2] By 1997 fully 40 percent of Americans were net recipients of government aid, he added. "That is to say, they suck more dollars out of the dish than they put in. Many of these people have the same relationship to our lords in Washington and other seats of government that a household pet has to its keeper." Over the next couple of decades, the magazine predicted, half of American would be net recipients.

How one measures the true size of government depends on where one sits. There is no doubt that the two magazines chose their measures to emphasize the growth of government. The numbers were not inaccurate per se, just not the only numbers available. Just as one can criticize Bill Clinton for declaring the era of big government over on the basis of civil service head counts, one can also criticize the *Economist* and *American Enterprise* analysts for declaring the era still alive by using gross domestic product or dependency ratios.

The two magazines were not the only ones to question the illusion of smallness, however. *Governing* entered the era-of-big-government debate in 1998 in studiously nonpartisan fashion with a detailed assessment of state and local head count. After noting that nothing seemed more certain in the wake of the 1994 Republican sweep than a wholesale downsizing of state government, *Governing* concluded that just the opposite had occurred, even in states headed by tough-talking Republican governors such as Michigan's John Engler and Texas's George Bush Jr. "In the mid-1990s, as the words 'freeze,' 'shrink,' 'cap' and 'cut' have become staples of the executive lexicon," wrote *Governing* reporter Jonathan Walters, "state government employment has continued to go up almost everywhere. Nationally, in the years from 1990 to 1996, it increased by 5 percent."[3] Local government employment went up, too, rising 11 percent. "All told, between 1990 and 1996, state and local government accounted for more than one-seventh of all the new jobs in the U.S. non-farm economy."

But for the shrinking of civil service employment, most of the promised cuts never took place. One can easily argue that the shadow of government includes a significant number of workers who would have been federal civil servants in the absence of head count constraints. If Washington could not cut its budget or reduce its mission, it most certainly could reduce its full-time-permanent head count, driving those jobs into service contracts, grants, and mandates, while creating a government that looks smaller but delivers at least as much.

This chapter will examine the political economy of smallness. Presidents have come to prefer the shadow of government because it appears to strengthen their control over government against an increasingly reform-minded Congress; Congress, because it provides an essential source of on-going campaign support and incumbency advantage; Democrats, because it provides a defense against their image as the party of big government; and Republicans, because it strengthens their base of business support. Even civil servants have incentives to favor the shadow, whether because it may increase public confidence or because it raises their performance appraisal ratings. Having a government that looks smaller but delivers at least as much also appears to increase incumbency advantages, whether that incumbent happens to be a Democrat or Republican, president or mayor. As the following pages will argue, keeping government looking small is the work force policy that satisfies almost every political preference. It is also the policy that caters to the public's core ambivalence about the size of government, which is the underlying currency that supports the political economy of shadow casting.

The Market for Smallness

The political economy of shadow casting starts with a simple conclusion: there would be no illusion of smallness if the American public were willing to accept a federal work force that is big enough to cover the government's mission. The fact is that Americans want at least as much, if not more, of virtually everything the federal government delivers, but they also believe that just about everything the federal government delivers is wasteful and inefficient. The vast majority of Americans want a high or very high priority given to almost anything the federal government runs, but they also believe that anything run by the federal government is doomed to create more problems than it solves. Before asking how the contradiction produces support for the illusion of smallness, however, it is first useful to understand the two sides of the contradiction.

A Government that Delivers at Least as Much

The first half of the contradiction is clearly revealed in a 1997 survey by The Pew Research Center for The People & The Press. If the sample of 1,762 respondents is representative, a significant majority of Americans wants the federal government to continue delivering at least as much as it ever has. Three-quarters of the Pew respondents said the federal government should be primarily responsible for ensuring that food and medicines are safe, two-thirds for managing the economy to prevent another recession or depression, three-fifths for ensuring that every American has access to affordable health care, and just over half for conserving the country's natural resources. Although some of the expectations have shrunk since the early 1960s when four out of five wanted the federal government to manage the economy, Pew Research Center director Andrew Kohut had ample reason to emphasize the stability in public support for what conservatives would label the era of big government.[4]

Moreover, Americans are mostly favorable toward both government employees and the agencies that deliver the goods. Roughly 70 percent of the Pew sample voiced a favorable opinion of government workers in general, a number that was up 15 points from 1981. When asked who they trusted more to do the right thing, politicians who lead the federal government or the civil service employees who run departments and agencies, the civil servants won hands down, by a margin of nearly five to one.

The Pew respondents also felt favorable toward most federal departments and agencies. The U.S. Postal Service topped the favorable ratings at 89 percent, prompting the postmaster general to run nationwide ads in late spring 1998 congratulating his work force on its performance, with the Park Service second at 85 percent, the Centers for Disease Control third at 79 percent, the Defense Department fourth at 76 percent, and the Food and Drug Administration fifth at 75 percent. Compared to ratings taken at the height of the Reagan war on waste in 1987, all but five of the nineteen agencies rated by Pew moved up, with the Defense Department being the biggest gainer of all, rising 19 points in the wake of its Gulf War victory.

Not only are Americans reasonably favorable toward their frontline departments, but they also are mostly confident that government can handle significant problems. A total of 60 percent of the Pew sample had a great deal or fair amount of confidence in the federal government's ability to handle domestic problems, up from 51 percent at the height of the Watergate crisis, while three-quarters had similar levels of confidence in the federal government's ability to handle international affairs, up only slightly from the mid 1970s. Confidence was up at the state and local level, too, where Americans were more confident in 1997 than they had been in twenty-five years. According to the Pew survey, 78 percent of Americans had a great deal or fair amount of trust and confidence in their local government to handle problems, a gain of 15 percent from 1972. State government did slightly better, with 81 percent of Americans having a great deal or fair amount of trust and confidence in 1997, up from 63 percent in 1972. The numbers confirm the longstanding notion that Americans are more trusting toward the governments they know, meaning the ones closest to home.

Overall, the numbers certainly help explain why most Americans want government to continue delivering goods and services on their behalf. Indeed, the nation remains remarkably steady in its view toward government power and activism, barely moving from its positions of nearly thirty years ago. Two-thirds of those polled by the Pew said that the federal government either had about the right amount of power for meeting today's needs or should use its powers even more vigorously to promote the well-being of all people. It is a division of opinion that has remained virtually unchanged since George Gallup first asked the question in 1964.

A Government that Looks Smaller

Americans may still support a mostly activist federal government, but they have serious doubts about how that government performs. They may love their bureaucrats and agencies, but they do not give government much credit for success. Asked how well the federal government is running its programs, only a quarter of the Pew respondents answered excellent or good, half said only fair, and a fifth said poor. Asked whether criticism of government was justified, three-fifths said yes. And asked whether something run by the government is bound to be wasteful and inefficient, two-thirds said yes, a number that has remained roughly constant since the Pew Research Center began asking the question in 1987 (the high was 69 percent in 1992, the low 63 percent in 1987). All in all, it was not a particularly enthusiastic portrait.

More troubling perhaps, the Pew respondents were mostly underwhelmed with the federal government's actual performance in delivering public value. Asked to rate the federal government's success on eight policy issues, they gave only one, ensuring that food and medicines are safe, an "excellent/good" endorsement. The other seven fell well short, with reducing poverty and juvenile delinquency each earning less than 15 percent of an "excellent/good" rating.

These performance ratings are particularly interesting when laid side by side with the favorability ratings of federal departments and agencies. Thus 75 percent of the Pew sample gave the Food and Drug Administration favorable marks, but only 58 percent said the federal government is doing an excellent or good job of ensuring that food and medicines are safe; 69 percent gave the Environmental Protection Agency favorable marks, but only 34 percent said the federal government is doing an excellent or good job of conserving the country's natural resources; 62 percent gave the Social Security Administration favorable marks, but only 26 percent said the federal government is doing an excellent or good job of providing a decent standard of living for the elderly.

The greatest favorability gap involved the Department of Education, which earned a 61 percent favorability rating as an organization, but earned only a 23 percent rating as an implementor on setting academic standards and an 18 percent rating on ensuring that all Americans can afford to send their children to college. Although the department is hardly solely responsible for either issue, the gap suggests a disconnection between how respondents rate favorability and how they rate performance, a disconnection that may reflect a host of intervening factors such as perceived tax burden.

When pressed to explain the poor performance on each of the eight policy issues, roughly half of the Pew respondents blamed the government while the other half said the given issue was just too difficult or too complicated to solve. There were only three areas where Americans said good performance was beyond the government's reach: ensuring an affordable college education, reducing juvenile delinquency, and reducing poverty. Juvenile delinquency was seen as the most difficult issue of all. Although only 11 percent of the Pew respondents said government was doing an excellent or good job on the issue, almost 70 percent of the critics said the issue was simply too difficult to solve. Where Americans place the blame depends in large part on how they rate the performance. "Americans who are mildly critical of government performance are more likely than others to fault the difficulty of the issues the government faces," Kohut argues. "Americans who are very critical of government performance are more likely to fault government itself."[5]

Alongside these general doubts about government performance, Americans also believe that government at all levels has the wrong priorities. Three-quarters of the Pew sample said the government should give high priority to ensuring access to affordable health care, for example, but only 15 percent said government had actually done so; 72 percent said the government should give high priority to providing the elderly a decent standard of living, but only 17 percent said government had done so; and 76 percent said the government should give high priority to conserving natural resources, but only 24 said the government had done so. This gap between the hoped-for priority and reality existed on all eight of the issues raised in the Pew survey, and it ranged from 60 percent (affordable health care) to 39 percent (ensuring everyone can afford college). Not surprisingly, the larger the perceived gap, the less an individual trusts government to do the right thing.

It is performance, not the priority gap, that has the most effect on public trust in government. Statistically, ratings of performance are almost seven times as powerful in explaining the distrust than dissatisfaction with government's priorities. Americans can disagree on the priorities, it seems, but not on the need for government to perform well on whatever priorities it sets. Performance does count. Given the relatively low ratings of performance discussed above, it is not surprising that confidence in Washington's ability to do the right thing all or most of the time was just 39 percent in 1997, up ever so slightly from a modern low of just 21 percent in 1994, but far below the modern high of 76 percent in 1964. If this is as good as confidence gets at the end of five years of unrelenting attention to reinventing government, perhaps Congress and the president are right to worry about how to convince the public that government can do good. Moreover, even the modest gains were gone after a year of unrelenting attention to stories of scandal and impeachment. By November 1998 the number of Americans who trusted Washington to do the right thing had fallen from 39 percent to 26 percent.[6]

The Core Constituents of Reinventing Government

The question is how the general contradiction described above might create a market for illusions. A first answer is that the positives tend to tone down the public's demand for radical reform. Americans may think government is bound to be inefficient and wasteful, but they do not think it needs much more than a tweak or two to work much better. Asked how much reform is enough, only 37 percent of the Pew sample said the federal government needs major reform, while 58 percent said the federal government is basically sound and needs only some reform. Granted, only 4 percent said the federal government does not need much change at all, but most prefer a more cautious course.

A second answer is that Americans are just as reluctant to hurt people as are Congresses and presidents. Asked what kind of reform might make them trust government again, most Americans recommend changing how government works, not who works there. Asked for their ideas on making government work in 1995, only 8 percent of Americans said government should change who the bureaucrats are, 29 percent said government should change how the bureaucrats work, and 27 percent said elected officials should change how they conduct themselves.[7] Moreover, according to the Pew 1997 survey, the vast majority of Americans think government is a good place to work. Although fewer than a quarter of the Pew respondents preferred government to the private sector as an employer, they are mostly positive about their bureaucrats.

The market for shadow government appears to reside, therefore, in the intersection between public demands for more of what government delivers, continued doubts about what government can actually deliver, and the general reluctance to undertake radical reform of any kind. Americans ask their government to do the impossible, as Charles Goodsell puts it, giving it "inconsistent, contradictory, and hence unachievable goals and tasks," demanding that it "achieve results indirectly, through the efforts of others," evaluating it "not by how much it *tries* to move ahead on an impossible front but whether or not 'success' is achieved," and "both overselling and underselling what it can do."[8] Under great pressure to deliver the goods without bulking up, government has little choice but to create shadows.

Not all Americans favor the shadow course, however. Indeed, the Pew survey suggests that there are at least four different philosophies of government reform. These four types are produced when two key questions from the survey are combined into a single measure. The first question asked respondents to place themselves on a six-point scale of government activism, the number one representing "someone who generally believes that, on the whole, federal government programs should be cut back greatly to reduce the power of government," and the number six representing "someone who feels that federal government programs should be maintained to deal with important problems." The second question asked respondents what they personally felt was the bigger problem with government: "Government has the wrong priorities, OR government has the right priorities but runs programs inefficiently?" After collapsing the first question into two categories, antigovernment (numbers one through three on the six-point scale) and progovernment (numbers four through six), respondents can be divided into four cells: (1) devolvers (antigovernment and wrong priorities), (2) realigners (progovernment and wrong priorities), (3) downsizers (antigovernment and right priorities, but inefficiency), and (4) reinventors (progovernment and right priorities, but inefficiency).[9] Table 3-1 shows the resulting combination.

Table 3-1. *Where the Public Stands on Reform*

Percent

Government reform philosophy	Bigger problem with government[a]	
	Has the wrong priorities	*Right priorities, but runs programs inefficiently*
Cut federal programs to greatly reduce government power (1–3 on 6-point scale)	*Devolvers* 16	*Downsizers* 22
Maintain federal programs to deal with important issues (4–6 on 6-point scale)	*Realigners* 14	*Reinventors* 39

Source: The Pew Research Center for The People & The Press, secondary analysis of data released in *Deconstructing Distrust: How Americans View Government* (Washington, D.C.: The Pew Research Center for The People & The Press, 1998), N = 1,762.

a. Percent of total respondents who occupy given cell; 9 percent of the total was in the don't know/not ascertained categories.

As the table shows, the number of Americans who might be moved by promises of a government that looks smaller and delivers at least as much is remarkably large. Four out of ten Pew respondents simultaneously expressed a demand for maintaining government programs to deal with important problems and believed the bigger problem with government was not the wrong priorities, but inefficiency. Although these reinventors would most certainly respond to the "works better and costs less" message of Vice President Gore's first reinventing government report, they would oppose any reduction in the core programs of government. They also would have been the first to criticize the back-to-back 1995 government shutdowns. Unlike the devolvers, who would have seen the shutdowns as a way to get government off their backs, if only for a moment, the reinventors would have seen peril in any effort to undermine essential services.

The devolvers and reinventors clearly define two archetypes of how best to reform government.[10] Devolvers would find comfort in the *Economist* and *American Enterprise* analysis of the true size of government, while reinventors would resonate to the illusion of smallness presented in federal head count policy. As the data presented in appendix B suggest, the two draw on similar demographic constituencies. Although there was a notable gender gap between devolvers (58 percent of whom were men, 42 percent women) and reinventors (42 percent of whom were men, 58 percent women), there was little variation between the two in race, region, and employment status.

It is on more traditional political attitudes where devolvers and reinventors draw on very different constituencies, creating two distinct packages of views toward government. The differences start with party identification, where devolvers were significantly more likely to identify themselves as Republicans, and reinventors significantly more likely to identify themselves as Democrats. This sorting is repeated when independents who lean one way or the other are assigned to their respective parties. As box 3-1 suggests, devolvers and reinventors formed the two ends of the continuum on a long list of issues, even as they shared a core confidence in state and local government.

Devolvers disliked almost everything about the federal government, from its bureaucracy to its leadership. They were the most likely of the Pew respondents to believe the federal government needs major reform, and they were clearly not willing to accept occasional downsizings as a sign of improvement. They were the most likely of the Pew respondents to know that federal employment had decreased under Clinton, but the most likely to have unfavorable views of most federal departments and agencies. Not surprisingly, therefore, devolvers are also the least likely by far of the four groups identified in table 3-1 to trust the government in Washington to do the right thing. Just 15 percent of devolvers said the federal government can be trusted just about always or most of the time, compared to 54 percent of reinventors.

Yet, even the devolvers wanted more of almost everything the federal government delivers. Granted, when asked how much the federal government should do about a list of eight policy issues, the devolvers were less likely than the reinventors to give a high or very high priority to all but two of the eight, the exceptions being a general agreement with the reinventors that the federal government should not give a particularly high priority to ensuring that Americans can afford to send their children to college and to reducing poverty. But when asked how much the federal government is doing about each of the eight, the devolvers systematically rated the actual priority as lower than their preferred priority. Subtract the actual from the preferred, and the devolvers wanted government to do more. Indeed, using this comparison of demand for the entire sample, it would be more accurate to describe the American public as wanting a government that looks smaller and delivers much more.

In contrast, reinventors liked almost everything about the federal government. They were far more confident in the federal government's ability

Box 3-1. *How Devolvers and Reinventors Divide*

Devolvers Are More Likely than All Other Groups to:	Reinventors Are More Likely than All Other Groups to:
Feel frustrated about the federal government	Feel basically content about the federal government
Believe the federal government is only doing a fair or poor job	Believe the federal government is doing an excellent or good job
Believe the federal government needs very major reform	Believe the federal government is basically sound
Agree the federal government controls too much of our daily lives	. . .
Know that federal employment has declined	. . .
Lack confidence in the federal government's handling of domestic and international problems	Have confidence in the federal government's handling of domestic and international problems
Believe state and local government should have more responsibility	. . .
Have unfavorable views of any federal agency, most notably the EPA and IRS	Have favorable opinions of most federal agencies, particularly the IRS and Department of Education
Have unfavorable views of elected federal officials, Congress, federal departments and agencies, Bill Clinton, and government workers	Hold favorable opinions of elected federal officials, Congress, departments and agencies, Bill Clinton, and government workers
Believe that anything run by the government is usually wasteful and inefficient	Disagree that anything run by the government is usually wasteful and inefficient
. . .	Believe the federal government should do more on most policy issues
Believe the federal government is doing a fair or poor job on most policy issues	Believe the federal government is doing an excellent or good job on most policy issues
Believe elected officials are not trustworthy	Believe elected officials are trustworthy
Rate the ethical and moral practices of officials as fair or poor	Rate the ethical and moral practices of officials as excellent or good
Blame government for its performance problems	Forgive government for its performance problems
Say the federal government today has too much power	Believe the federal government should use its powers more vigorously
Believe they are paying more than their fair share in taxes	Believe they are paying about the right amount in taxes
Want their son or daughter to go into politics	. . .
. . .	Have confidence in the wisdom of the American people
Think government is not a good place to work	Think government is a good place to work

Box 3-1 *(continued)*

Devolvers and Reinventors Are Almost Equally Likely to:

Have a great deal or fair amount of confidence in state and local government
Be upset if someone claimed government benefits they were not entitled to or had not
  paid all the income taxes they owed
Care if someone had gotten out of jury duty
Have favorable opinions of the Postal Service and Social Security Administration, the
  military, and state and local government
Have favorable opinions of public employees, and state and local government officials
Mostly believe the federal government should do more of everything, most notably
  ensuring that food and medicines are safe, and reducing juvenile delinquency and
  poverty
Trust civil service employees more than politicians to do the right thing
Believe that people will mistrust the government no matter what

Source: The Pew Research Center for The People & The Press, secondary analysis of data released in *Deconstructing Distrust*, N = 1,762.

to handle international and domestic problems, more favorable toward individual departments and agencies, most notably the IRS. They were also more likely to see a federal role in almost all of the issues tested by Pew, with their top five being ensuring that food and medicines are safe (74 percent), managing the economy to prevent a recession (72 percent), ensuring that every American has access to affordable health care (65 percent), conserving the country's natural resources (56 percent), and providing a decent standard of living for the elderly (54 percent). They were also more confident toward Congress, elected officials, Bill Clinton, and government workers, and more forgiving toward government's performance problems. Little wonder, therefore, that reinventors were simultaneously the most contented and least angry of all Pew respondents toward government.

The question is why reinventors would favor any reforms at all. The answer can be found in their steady complaint about waste and inefficiency. Although reinventors disagreed with devolvers that the federal government needs major reform, only 7 percent said the federal government does not need much change at all. Over half also agreed that when something is run by the government, it is usually wasteful and inefficient. It would be a mistake, therefore, to assume that reinventors will meekly accept occasional reassurances that government is getting better absent more convincing evidence about eliminating waste, evidence that includes constraints on total civil service head count.

Despite their disagreements, devolvers and reinventors shared a set of common views of government. They were both likely to have confidence in state and local government, be angry at fellow citizens who cheat government, and trust civil service employees more than politicians to do the right thing. Both shared a high regard for the Postal Service, the Food and Drug Administration, and the military. As for the effect of word choice on public opinion, both groups were almost equally likely to have favorable opinions of public employees, even though devolvers were far less favorable when asked about government workers. Although overwhelming numbers in both groups said that government can become more efficient, one should not doubt the resistance among devolvers. Cutting civil service employment will never be enough to move them to greater confidence. They are true believers in a resorting of responsibilities and would have scoffed at Clinton's assurances that the era of big government is over. Among the other three groups, however, a more modest reform agenda would clearly work. Congress and the president could easily build a significant public majority for imposing head count ceilings, hiring freezes on the one hand (looks smaller), while streamlining internal procedures and measuring performance on the other (deliver at least as much). In doing so, they would easily isolate the devolvers, who would have little recourse but to read the *Economist* and *American Enterprise* for solace.

The Core Leaders of Reinventing Government

Even if the public were to resolve its ambivalence in favor of deep cuts or vast expansions, Congress and the presidency would still face substantial institutional incentives for creating the illusion of smallness. As will be discussed shortly, the illusion of smallness allows Congress and the president to have their cake and eat it too. They can claim a shrinking government, even as they satisfy the demand for government goods and services.

Gore certainly understood that reinventing government was good politics when he accepted the reinventing government assignment in 1993. According to journalist Elizabeth Drew, Gore had been given the reinventing government issue in March as a "consolation prize" instead of the lead role on welfare reform.[11] If Gore was disappointed by the outcome, he never showed it. He approached the National Performance Review with unprecedented fervor, collecting a staff of nearly a hundred federal managers to investigate every facet of federal management. "There are not going to be any sacred cows," Gore said at the outset, "At the end of the month, we'll have real results and real proposals to offer. Write it down. Check back with us."[12]

Six months later, the National Performance Review produced the first of what would become annual reports. Standing next to Clinton and backed by two forklifts piled high with government regulations, Gore said "Mr. President, if you want to know why government doesn't work, look behind you."[13] Whatever the impact on Gore's national standing, which grew with appearances on the *Today* show, *Larry King Live*, and *Late Night with David Letterman*, the event created a short-lived rise in public support for the administration's health-care package. That is precisely why reinventing won the post-Labor Day time slot. The president's pollster, Stanley Greenberg, had been warning all summer that the public had little sympathy for the kind of health care bureaucracy envisioned in the emerging plan. A frontal assault on wasteful government might just give the president a moment of forgiveness. As such, the reinventing release became a kind of inoculation against public skepticism. Although the health-care plan eventually succumbed to the antibureaucracy argument, reinventing government gave it a moment of hope in what was an extraordinarily hostile environment.[14]

Reinventing government involved more than pure politics, however. Clinton and Gore shared a common concern about making government more effective. Both also shared an interest in restoring their party after twelve years of Republican tax-and-spend pounding. As the *Wall Street Journal* reported on the day of the release, "Much as it was easier for Republican President Nixon to overcome conservative opposition and go to China, an attempt to streamline government is more powerful coming from a Democrat, whose party generally likes government. President Clinton will be especially eager to push his plan to remake government as a way of offsetting the image that he is just an old-fashioned tax-and-spend democrat, an image some Republicans tried to pin on him during the summer budget debate."[15]

Nevertheless, as table 3-2 suggests, reinventing government fits with the prevailing view of government reform among the presidential appointees, senior civil servants, and members of Congress interviewed by the Pew Research Center in 1997, as well as among the public employees at all levels of government interviewed at roughly the same time. Devolution has even less support in the halls of Congress or executive branch than it does in the general public writ large. (Readers are cautioned that the sample of leaders interviewed by Pew had a higher percentage of refusals to answer the two questions that form the basis of the typology than of responses.)

Table 3-2. *Where Government Officials Stand on Reform*

Percent

| | Bigger problem with government[a] | |
Government reform philosophy	Has the wrong priorities	Right priorities, but runs programs inefficiently
Cut federal programs to greatly reduce government power (1–3 on 6-point scale)	*Devolvers*	*Downsizers*
All leaders[b]	6	14
Only executive	3	9
Only Congress	14	28
Public employees	13	21
Maintain federal programs to deal with important issues (4–6 on 6-point scale)	*Realigners*	*Reinventors*
All leaders	8	46
Only executive	13	50
Only Congress	4	31
Public employees	16	39

Sources: For leaders, The Pew Research Center for The People & The Press, secondary analysis of data released in *Washington Leaders Wary of Public Opinion* (Washington, D.C.: The Pew Research Center for The People & The Press, 1988), N = 98 presidential appointees, 81 members of Congress, and 151 members of the career Senior Executive Service; for public employees, The Pew Research Center for The People & The Press, secondary analysis of data released in *Deconstructing Distrust: How Americans View Government* (Washington, D.C.: The Pew Research Center for The People & The Press, 1998), N = 542.

a. Percent of total respondents who occupy a given cell; figures do not include don't knows/not ascertained.

b. All leaders includes members of Congress, presidential appointees, and career members of the Senior Executive Service; "only executive" includes presidential appointees and career members of the Senior Executive Service.

It is impossible to know, of course, whether Congress and the president are leading or following public opinion on government reform.[16] What is clear is that there is a remarkable coincidence of opinion between the governed and the government. Interestingly, however, all three sets of leaders interviewed underestimated the public's trust in government while overestimating the degree to which the public would say government could act to increase trust.

Whether more accurate readings on their part would change their general position on government reform is doubtful, for the illusion of smallness reflects institutional incentives that go deeper than short-term variations in public opinion. As the rest of the chapter will show, presidents, Congress, the political parties, and civil servants all have at least some incentive to promote a government that looks smaller and delivers at least as much.

Presidential Incentives

Ordinarily, presidents have good reason to keep every last person delivering services within government. To the extent shadows dilute their control, presidents must theoretically resist. "While legislators eagerly delegate their powers to administrative agencies, presidents are driven to take charge," writes Terry Moe in outlining his theory of public bureaucracy. "They do not care about all agencies equally, of course. . . . But most agencies impinge in one way or another on larger presidential responsibilities—for the budget, for the economy, for national defense—and presidents must have the capacity to direct and constrain agency behavior in basic ways if these larger responsibilities are to be handled successfully."[17]

The desire for control is why presidents have long supported what organizational theorists call scientific management, which favors what Moe describes as the presidential ideal of "a rational, coherent, centrally directed bureaucracy that strongly resembles popular textbook notions of what an effective bureaucracy, public or private, ought to look like."[18] Given its focus on the president as the one true master of government, as Luther Gulick once described the chief executive, it is not surprising that scientific management would be the tide of reform most likely to emanate from the White House.

The desire for control is also why presidents have long resisted efforts to cut the number of political appointees. They simply believe in leadership by layering. Whether Democrat or Republican, they adamantly defend the penetration of political appointees ever deeper into the executive hierarchy. To paraphrase Senator Daniel Patrick Moynihan (D-N.Y.), they have defined leadership downward. The result has been a steady thickening of government. More layers of leaders, more leaders at each layer. Occurring under head count pressure, the thickening gives agencies cause to cast shadows. Given a choice between expanding the middle- and senior-level hierarchy or casting a shadow, however, presidents and their lieutenants will pick the former. It is in their political and institutional self-interest to do so.

Finally, the desire for control is why presidents resisted the head count pressure for as long as they did. As the next chapter will clearly demonstrate,

Congress, not the president, was the source of most head count ceilings and hiring freezes during the 1950s and 1960s. Presidents resisted and Congress insisted.

Ordinarily, therefore, we would expect presidents to fight any efforts to flatten the hierarchy, decentralize control, and impose head counts. Such resistance fits perfectly with the prevailing incentives described by Moe's theory of public bureaucracy. "Governance is the driving force behind the modern presidency," Moe writes. "All presidents, regardless of party, are expected to govern effectively and are held responsible for taking action on virtually the full range of problems facing society. To be judged successful in the eyes of history—arguably the single most important motivator for presidents—they must appear to be strong leaders, active and in charge." They must have organizations that appear to work.[19]

These are not ordinary times, however. Recent presidents have done all of the above: they have fought at least two battles of the bulge (Reagan and Clinton), pushed for decentralization (Nixon and Clinton), and become steadfast advocates of reducing overall head count (Nixon, Carter, Reagan, and Clinton). Even when they have abandoned head count as a budget-making tool, as the Clinton administration did in the mid 1990s, they have only done so because they knew that departments and agencies did not have the money to hire the employees to threaten the head count ceilings they had established. But for their continued support for politicization, which may be weak evidence of affection for centralization, they have behaved as if they are adversaries of the very organizations they lead.

Congress Now Proposes

The question is what might lead presidents to favor organizational structures that are contrary to their hypothetical self-interest. The answer may be that Congress, not the presidency, has become the central force in government reform. At least as far as statutory efforts go, Congress now proposes and the president disposes.

My own research on past reform efforts reveals Watergate was the unmistakable turning point.[20] Congress authored ten of the thirteen management reforms passed in 1974, including the Congressional Budget and Impoundment Control Act, marking a successful resurgence after nearly a half century of decline. As James Sundquist argues, the resurgence involved more than just the power of the purse. "It was not enough for the Congress to reclaim powers that had been allowed to drift away or had been usurped.

...The Congress felt impelled, also, to move in whatever ways it could to assert tighter control over the executive branch in the exercise of the still vast authority that the executive of necessity retained."[21]

Congress hardly needed to learn how to legislate on government management, however. It had already established itself as a steady source of war on waste and of watchful-eye reforms. All it needed to do was add the scientific management and liberation management philosophies to its agenda, which is exactly what it did. From 1945 to 1974 presidents accounted for three-quarters of all management reforms enacted into law, drawing heavily on scientific management for their legislative inspiration. From 1974 to 1995, however, Congress became the dominant source of reforms, accounting for three-quarters of all reform ideas in the wake of Watergate. Adding in the eleven statutes passed in the 1993–96 period, Congress accounted for seventy of the ninety-three reforms enacted since Nixon's resignation.[22]

The trends actually accelerated after Reagan entered office. Of the sixty management reforms enacted since 1981, fifty originated in Congress, including a host of reforms more traditionally associated with presidential control. It was Congress, not the president, that authored the 1990 Chief Financial Officers Act, which created chief financial officers across government and mandated annual financial statements for every department and agency. It was Congress, not the president, that authored the 1993 Government Performance and Results Act, which established an entirely new binding process for holding individual departments and agencies to a government-wide process. And it was Congress, not the president, that authored the 1996 Information Technology Management Reform Act, also called the Clinger-Cohen act in honor of its House and Senate cosponsors, which established chief information officers across government and imposed a new process for integrated information planning.

Fifty years ago these statutes would have almost certainly come from the president—indeed, post–World War II commissions headed by Herbert Hoover recommended elements of all three. Today Congress is the author in what is becoming a presidential spectator sport.

The consequences of the growing congressional involvement are clear. Making government work has become a distrustful business, focusing on procedural compliance with tightly written statutes. "No longer willing to defer to the president or blue-ribbon commissions," I have argued, "Congress opened its own legislative assembly line. It is not clear that Congress will ever go back, particularly given the persistent levels of public distrust, or that the presidency is equipped to stake a claim to its once singular leadership of government reform."[23] Whether for good or ill, Congress has built its own vision of the ideal bureaucracy, building what Moe describes as "the kind of bureaucracy interest groups incrementally demand in their structural battles. This 'congressional bureaucracy' is not supposed to function as a coherent whole. Only the pieces are important. That is the way groups want it."[24]

Presidents still pursue reform from time to time, of course, just not with the traditional elements of rational, centralized scientific management. Liberating government from the rules has become the president's preferred reform, represented by the 1994 Acquisition Streamlining Act. The act produced a sharp reduction in procurement paperwork, while raising the threshold for simplified procurement from $25,000 to $100,000 and encouraging departments and agencies to become smarter buyers of goods and services. But for occasional congressional forays into the tide, scientific management has been out of fashion for the better part of two decades. My research suggests that scientific management had mostly played out in the 1940s and 1950s with the two Hoover commissions. The days of department and agency building are now over, as are the days of tight central control.

As Congress has become more dominant in shaping government reform, presidents have struggled to regain a semblance of control. But for occasional looks back at scientific management, the latest example being Gore's endorsement of chief operating officers in 1993, presidents have been led away from scientific management and toward a new set of tactics. Their strategic advantage today lies with informal networks and exhortative demands that render statutes less important for shaping organizational structure. If they cannot subvert compliance, they can most certainly give departments and agencies the permission to "satisfice" the law, as Richard Cyert and James March would put it, by creating a largely unregulated universe of highly informal reinventing activities and laboratories.

If not quite adversaries of the agencies they oversee, presidents are no longer quite allies, either. To win control of government, presidents must dismantle the very control structures that have served them so well over the years, even if that means pushing work outward and downward, while embracing the head count ceilings of the war on waste. In short, they must adopt a new set of tactics that weaken congressional control largely through deregulation, decentralization, and, where necessary, shadow casting.

Thus Gore has argued strenuously against the very systems that once assured presidential responsiveness: "In Washington's highly politicized world, the greatest risk is not that a program will perform poorly, but that a scandal will erupt. Scandals are front-page news, while routine failure is ignored. Hence control system after control system is piled up to minimize the risk of scandal. The budget system, the personnel rules, the procurement process, the inspectors general—all are designed to prevent the tiniest misstep."[25]

Gore has also supported decentralization, a favored tool of those out of power. According to Moe, it is opponents of those in power who "like fragmented authority, decentralization, federalism, checks and balances, and other structural means of promoting weakness, confusion, and delay."[26] Edit out the weakness, confusion, and delay, and Moe has the first principle of reinventing government: cutting red tape. As Gore argued,

> Effective, entrepreneurial governments cast aside red tape, shifting from systems in which people are accountable for following rules to systems in which they are accountable for achieving results. They streamline their budget, personnel, and procurement systems—liberating organizations to pursue their missions. They reorient their control systems to prevent problems rather than simply punish those who make mistakes. They strip away unnecessary layers of regulation that stifle innovation. And they deregulate organizations that depend upon them for funding, such as lower levels of government.[27]

Freedom, not control, is the preferred option.

Finally, Gore has championed the concept of the creation of dozens of performance-based organizations, which would be freed from government control systems under performance-based contracts. Creating agile, highly responsive organizations headed by senior executives on short-term contracts might give the president maximum short-term authority, but it would also expose the agency to immediate manipulation by adversaries who might win a future election. A similar critique could be made of Gore's focus on customer satisfaction, which opens an agency to the kind of external sunshine that adversaries favor. Can it be that the theory of public bureaucracy simply cannot tolerate reality?

Before rejecting the theory, however, it is useful to note that party politics and public opinion also play a significant role in shaping presidential incentives for action. Gore entered office first and foremost a Democrat who wanted to be part of an activist administration. Given his own desires to ascend to the presidency and his party's lingering reputation for tax-and-spend government, his political fortunes rested heavily on proving to the public that government could perform. The political incentives thus far outweighed the traditional structural pressures that Moe describes. Decentralization makes perfect sense, therefore, as a defense against further congressional encroachment on executive prerogative. Far better to hide the work force or diffuse authority than to risk congressional meddling, which has been growing under Republican and Democratic majorities alike, and under divided and unified party control of the two branches.

One can also argue, as Moe probably would, that the performance-based organizations and customer service actually fit quite nicely with presidential control. By changing the basis of the relationship with Congress from one of budgets and incremental adjustment to hard measures of performance, the performance-based organizations would gain significant control of their own destinies. And who would select and negotiate the contracts at hand? The president, of course. The very first contracts written would establish precedents of their own for the future. Little wonder then that the new Republican Congress would reject the performance-based organization concept out of hand. Democrats would have, too.

Politics is very much a part of Moe's theory of public bureaucracy. As he writes, "Winning groups, losing groups, legislators, and presidents combine to produce bureaucratic arrangements that, by economic standards, appear to make no sense at all. Agencies are not built to do their jobs well. Strange and incongruous structures proliferate. Presidential bureaucracy is layered on top of congressional bureaucracy. No one is really in charge."[28] If that is not a description of the tides of reform, what is? Offensive though such organizations might be to economics, they are perfectly comfortable for democracy, which writes its conflicts in the structures of government just as certainly as it does in the statute books.

Moreover, even decentralizers have been known to favor uniformity. That is why, for example, the Gore reinventors wanted every federal department and agency to create a chief operating officer. "Transforming federal management systems and spreading the culture of quality throughout the federal government is no small task. To accomplish it, at least one senior official with agencywide management authority from every agency will be needed to make it happen."[29]

Gore was hardly the first to propose what the new institutional sociologists would call coercive isomorphism. The chief operating officer title joined a long list of government-wide officers, including chief financial officers, chief information officers, and inspectors general, that have been created to strengthen government management. What makes chief operating officers different is their potential evolution in a more senior version of the assistant secretaries for administration recommended by the first Hoover Commission on Organization of the Executive Branch of Government almost a half-century ago. The notion of a single high-level officer, preferably a career civil servant, who would continue from administration to administration as a source of internal leadership makes eminent sense however and whoever recommends it.

Still Thickening after All These Years

Not everything in the illusion of smallness is contrary to Moe's theory of political bureaucracy. Even as presidents invent new tactics for wresting control from Congress, they continue to heed the bureaucratic incentives on political appointments. The definition of leadership by layering began with Franklin Roosevelt's 1937 Brownlow Committee, which argued that the president needs help, and continued into the Eisenhower administration, which created Schedule C of the federal general service to give cabinet officers greater freedom to hire their own personal and confidential assistants, through Nixon's unprecedented effort to pack the executive branch with loyal aides, and into the more recent centralization of all political appointments in the White House Office of Presidential Personnel. Although the politicization has prompted a substantial amount of lower level layering, as departments and agencies follow Moynihan's Iron Law of Emulation, the incentives for centralization are overwhelming. Much as I still believe that thickening undermines presidential leadership, it continues to exist because it allows presidents to simultaneously fulfill their perceived constitutional obligation to command the government and their political obligation to reward contributors and allies.

Presidents are right to believe that their appointees can make a difference, a point well made by B. Dan Wood and Richard Waterman. Examining Reagan's efforts to dominate administrative decisionmaking in seven agencies—EPA, Equal Employment Opportunity Commission, FTC, FDA, National Highway Traffic Safety Administration, Nuclear Regulatory Commission, and Office of Surface Mining—Wood and Waterman concluded that presidential appointees can have "extraordinary influence" over agency policy. "In five of the seven programs we examined, agency outputs shifted immediately after a change in agency leadership. In four of these cases (the NRC, the EEOC, the FTC and the FDA), change followed an appointment at the beginning of a presidential administration. The direction and magnitude of these responses reflects the increased power of a chief executive in the period after a presidential election."[30] Presidents can hardly be expected to give up that kind of influence.

Although the Gore reinventors considered a token cut in the number of presidential appointees as part of what would become a downsizing of 272,900 jobs under the Workforce Restructuring Act of 1994, the White House Office of Presidential Personnel scuttled the recommendation, eventually leading the effort to defeat a Senate-passed bill that would have imposed a more substantial cut from 3,000 to 2,000 appointees.[31] Once again, the desire for presidential control outweighed all arguments for what would have been at most a symbolic thinning at the top of the hierarchy.

Despite this defense of the presidential appointments process, the number of vacancies at the top of government began to rise as the Clinton administration aged. As of 1 September 1997, only seven months into the administration's second term, nearly 30 percent of the 470 top political jobs were still vacant, prompting the Senate to take the administration to task for violating the 1868 Vacancies Act. Under the act, which was revised in 1988, presidents had exactly 120 days to submit nominations to fill vacancies in Senate advise-and-consent positions.

The obvious violation of the act, particularly by the Department of Justice, prompted Senator Robert Byrd (D-W.Va.), the chamber's self-appointed guardian of the separation of powers, to wax eloquent about the constitutional system. Clutching a copy of the Constitution in one hand, the 80-year-old senator attacked the Department of Justice for its "unmitigated arrogance" and warned his colleagues of yet another breach of constitutional prerogative. "Each time a vacancy is filled by an individual in violation of the act, yet another pebble is washed off the riverbank of the Senate's constitutional role. As more and more of these pebbles tumble downstream, the constitutional riverbank weakens until, finally, it will collapse."[32] In a classic cake-and-eat-it-too defense of both the number of appointees and high vacancy rates, White House personnel director Bob Nash vehemently disagreed with "any assessment that indicates the executive branch is not functioning because of a few vacancies. The president has been and continues to be very successful in implementing his legislative and administrative agenda."[33] Every last position was necessary, even if it remained vacant for years at a time.

Given the prevailing incentives, it is no surprise that the Clinton administration would fight any cuts. What is more surprising perhaps is the degree to which the Clinton administration lost control of the senior hierarchy through a steady and largely accidental title creep. Notwithstanding its rhetoric about leaner, meaner bureaucracy and its determined attack on the midlevel bulge, the administration added as many new titles to the senior-most levels of government in its first five years as the seven administrations before it had added over their three decades combined. Table 3-3 shows the changing height (number of layers) and width (number of occupants) between 1960, 1992, and 1996.[34]

Before turning to the titles themselves, it is important to note that the Clinton administration slowed the growth in the number of senior-level positions. The numbers may not have gone down, but they did not go up by much either. As table 3-3 shows, the total number of positions barely climbed at all. By comparison, the Bush administration added 641 positions to the senior hierarchy, for a 37 percent increase, while the Reagan and Carter administrations added 173 (11 percent) and 600 (61 percent) respectively. Although the Clinton administration rejected the Senate's proposed cut in total political appointees, it held the line on the width of the senior hierarchy. It did so evenly from the very top of the senior hierarchy in the secretary, deputy secretary, under secretary, and assistant secretary compartments, where Republican presidents have historically done their packing to reduce agency activism, and in the administrator compartment, where Democrats have historically done their widening to enhance agency delivery. Although the Clinton administration could have easily hidden small increases in the senior-most layers, it clearly took the head counts seriously.

What is remarkable, therefore, is the extraordinary growth in the height of the senior hierarchy. The Clinton administration oversaw the creation of sixteen new titles in government, including a stunning number of new "alter ego" deputy posts, almost all of which were occupied by career civil servants. Among the new titles were deputy to the deputy secretary, principal assistant deputy under secretary, associate principal deputy assistant secretary, chief of staff to the assistant assistant secretary, deputy associate deputy secretary, assistant chief of staff to the administrator, and chief of staff to the assistant administrator, all classic deputies whose primary responsibilities are to stand in for their principal. The Clinton totals would have been even higher had three titles not disappeared between 1992 and 1998: the principal associate deputy under secretary (which had existed in Energy), the associate deputy under secretary (which had existed in six departments and appears to have moved up into the deputy secretary compartment), and associate assistant administrator (twelve of which had existed in Commerce). All totaled, the Clinton administration witnessed the creation of nineteen

Table 3-3. *The Thickening of Government, 1960–98*

Title[a]	Number of departments where title exists			Number of positions open for occupancy		
	1960	1992	1998	1960	1992	1998
Secretary	10	14	14	10	14	14
Chief of staff to the secretary	...	11	13	...	11	13
Deputy chief of staff to the secretary	...	2	9	...	2	10
Deputy secretary	3	14	14	6	20	23
Chief of staff to the deputy secretary	...	2	5	...	2	5
Deputy deputy secretary	...	...	3	...	...	4
Principal associate deputy secretary	1	...	1	2	13	1
Associate deputy secretary	...	6	6	...	...	12
Deputy associate deputy secretary	...	...	1	...	...	1
Assistant deputy secretary	...	...	3	...	...	5
Under secretary	8	9	10	15	32	41
Chief of staff to the under secretary	...	...	4	...	...	4
Principal deputy under secretary	1	2	2	1	8	2
Deputy under secretary	4	11	8	9	52	8
Principal associate deputy under secretary	...	1	...	...	1	...
Associate deputy under secretary	...	6	...	...	11	...
Principal assistant deputy under secretary	...	...	1	...	...	1
Assistant deputy under secretary	...	1	1	...	11	1
Associate under secretary	...	1	1	...	1	1
Assistant under secretary	...	...	1	...	...	1

Assistant secretary	10	14	14	87	225	212
Chief of staff to the assistant secretary	..	4	8	..	5	21
Principal deputy assistant secretary	1	8	7	1	76	64
Associate principal deputy assistant secretary	..	..	1	..	..	1
Deputy assistant secretary	7	14	14	78	518	484
Principal deputy deputy assistant secretary	..	..	1	..	..	5
Deputy deputy assistant secretary	5	..	1	..	..	1
Associate deputy assistant secretary	..	4	6	20	50	42
Assistant deputy assistant secretary	..	3	2	..	26	16
Principal associate assistant secretary	1	..	2	..	..	6
Associate assistant secretary	..	14	12	4	208	148
Chief of staff to the associate assistant secretary	..	..	1	..	..	2
Deputy associate assistant secretary	3	..	8	..	121	66
Assistant assistant secretary	..	14	14	16	177	220
Chief of staff to the assistant assistant secretary	..	..	1	..	..	1
Deputy assistant assistant secretary	..	11	13	..	57	82
Administrator	9	11	9	90	128	140
Chief of staff to the administrator	..	2	5	..	7	12
Assistant chief of staff to the administrator	..	..	1	..	..	1
Principal deputy administrator	..	3	2	..	9	4
Deputy administrator	8	10	9	52	190	193
Associate deputy administrator	..	1	2	..	15	30
Deputy associate deputy administrator	..	..	1	..	..	1
Assistant deputy administrator	1	4	3	2	48	42
Deputy assistant deputy administrator	..	..	1	..	..	1

(Table continues)

Table 3-3 *(continued)*

Title	Number of departments where title exists			Number of positions open for occupancy		
	1960	1992	1998	1960	1992	1998
Associate administrator	2	9	9	3	105	138
Chief of staff to the associate administrator	...	...	1	...	...	1
Deputy Associate Administrator	...	6	4	...	28	24
Assistant administrator	7	8	8	55	159	146
Chief of staff to the assistant administrator	...	...	1	...	...	1
Deputy assistant administrator	...	8	5	...	66	54
Associate assistant administrator	...	1	...	...	12	...
Total	17	33	49	451	2,408	2,462[b]
Absolute increase	...	16	16	...	1,957	54
Percentage increase	...	88	49	...	434	2.2

Sources: 1960 and 1992 data are from Paul C. Light, *Thickening Government: Federal Hierarchy and the Diffusion of Accountability* (Brookings/Governance, 1995); 1998 data are from further coding of the *Federal Yellow Book*, Winter 1998 edition.

a. This table includes all titles in the 14 federal departments that are listed at Executive Levels I, II, III, IV, and V of Title 5, United States Code, as well as titles that are variations of all titles at Executive Level II, including, for example, the secretaries of the Army, Air Force, and Navy, Administration and Federal Highway Administration at Executive Level II, and assorted commissioners, directors, administrators, inspectors general, general counsels, chief information officers, and chief financial officers at Executive Level IV.

b. 1996 figures include the Social Security Administration, which was elevated to independent status in 1994, but was part of the Department of Health and Human Services until then. With Social Security excluded, the totals for 1996 would have fallen by 54 to 2,384, for a decrease of 24 positions or 1 percent from 1992.

new titles and the elimination of three, yielding the net increase of sixteen. Box 3-2 shows the inventory of titles open for occupancy across all departments and agencies in winter 1998.

There is considerable evidence in table 3-3 that much of the layering that occurred in the assistant secretary and administrator compartments was accidental, more a product of not paying attention than a deliberate expression of traditional control incentives. Of the nineteen new titles, only five existed in more than one department. Although history suggests that most of the titles will eventually spread to other departments, there is little evidence of the kind of breakthrough layering witnessed in the creation of entirely new compartments such as the deputy secretary compartment, which first appeared in 1952 and which had spread to all departments by 1992; or new titles such as chief of staff to the secretary, which first appeared at Health and Human Services in the early 1980s and which had spread to all but one department by 1998; or principal deputy assistant secretary, which first appeared at the Department of Defense in 1960 and which had spread to seven departments by 1998. Once created, a new title can spawn its own title riders. Even as new chief of staff titles spread to other departments in the late 1980s and early 1990s, the existing chief of staff titles began sprouting new alter ego deputies. The first deputy chief of staff to the secretary popped up at HHS in the late 1980s, then spread outward with inexorable force to seven more departments by 1998.

The growth in titles was most certainly not the result of deliberate title making by the president or Congress. None of the new titles were created through executive memoranda or statute. Rather, they appear to have been created almost entirely by individual administrators deep within their agencies. But for the deputy chief of staff to the secretary and the new deputy to the deputy secretary titles, which would surely have been noticed by the senior-most officials, the rest of the new titles would be mostly invisible within their agencies.

Traditionally, the Office of Personnel Management would have stopped the proliferation. But not only was its staff decimated by the downsizing, but also its role in position management was always weak. Nor is it clear that OPM could have stopped the growth had it wanted to. Central control was clearly out of fashion under Gore's liberation philosophy, and agencies have long been free to create layers of management as they wish. Left to their own devices, administrators will create alter ego deputies, whether because having such deputies convey a certain status in the administrative pecking order or because such titles are marks of one's own professionalization.

Box 3-2. *Titles in Federal Government, Winter, 1998*[a]

Secretary Chief of staff to the secretary Deputy chief of staff to the secretary **Deputy secretary** Chief of staff to the deputy secretary Deputy deputy secretary Principal associate deputy secretary Associate deputy secretary Deputy associate deputy secretary Assistant deputy secretary **Under secretary** Chief of staff to the under secretary Principal deputy under secretary Deputy under secretary Principal associate deputy under secretary Associate deputy under secretary Principal assistant deputy under secretary Assistant deputy under secretary Associate under secretary Assistant under secretary **Assistant secretary** Chief of staff to the assistant secretary Principal deputy assistant secretary Associate principal deputy assistant secretary Deputy assistant secretary Principal deputy deputy assistant secretary	**Assistant secretary** *(continued)* Deputy deputy assistant secretary Associate deputy assistant secretary Assistant deputy assistant secretary Principal associate assistant secretary Associate assistant secretary Chief of staff to the associate assistant secretary Deputy associate assistant secretary Assistant assistant secretary Chief of staff to the assistant assistant secretary Deputy assistant assistant secretary **Administrator** Chief of staff to the administrator Assistant chief of staff to the administrator Principal deputy administrator Deputy administrator Associate deputy administrator Deputy associate deputy administrator Assistant deputy administrator Deputy assistant deputy administrator Associate administrator Chief of staff to the associate administrator Deputy associate administrator Assistant administrator Chief of staff to the assistant administrator Deputy assistant administrator Associate assistant administrator

a. This box includes all titles in the 14 federal departments that are listed at Executive Levels I, II, III, IV, and V of Title 5, United States Code, as well as titles that are variations of all titles at Executive Levels I-V, including, for example, the secretaries of the Army, Air Force, and Navy, director of the Federal Bureau of Investigation, and the administrators of the Federal Aviation Administration and Federal Highway Administration at Executive Level II, and assorted commissioners, directors, administrators, inspectors general, general counsels, chief information officers, and chief financial officers at Executive Level IV.

Ironically, even as departments and agencies labored under the president's order to de-layer the middle levels of government, the upper levels were mostly immune. With no one watching, a handful of administrators did what sometimes comes all too naturally: they bulked up their own units.

Because titles are rather like kudzu, the best time to kill a new title is when it is only barely established. Of the six titles that disappeared between 1960 and 1992, four had existed in just one department, while the other two had existed in just two. Now would be the time to kill the new titles. Unfortunately, new titles have a remarkable survival rate. Of the six titles that were killed, five came back in the very next administration and survive to this day. Absent a sustained attack and tough weed control, most of the new Clinton titles will come back. That is the nature of administrative kudzu.

By itself, the new height will not lengthen the shadow of government. The new titles simply have not spread far enough to cast light. Nevertheless, the height does confirm the central incentives for thickening, whether driven by the president's own demand for control or by agency preferences for institutional similarity. As those sixteen new titles start to spread, as they most certainly will given the hostility of liberation management toward meddlesome central oversight, the federal hierarchy will continue to go circular.

Congressional Incentives

Unlike the presidency, where casting shadows is a mostly counterintuitive expression of institutional self-interest, Congress has ample incentive to favor a government that looks smaller and delivers at least as much. Simply stated, head count constraints give individual members substantial electoral advantages back home, whether by providing protection against opponents who charge that members have been captured by the federal bureaucracy, creating significant opportunities for crediting nonfederal jobs with federal dollars, and generating a steady flow of the campaign funding needed for reelection. In short, shadow casting is a substantial source of incumbency advantage.

Before turning to the argument in more detail, however, it is important to note that the shadow of government fits perfectly with the incentives described by Moe's theory of public bureaucracy. Unlike presidents, who must balance short-term pressures to produce against longer term incentives to balkanize, legislators have a very simple incentive to do what interest groups want by way of structural choice. Because of what Moe describes as "their almost paranoid concern for reelection," and because "interest groups, unlike voters, are not easily fooled," legislators are not given to "flights of autonomous action or statesmanship."[35] Harsh and unforgiving as Moe's characterizations might be, his description fits well with the history of head counts described in the next chapter. Most of the early thaws in the head count freezes were prompted by heavy lobbying from the postal unions, while most of the resistance to a more deliberate work force policy reflected continuing pressure from private contractors and consulting firms.

It is easy to understand why interest groups, both those that are favorable toward an agency and those that are unfavorable, would endorse the use of shadows. Those that favor a given agency or program can do everything Moe recommends by way of complicating administrative systems, even as they use shadows to produce the desired goods. To protect their agency from outside influence, they can write detailed legislation that constrains future action, impose specific deadlines for action as a device for front-loading benefits, demand greater professionalism than technically justified, limit congressional opportunities for oversight, and enhance judicial review of agency decisionmaking.

Such tactics can also be applied to contracts, grants, and mandates. What better way to assure long-term protection than to give a favored program to intensely loyal, self-interested firms? What better way to confuse congressional overseers than to place a favored program deep within a web of contracts, subcontracts, grants, and mandates? What better way to judicialize the delivery of public goods than to write a legally binding contract that can be defended in court? The very things that allies would favor, meaning "designs that place detailed formal restrictions on bureaucratic discretion, impose complex procedures for agency decisionmaking, minimize opportunities for oversight, and otherwise insulate the agency from politics," fit perfectly with a shadow work force governed by tight performance-based contracts, grants, and mandates.[36] Shadow casting is an obvious defense strategy.

At the same time, groups that oppose a given agency or program can use the shadow of government to weaken delivery. Adversaries can fragment internal structures, write ambiguous mandates that confuse more than clarify, resist formal deadlines, open the agency to maximum external inspection, pursue appointment and personnel policies that enhance political direction of the agency, impose time-consuming procedures for making decisions, require endless justifications for even minor action, and demand procedures that allow them to participate, appeal, and delay.

Such tactics can easily produce an increase in shadow casting. What better way to drive an agency to contracting than to set the price of internal action so high that nothing can be done in house? What better way to frustrate accountability and create the potential for scandal than to load an agency with so many regulations that it cannot properly oversee the contracts it lets? What better way to assure maximum feasible conflict than to impose head count constraints that might lead to unfunded mandates? The very things adversaries favor, meaning "fragmented authority, labyrinthine procedures, mechanisms of political intervention, and other structures that subvert the bureaucracy's performance and open it up to attack," inevitably create incentives for casting shadows as agencies struggle to fulfill their missions.[37]

Even if interest groups were agnostic about bureaucratic structure, which they most certainly are not, shadow casting creates enormous congressional benefits back home. For most members of Congress, as Thomas Mann argues, elections will always be *Unsafe at Any Margin*. The fear of defeat is so great that members do all they can to assure reelection. If that means creating an occasional shadow through pork barrel legislation, no problem.

That Congress cares about credit claiming back home is hardly in dispute. A host of political scientists have written about the phenomenon, none ever so persuasively as Richard Fenno in *Home Style*. Nor is there any doubt that pork barrel projects, and the shadows they create, generate credit-claiming opportunities. As Morris Fiorina writes, "The average constituent may have some trouble translating his congressman's vote on some civil rights issue into a change in his personal welfare. But the workers hired and supplies purchased in connection with a big federal project provide benefits that are widely appreciated."[38]

That is why, for example, all fifty governors, the American Automobile Association, environmental groups, the Chamber of Commerce, and even the American Planning Association (highways need planners, too) endorsed the $217 billion transportation bill passed by Congress in May 1998. Congress most certainly understood that the Transportation Equity Act for the Twenty-First Century (TEA 21) would create jobs back home. Although never discussed as anything but good old fashioned pork, the shadow effects featured prominently in the House debate leading to final passage. It was a debate led by twelve-term House member E. G. "Bud" Shuster (R-Pa.), chairman of the House Transportation and Infrastructure Committee and arguably the most effective pork producer since Jamie Whitten (D-Miss.).

Shuster was unapologetic about the size of the measure, which increased federal transportation spending by nearly half, warning his colleagues not to believe "this baloney that we somehow break the budget, that we somehow create a deficit." Not only would the bill save lives, cut the federal debt, improve productivity, and restore American competitiveness, it would create 42,500 jobs for every $1 billion spent. (Applying Schuster's calculation, which appears to be based more on hunch than science, to the $228 billion the federal government spent on contracts and grants in 1996 would produce nearly 9.7 million shadow jobs, or roughly 1.7 million more than generated through the methodology used in chapter two.)

Shuster also defended the $9 billion reserved for special demonstration projects hand picked by individual members of Congress. "Who knows better what is most important in their district than the Members of Congress from that district?" he asked those who questioned the 1,400 earmarks. "I would respectfully suggest there is a bit of arrogance in those who say that somehow they know better what is important in their congressional districts than Members know. Indeed, I would suggest that if Members do not know what is really important to people in their congressional district, they are not going to be here very long." Shuster reserved special words for House colleagues who simultaneously attacked the projects even as they pushed for "multimillion dollar projects in their own congressional districts." "How I envy the pious," Shuster paraphrased James Michener's *The Hawaiians*, "They can be such hypocrites and never even know it."[39]

The last-minute negotiations surrounding the bill proved his point. The Senate, which had long protested the pork, weighed in with 360 projects worth $2.3 billion just hours before the Memorial Day recess would begin. "The Senate castigates projects," Shuster had predicted in March. "But when they come to conference at about 2 a.m. on the 21st day, they reach in their pocket and pull out a list."[40] The Senate did just that late on May 22, only hours before the final conference report was to come up for a vote. Packing in the new projects, the bill passed the Senate 88 to 5.

There is nothing new about transportation pork, of course. Congress has been taking home the projects for decades, usually through funding formulas that allow each member to claim a fair share of the credit for new highways and the jobs they create. What makes the past decade interesting perhaps is the growing use of earmarks to make the credit claiming easier. Both the number and amount of earmarks has been rising steadily, whether in transportation, higher education, veterans health care, or environmental protection. The number of transportation earmarks has gone up from just 10 projects and $362 million in 1982 to 152 projects and $1.4 billion in 1987, 538 projects and $6.2 billion in 1991, and 1,850 projects and $9.3 billion in 1998. Although higher education pork dipped briefly in the mid-1990s because of a determined campaign by California Democrat George Miller, it appears to be on its way back up, too.

No one talks about the shadow-casting effects of such legislation in explicit terms, of course, and no one would ever recommend that the highway construction jobs be nationalized. Even staunch critics of the federal downsizing such as Eleanor Holmes Norton (D-D.C.) can find ample reason to support transportation earmarks. "Mr. Speaker, this is not pork," Norton argued in support of the transportation package. "This is steak. If we want to continue to be a prime rib country, we better pass this bill quick."[41] But the shadow-casting effects exist nonetheless. Assuming that all $217 billion goes directly into grants to state and local government, TEA 21 will create almost six million shadow jobs with its six years of funding.

Debt Acknowledged?

If Congress had any hope that such shadow casting might make contractor and grantee employees more forgiving, or at least less distrusting, toward government or politics, there is no evidence of the effect. To the contrary, the limited available evidence suggests that Americans who work in the nongovernmental shadow under contracts or grants are just as distrusting as the rest of the country. According to the Pew Research Center's 1997 trust-in-government survey, 14 percent of Americans either worked for a nongovernmental employer that received government funds for its work or lived in a household with someone who did. Put that number together with the 28 percent of Pew respondents who either worked for federal, state, and local government or lived in a household with someone who did, and over four out of ten Americans have come to rely on the federal government for all or part of their wages. As table 3-4 shows, these beneficiaries were no more likely to trust government than were their nongovernmental peers.

To the contrary, compared to the Pew Research Center respondents who either worked for government or lived in a household with someone who did, those who worked for nongovernmental employers under contracts and grants were usually the most distrusting of all. They were significantly less likely than government employees and family members to trust the government in Washington to do what is right and were the most frustrated with the federal government overall. They also gave the federal government the worst overall rankings and had the least favorable opinion of elected federal officials. Not only were they consistently negative toward actual government performance, but they also were the most likely to say the poor performance was the government's fault. Asked who they trusted more, civil servants or politicians, they were the most likely of any group to give the nod to politi-

Table 3-4. *A Sampling of Opinion on Government among Americans Who Work for, under, or on behalf of Government, 1997*

Percentage of respondents who agree with statement

	Does respondent or member of household work for government?			
	No	Yes: at any level	Yes: self only at federal level	Yes: for private employer under contract/ grant
Trust the government in Washington to do what is right just about always or most of the time	37	40	44	32
Feeling about the federal government				
Basically content	29	32	37	31
Frustrated	56	57	52	59
Angry	13	9	9	9
Federal government is doing only fair or poor job	74	71	66	73
Government often does a better job than given credit for	32	37	33	31
Number of people employed by federal government has decreased	32	38	56	40
Favorable opinion of elected federal officials	55	61	64	54
Favorable opinion of federal departments and agencies	56	65	58	62
Favorable opinion of government workers[a]	65	80	. . .	70
Favorable opinion of public employees[a]	69	82	. . .	72
Favorable opinion of state and local government officials[a]	69	73	. . .	67
Trust politicians or civil service employees to do right thing				
Politicians	16	17	23	27
Civil service employees	65	70	62	71

(Table continues)

Table 3-4 *(continued)*

| | Does respondent or member of household work for government? | | | |
	No	Yes: at any level	Yes: self only at federal level	Yes: for private employer under contract/ grant
Federal government is bound to be inefficient no matter what	8	6	5	7
View that is closest to own				
The federal government today has too much power	34	29	29	34
The federal government is using about the right amount of power	30	37	33	33
The federal government should use its powers even more vigorously	34	32	37	32
Have a great or good deal of confidence in American people	62	67	74	58
Prefer government to private sector as an employer	19	33	46	19
Want son or daughter to go into politics as a life's work	27	27	13	24
Recommend that young people start their careers in politics or government	36	51	53	45
Think government is a good place to work	69	76	79	70

Source: The Pew Research Center for The People & The Press, secondary analysis of data released in *Deconstructing Distrust: How Americans View Government,* N = 1,210 for those who do not work for government; N = 546 for those who worked for government or whose family member worked for government; N = 88 for those who worked for the federal government; N = 259 for those who work for a nongovernment employer who receives funding from the government under a contract or grant

a. The question was asked of a split sample, rendering the federal employee subsample too small for meaningful interpretation.

cians. Finally, they were the least trusting toward the Congress, the source of so much of their support.

Notwithstanding their general distrust as citizens, federal employees were clearly more forgiving toward government than other respondents, which is to be expected. But even here, the Pew survey found that federal employees had plenty of bite toward their own employer. They were less trusting toward their civil service brethren than any other group in table 3-4, and they had surprisingly unfavorable opinions of federal departments and agencies. They were highly critical of government performance on all but ensuring safe food and medicines, and they were almost as negative about government inefficiency as other respondents. Nevertheless, federal employees were the most positive toward government as an employer, the most likely to recommend that young people start their careers in politics or government, and the most likely to believe that government is a good place to work. Government employees think as citizens when asked about trust in government, but they think as employees when asked about their jobs.

A Debt Repaid?

The shadow work force may not be particularly grateful for their federal support, at least as measured by trust in government, but contractors most certainly are. Looking back over the past decade, the top contractors have showered both lobbying attention and campaign contributions on Congress and the presidency. In the first half of 1997, for example, the top twenty-five federal contractors spent over $38 million on lobbying, with General Motors at $5.2 million in lobbying expenditures, United Technologies at $4.2 million, General Electric at $4.1 million, Northrop Grumman at $3.6 million, and Boeing at $2.9 million. Although it is impossible to know how much or little was spent lobbying Congress for specific products such as new fighter jets or new computer systems, the more general purpose of the lobbying was to create a generally favorable climate toward the individual corporations involved, which in turn might create a specifically favorable climate toward their products and services.

The top twenty-five contractors also provided significant amounts of campaign support to candidates for federal office. Although there is no evidence that such campaign financing purchases specific votes on legislation, there can be little doubt that the dollars helped remind incumbent members of Congress that contractors care about their reelection. As table 3-5 shows, the top twenty-five contractors contributed just over $10 million in

Table 3-5. *Contractor Campaign Contributions, 1992 and 1996*

Percent, unless otherwise specified

Measure	1992	1996
Total contributions from the top 25 contractors (dollars)	10,023,000	15,137,000
Political action committee and individual contributions to Democrats	53	35
Political action committee and individual contributions to Republicans	46	65
Political action committee and individual contributions to incumbents	86	86
Political action committee and individual contributions to House candidates	67	70
Political action committee and individual contributions to Senate candidates	31	27
Political action committee and individual contributions to presidential candidates	2	3
Total contributions from political action committees	80	55
Total contributions in soft money	13	38
Total contributions from individuals	7	7

Source: Analysis of databases maintained by the Center for Responsive Politics.

1992 and $15 million in 1996. AT&T led the group on campaign contributions at almost $4 million, followed by Lockheed Martin at $2.5 million, General Electric at $1.8 million, Northrop-Grumman at $1.5 million, and Boeing at $1.3 million.[42]

As the contribution figures show, contractors clearly favor incumbents. Congress may have changed majority parties in 1994, but incumbents got exactly 86 percent of top twenty-five contributions immediately before and after the congressional elections. The major difference between 1992 and 1996 is the rising tide of soft campaign contributions. Because soft money contributions are unregulated, contributions can rise well beyond the meager limits imposed on political action committees and individual contributions by the Federal Election Campaign Act. That means that contributors can make themselves even more visible. That the top contractors would drift toward more soft money is merely a reminder that campaign cash is a potent tool for thanking incumbents for what they may have done in the past and for creating a favorable climate in the future.

Party Incentives

Americans clearly believe the two political parties have very different positions on the structure of government. Republicans have long been given the benefit of the doubt regarding government management, for example. Americans not only believe Republicans would do a better job attacking fraud, waste, and abuse, while increasing bureaucratic efficiency, but they also believe that Republicans have a better understanding of just what might make government run more like a business.

Republicans have also historically enjoyed the public's confidence in their ability to manage the federal government well. In August 1995, for example, 49 percent of the public said Republicans would do a better job managing the government, compared to just 30 percent for the Democrats and to 13 percent who said neither party would do well. By August 1997 the gap had narrowed to just 6 percent—39 percent for the Republicans and 33 percent for the Democrats, with 16 percent choosing neither. The gap closed not because of reinventing government, for the Democrats gained only 3 percent over the two years, but because of increasing doubts about Republican competence in the wake of the back-to-back government shutdowns in late 1995.[43]

As for reforming the government, Americans divide almost equally in their rating of which party would do a better job in actually making government work better. In a March 1998 Pew Research Center survey, for example, 37 percent of respondents said the Republican Party would do a better job, 35 percent said the Democrats, 8 percent said both would do equally well, and 10 percent said neither would do well.[44]

Presidential elections rarely turn on debates about bureaucratic reform, of course. Looking back over the years, the size and structure of government have never come close to making the list of most important problems about which citizens care. Jobs, inflation, international crisis, war, scandal, schools, children, the elderly, health care, the environment, and a host of other issues are infinitely more interesting to most voters than government operations.

Nevertheless, campaigns do help explain why both parties might favor shadow government. In theory, Democrats should seek to advertise the benefits of activist government, while Republicans should keep the focus on inefficiency and the need for solid business sense. Given their support from organized labor, it would be surprising if Democrats talked much about the need for contracting out. And given their support from big and small business alike, it would be equally surprising if Republicans promised to create new departments and agencies, increase government pay, or improve life in the career civil service.

Until just recently, however, there has been almost no systematic evidence to support either hypothesis. Lacking solid data to the contrary, most public administration and management scholars have concluded that bureaucrat bashing is on the rise in both parties. "Countless politicians run for office (including the highest posts in the land) on platforms that blame society's problems on 'the bureaucrats' and their burdensome rules, lack of entrepreneurship, wasteful extravagance, social experimentation, intervention in business , and whatever else nettles." writes Charles Goodsell in *The Case for Bureaucracy.* "Candidates promise that when elected they will sternly deal with the bureaucratic enemy. When, after the election, neither the bureaucrats nor the problems disappear, voters conclude that the survival of the former has caused the perpetuation of the latter."[45]

Goodsell is quite right in emphasizing the political benefits of bureaucrat bashing. Incumbents and challengers have long seen the value in running against government. In reality, however, the actual rhetoric from the 1960, 1980, 1992, and 1996 presidential campaigns suggests a more nuanced message. Looking at the inventory of every campaign advertisement, speech, and debate in each campaign, all of which have been collected and coded by the University of Pennsylvania's Annenberg School for Communication, the conversation about government appears to have changed radically twice: first in 1980 and again in 1992. As table 3-6 shows, whereas Republicans owned the antigovernment issue in 1980, Democrats were able to shift the conversation to much safer ground by 1992, even to the point of making bureaucracy almost lovable again.[46]

The patterns revealed in the table will almost certainly deepen as more of the Annenberg data come on line. Carter talked at length about leaner, meaner government in 1976, for example, promising grand reorganizations and deep cutbacks, creating an easy target for Reagan's 1980 war on waste counterattack. For now, readers must be satisfied with the available data, which clearly illustrate the ways in which campaign promises can create pressures for shadow casting.

Toward that end, the 1960 campaign should be taken as a baseline against which to measure the 1980, 1992, and 1996 contests. The government simply was not a major focus of conversation. Together, Kennedy and Nixon

Table 3-6. *Presidential Campaign Rhetoric about Government, 1960, 1980, 1992, 1996*
Number of words

Word spoken about government	1960 Dem	1960 Rep	1980[a] Dem	1980[a] Rep	1992[a] Dem	1992[a] Rep	1996 Dem	1996 Rep	Total
Bureaucrat	0	3	0	2	2	23	0	15	45
Bureaucratic	0	2	2	9	9	10	16	0	48
Bureaucracy	6	0	1	6	54	33	16	37	153
Waste, fraud, or abuse	0	0	1	82	28	20	6	31	110
Size of government	0	2	0	4	0	0	28	6	40
Big government	4	0	1	2	17	27	11	21	83
Public employee/employment	0	0	2	1	1	0	0	0	4
Civil servant/service	1	0	1	1	1	0	0	0	4
Public servant/service	2	0	8	2	10	5	15	4	4
Total words spoken	13	7	16	109	122	118	92	114	533
Total campaign speeches, ads, and debates in which references could have occurred	173	57	179	88	106	145	161	111	1,020

Source: Annenberg Campaign Data Base.
a. Does not include third party candidates.

uttered the words listed in table 3-6 only twenty times in the 230 speeches, advertisements, and presidential debates recorded in the Annenberg archive.

Kennedy was the more active of the two candidates, using the word bureaucracy six times. He was hardly a bureaucracy lover, however. Two of his mentions came in a stump speech defending himself against traditional Republican attacks. "I do not believe in a super state. I see no magic to tax dollars which are sent to Washington and then returned [to the states]. I abhor the waste and incompetence of large-scale Federal bureaucracies in this administration, as well as in others," Kennedy told supporters in New York City on September 14, 1960. "But I do believe in a government which acts, which exercises its full powers and its full responsibilities. Government is an art and a previous obligation; and when it has a job to do, I believe it should do it."

Ironically, given his later efforts to politicize the bureaucracy, Nixon actually made the more spirited defense of federal bureaucrats, albeit in a broad attack on big government. "Now why am I so concerned about [local] control of education?" he asked an audience in Dallas on September 12, 1960. "It isn't that I have a great suspicion of Federal bureaucrats. They're very honest, very loyal, hundreds of thousands of them. I've worked with them; I'm one of them as a matter of fact. The point is this: the greatest guarantee of freedom is diversity of control, local control." By distinguishing between bureaucrats and their bureaucracy, Nixon laid the rhetorical basis for Clinton's 1992 rescue of activist government. Whatever the reason, Nixon felt obligated to defend the people of government, even as he excoriated their antiquated management systems. It was a pattern to be repeated in 1970 when he explained his decision to create a new Office of Management and Budget.[47]

By 1980 the campaign climate had clearly changed. Reagan went on the attack against the incumbent president, devoting an entire stump speech to his view of government as a bastion of fraud, waste, and abuse. He had started the campaign in September by promising billions in savings from a sustained effort to end "waste, extravagance, abuse and outright fraud" in federal agencies and programs, and ended it on November 3, 1980, with a broad appeal to Americans who "feel burdened, stifled, and sometimes even oppressed by government that has grown too large, too bureaucratic, too wasteful, too unresponsive, too uncaring about people and their problems."

In between he kept the Carter administration on the defensive. Speaking before a Columbia, South Carolina, crowd on October 10, 1980, Reagan returned again and again to the savings to be gained by controlling the waste inherent in bureaucracy. "Early in this campaign, I challenged this administration to acknowledge the enormity of the problem of waste and fraud in the federal government. I asked them to account for their three-and-a-half-year failure to cope with this unrelenting national scandal. The Carter administration has ignored that challenge." Ridiculing Carter for having promised to abolish and consolidate hundreds of departments and programs, Reagan focused on contractor fraud at the General Services Administration, which he characterized as a fight between a heroic administrator and an entrenched, corrupt bureaucracy. Although Reagan mostly talked about the failings of big bureaucracy, his two personalizations were tough. One came in a speech, the other in an advertisement promising a freeze on federal hiring and the elimination of "any program that serves the bureaucrats and not the needs of the people."

It is not at all clear why the Carter administration did not rise in its own defense. After all, it led the effort to reform the civil service and could have easily taken credit for the 1978 Ethics in Government and Inspector General Acts. It was most certainly not a lack of opportunity. Despite the Iranian hostage crisis, the Democratic presidential campaign generated twice as many speeches and advertisements as the Republican campaign did.

But even when the Carter campaign did rise in response to Reagan, the answer was tepid at best. Speaking at the annual convention of the Civil Service Employees Association (CSEA), a collection of government employee unions, he welcomed endorsement by the CSEA, "because I know that this country has the best and most productive public employees—federal, state, and local—of any nation on Earth. I've worked at every level of government for the past quarter-century. I know from personal experience the dedication that you bring to your careers, public service. Most people know that public employees keep our Nation safe, our roads in good condition, our schools open, our water and air clean, our work places healthy and safe, our elderly and our sick cared for, our laws enforced, and perform countless other necessary services day and night. And I'm glad to give thanks where it's due." Absent from that speech, or any other speech or advertisement for that matter, was an answer to the Reagan charges. Carter's only advertisement that mentioned bureaucracy was a classic biographical piece in which he complained about bureaucracy as a segue into a backyard conversation with a small group of ordinary Americans.

It was up to Bill Clinton to redefine the bureaucracy in 1992. It is not at all surprising that he would seek to neutralize fraud, waste, and abuse as an issue or to offer a new vision of lean and mean government. He had every incentive to reposition the party. What is perhaps more surprising is how easily he put the Bush campaign on the defensive. By early September Bush was forced to state his own position as the true candidate of small government. "I'm the one that stands for freedom and democracy," he told a September 15 rally in Marysville, Ohio, "freedom through strength, freedom from big government, freedom from the arrogance of the bureaucrat, and freedom from the long arm of the tax man. I stand for these things because they are the way we can build a safer and more secure America so that you can fulfill your dreams."

Unlike Reagan, who almost never personalized his attacks on bureaucracy, Bush featured the arrogant bureaucrat in speech after speech. Delivering a new stump speech before a group of private-sector employees earlier in September, Bush characterized the election as a choice between "a big government that thinks it knows best and a smaller government that believes you know better." Clinton was the candidate of bureaucrats, not the people. "Governor Clinton wants to give Government more power. And I want to give you, the American people, more power. Governor Clinton wants to make the bureaucrat's life easy, to provide one-size-fits-all service in schools and in day care. I want you to be able to choose your schools and choose your day care so that we make your lives easier." Alongside criticizing Clinton for waffling on the issues—"He's been spotted in more places than Elvis"—Bush also made every effort to tie Clinton to his Democratic predecessors, arguing in late September that "we've heard that song before. Jimmy Carter sang it. Walter Mondale sang it. Michael Dukakis sang it. They're going after the rich, but the middle class always gets up singing the blues. Big government gets the gold, and you get the shaft."

Clinton easily blunted the attacks by distinguishing between bureaucrats and bureaucracy. The only time Clinton used the word "bureaucrats" was when he promised to fire them. "He won't streamline the federal government and change the way it works," Clinton said of Bush. "Nor will he cut a hundred thousand bureaucrats and put a hundred thousand new police officers on the streets of American cities. But I will." Clinton focused instead on big bureaucracy, embracing the war on waste, while crafting an alternative vision of an activist government shorn of bureaucratic excess. His most important statement on the issue came in a September 25 stump speech delivered at the University of Connecticut. He started by acknowledging his party's history. "I know that the Democratic Party in Washington has been in the past too identified with tax-and-spend, big government, bureaucratic solutions. . . . But I have worked hard to be a different kind of

Democrat and to give the American people a different kind of Democratic Party.... My fellow Americans, contrary to the rhetoric of my opponent, the issue is not more or less government, the question is what kind of government. I want a government that works to spur growth, create jobs, increase incomes; a streamlined government that still plays a central role, because in every advanced country in the world, whether governed by conservatives or liberals, there is an aggressive role for a government working to promote private sector economic growth."

Bush had no answer. Much as he pounded away on the traditional fraud, waste, and abuse theme, his attack was clearly limited by his own incumbency. He could blame Congress for wasteful programs, which he did, ask for the line item veto as a way to eliminate pork barrel projects, which he also did, even promise to wring out the waste and excess in the health-care system, which he did. But he could not make the fraud, waste, and abuse label stick to the Democrats. Clinton had already admitted that the old Democrats were the party of fraud, waste, and abuse, clearly dampening the charge against New Democrats like him.

Remarkably, Dole could not make the fraud, waste, and abuse issue stick to Clinton four years later. It was most certainly not for a lack of trying, however. Dole mentioned government waste thirty-one times during the campaign, featuring waste in one of his most visible attack advertisements:

> ANNOUNCER: The truth. 484 spending proposals. Costing us $432 billion in bigger government. A massive health-care bureaucracy. Thousands of wasteful projects like $2.5 million for alpine slides in Puerto Rico. $76 million for programs like midnight basketball. The largest tax increase in history. Yet Clinton says....
> CLINTON: But I don't think that qualifies me as a closet liberal.
> ANNOUNCER: That's not what the facts say, Mr. Clinton. The real Bill Clinton? A real spend-and-tax liberal.

Dole also took on fraud, waste, and abuse on the stump, increasing the volume later in the campaign as he searched for some way to reduce Clinton's substantial lead. In Selma, California, for example, he promised to fund his tax cut by harnessing the three horsemen again: "There's enough waste in the government to give you the tax cut, enough waste, enough fraud, enough abuse, enough people flying around the world. Hazel O'Leary [Clinton's Energy Secretary] only lands for refueling. She's gone all the time. Why can't you take a vacation?"

Dole's attacks were easily deflected by the downsizing of government. Having promised a leaner government in 1992, Clinton never missed an opportunity to tell voters that he had delivered. The reference rarely varied from the following paragraph, which he first delivered in St. Louis on September 10.

> Our friends in the Republican Party often attack government, but I found they hadn't done much reforming in the last several years. So we did. The government is now smaller by about 250,000 than it was the day I took office. It will be down by about 270,000 by the end of this year. The last time it was this size was when John Kennedy was president. As a percentage of our workforce, your federal government is now the same size it was in 1933 when Franklin Roosevelt took the oath of office before the New Deal.

Much as Dole argued that Clinton had been "doing everything in his power to make sure the government stays big and gets bigger," Clinton had the numbers on his side. Much as Dole attacked the arrogant bureaucrats in Washington, Clinton answered with the numbers. "Yes, the government cannot solve all your problems with a big bureaucracy," he told a crowd in Albuquerque on October 13. "That government is gone. It was our administration—not our friends in the other party . . . that cut the size of the federal government to its lowest since John Kennedy was president."

On and on it went. The bad bureaucrats were gone with the downsizing, the bad bureaucracy was gone with the reinventing. What remained was closer to the people, more customer friendly, slimmer, tougher, faster, smoother, more flexible, and filled with dedicated public servants. Speaking to young people in Atlanta in late October, Clinton referred to "how bad big old federal government was, but it's our administration working with our allies in Congress [that] has cut the size of the federal government, the number of regulations, the number of government programs, and we have privatized more government operations than the last two Republican administrations did in 12 years combined. That's the truth." By embracing the war on waste in 1992, he was able to blunt Republican attacks on his own administration in 1996. Clinton had made bureaucracy lovable again by attacking it, disparaging it, and, ultimately, cutting it. It is impossible to know whether he would have been as successful in restoring government during poor economic times. But by delivering a government that most certainly looked smaller and delivered more, Clinton blunted the traditional antigovernment attack. Future Democratic candidates will likely follow his lead, even if that means conflict with their own supporters in the government employee unions.

The question is how future Republican candidates might recapture the issue. One option is to continue the war on waste campaign, only with better data and a more systematic focus. It would be a mistake, however, to blame the ineffectiveness of the issue simply on Dole. The war on waste issue did not work because the incumbent administration embraced it, as Vice President Gore will most certainly do if he gets a chance to run for the presidency in his own right. One suspects, therefore, that Republicans will up the ante. If Democrats can cut government back to the Roosevelt years, do not be surprised if Republicans promise to take it back to the Harding days. It would be relatively simple to cut government another 300,000 jobs without closing a single agency. Having gone to school on the shadow making under Reagan, Bush, and Clinton, the next Republican administration could easily push the lost jobs outward and downward. Democrats would be hard pressed to meet such a call without a backlash from organized labor.

Civil Service Incentives

There is one last player in the political economy of shadows: the civil servants who survive the downsizing. Although one can feel sympathy for the relatively small number of employees who lost their jobs through reductions in force, the managers who have lost their titles, and, most significantly, the civil servants who had to pick up the slack from the mostly random cuts, there is some evidence that the federal employees left behind after the downsizing are doing better than they could have expected. If not quite ready to endorse shadow making, they have at least some reason to keep quiet.

That civil servants have incentives to care about structure is obvious. As Moe argues, career officers have a variety of tools for insulating themselves against the vagaries of political uncertainty, not the least of which is the coming and going of political appointees: "They can promote further professionalization and more extensive reliance on civil service. They can formalize and judicialize their decision procedures. They can base decisions on technical expertise, operational experience, and precedent, thus making it 'objective' and agency-centered."[48] Comfortable as big numbers might be, Moe suggests that the civil service may actually be strengthened as its numbers fall. The fewer the managers, the greater the power of the managers who remain; the fewer the technical experts, the greater the power of those who control the expertise. Just as a contractor's bargaining leverage is increased when there are fewer bidders, which explains the flurry of defense mergers over the past ten years, a civil servant's bargaining strength is increased as more work is moved out of house, provided, of course, that civil servant can provide the needed expertise.

All Above Average

The limited available evidence confirms at least one part of the pattern: the civil servants who survived the Workforce Restructuring Act are both more satisfied and better paid. Consider two sources of data on the issue.

The first comes from the Merit Systems Protection Board, which has conducted five massive surveys of federal workers over the past fifteen years. The most recent survey involved a sample of 9,710 federal employees and revealed deep concerns regarding downsizing and reinventing.[49] Among supervisors, for example, nearly three out of five reported that there had been a noticeable reduction in the number of supervisor positions in their agencies, with parallel increases in both the number of subordinates and the workload among those who survived. Among all of the respondents, supervisors and nonsupervisors, nearly half said their jobs had changed since 1993, most of whom thought the change had been negative. Although four out of five said that the work performed by their unit both gave the public a worthwhile return on their taxes and could not be performed as effectively by a private sector company, only one-fifth agreed that the Gore reinventing effort had made a positive impact on improving customer service to the public, exactly half the number who disagreed.

Among respondents who worked in agencies that had made reinventing an important priority, the numbers were significantly higher. But even in such organizations, the number of respondents who said reinventing had made a positive impact in bringing change to government managed to creep up to only 35 percent. Overall, 75 percent said downsizing had not helped their agencies achieve their missions more effectively, while just over half said downsizing had seriously eroded the institutional memory or knowledge in their organization. Even when the Workforce Restructuring Act targets expire, the downsizing may still exert some force. Roughly 40 percent of the survey respondents said that worries about a future wave of reductions in force and budget cutbacks were reducing their productivity.

None of these responses is particularly shocking, given the intensity of the reinventing pressure. But perhaps what is more interesting, given the theory of public bureaucracy, is the surprisingly high numbers of respondents who nonetheless declared themselves satisfied with both their jobs and their pay. Despite all the negativity described above, 70 percent said they were satisfied with their jobs, a number that remained virtually unchanged from the 1989 and 1992 surveys. And despite all the fears of the future, exactly half were satisfied with their pay, a number that had climbed from 28 percent in 1989 and 42 percent in 1992. Even more important for the long-term health of the career service, the gap between the perceived quality of employees who left and those who took their place was closing rapidly. In 1989, for example, 56 percent of supervisors rated the quality of the leavers as average or above average, while only 36 percent rated the quality of new hires the same. By 1996 the gap between leavers and new hires had closed to just 8 percent, 53 percent to 45 percent.

Before confirming Moe's notion that smaller numbers of civil servants would have greater power and, therefore, higher satisfaction, it is important to note the methodological difficulties in drawing a link between downsizing and happiness. It is entirely possible that the less-satisfied employees simply left government. After all, the downsizing campaign was driven mostly by attrition and voluntary separation. In theory, those who left would be the ones most dissatisfied with government. Their departure would leave the more satisfied behind. Moreover, there is every indication that satisfaction would be lower at the bottom of organizations, where pay is lower and stress may be greater. Sawing off the bottom, as the downsizing most certainly did, would inevitably leave more satisfied employees behind. It would also leave government with more highly paid employees.

Nevertheless, there is at least some evidence of a link between downsizing and happiness in the annual performance appraisal process. As table 3-7 shows, the federal performance ratings have made startling gains since 1990, the last year for which data is easily accessible from the Office of Personnel Data files. The trends are up across the board, whether for the most senior managers and supervisors or for blue-collar employees. The supervisors who do the ratings have made their findings clear: all federal employees are now above average. Indeed, federal employees are not only well above average, they are close to becoming outstanding.

The higher the position, the better the ratings. At the very top of the General Schedule in 1996, 56 percent of the 130,000 managers and supervisors won outstanding grades, an increase of 25 points in just seven years. At the next highest category, nearly half of the 135,000 General Schedule 13-15 nonmanagers and nonsupervisors wound up in the outstanding category, an increase of 21 points over the period. Although the trend was the same

Table 3-7. *Government Above-Average Performance Ratings, 1990–96*

	Percent rated fully successful/exceeds fully successful/outstanding			
Fiscal year	*General Schedule 13–15 managers and supervisors*	*General Schedule 13–15 nonmanagers and nonsupervisors*	*General Schedule 1–12*	*Federal wage system employees*
1990	20 / 50 / 31	26 / 45 / 28	36 / 39 / 25	39 / 41 / 20
1991	18 / 47 / 35	23 / 45 / 32	31 / 41 / 27	34 / 44 / 22
1992	17 / 46 / 37	23 / 45 / 32	30 / 41 / 29	31 / 45 / 25
1993	14 / 45 / 41	21 / 46 / 33	27 / 42 / 31	26 / 45 / 29
1994	12 / 42 / 46	18 / 40 / 42	24 / 42 / 34	24 / 45 / 31
1995	10 / 38 / 52	15 / 39 / 46	23 / 40 / 37	22 / 42 / 36
1996	11 / 33 / 56	16 / 35 / 49	22 / 38 / 39	21 / 40 / 39

Source: Office of Personnel Management, *The Fact Book*, 1997 ed.

further down the hierarchy, the 1.1 million General Schedule 1-12 and 240,000 Federal Wage System employees (blue collar) both ended up at the same place, 39 percent rated outstanding, with wage system employees moving up a bit faster over the seven years. Interestingly, the gap between senior managers and frontline employees increased during the period, rising from 11 percentage points in the outstanding category in 1990 to 17 points in 1996. Frontline employees just could not keep up with their higher level peers.

The ratings obviously measure more than actual performance, if they measure performance at all. Indeed, the performance ratings may be the perfect barometer of downsizing stress. Under the rules governing the reductions in force that took place early in the Clinton administration, civil servants received seniority credits based on their annual performance rates. Because seniority gives employees bumping rights when a reduction in force takes place, the easiest way for a manager to protect his or her staff is to overrate prized employees. Thus much as one can criticize random downsizing for its lack of precision, one can also criticize targeted downsizing for its unintended effects on the performance appraisal system. Although the vast majority of federal employees are doing good work, even the most tireless booster would have trouble defending a five-point rating system in which the average score is already above the fourth mark and rising fast. If the current trend holds, and OPM remains either unwilling or unable to stem the inflation, all federal employees will be outstanding in the year 2020.

Ultimately, it would be impossible to interpret either the Merit System Protection Board survey or the performance ratings as proof positive that civil servants somehow favor shadow casting, if only because the ratings increase began well before candidate Clinton promised a cut in federal personnel. Moreover, those who got the higher ratings and pay most certainly paid a price. Nevertheless, the data do suggest that downsizing and budget cuts do provide some rewards to ease the pain. Civil servants may rightly worry about the effect of downsizing on the institutional memory and knowledge base of government, but they also reap at least some benefits as a result. The incentives most certainly condition what might be a more intensely negative reaction.

Union Incentives

In theory, no group should be more self-interested in opposing the shadow of government than federal employee unions. After all, each job that leaves the federal government for a contractor, grantee, or state and local entity is a job lost from potential membership.

Interestingly, however, the federal employee unions have been historically less actively opposed to the shadow of government than self-interest might predict. But for occasional exceptions such as the American Postal Workers Union spring 1998 "Save Our Service" campaign against further contracting out of mail sorting, the federal unions have generally accepted the downsizing pressure.[50] Indeed, the House legislative report on the Workforce Restructuring Act even went so far as to describe union support for downsizing as "widespread."[51]

That support came from two sources. First, the federal unions clearly believed that most of the proposed cuts involved middle-level managers, an assumption that proved false, as the next chapter will show. Nevertheless, as John Sturdivant of the National Association of Government Employees explained in November 1993, as the Workforce Restructuring Act moved forward, "The understanding is this 252,000 reduction is going to be mostly managers because those are the folks that would be reduced under the National Performance Review. . . ." Moreover, as Sturdivant continued, "as employees we have two choices: either to sit there and watch it happen and have no say about it and experience detrimental impact on the employees that we represent . . . or come to the table and have some say about it in a way that our knowledge and our experience ultimately will result [in improvements]—because we are the ones who will be asked to do more work with less people."[52]

Second and more important, union support for downsizing was clearly linked to establishment of a new National Partnership Council that gave the unions a greater opportunity to shape federal work force policy. Although Sturdivant could not recall whether the quid pro quo was ever explicitly discussed, he did recall two face-to-face meetings with the vice president and a tough conversation about the need to protect union workers from the cuts. "We told them that up front, that we want to change the way we do business; we want to be part of the solution, not part of the problem, but we certainly are not going to change the way you do business if it means the people that we represent are going to be out on the streets."[53]

It is not clear, however, that the federal unions could have stopped the downsizing had they wanted to. They had the first Democratic president in twelve years, ample congressional support for downsizing, and enormous pressure to join the reinventing campaign. They also had at least some promise of protection and a new forum for influencing the course of future reform.

The federal unions did not give away their rights to oppose occasional efforts to expand privatization and contracting out—rights that they most certainly exercised in weakening a 1998 effort to force departments and agencies to provide a list of activities that are not inherently governmental functions. They may be able to stop further erosion of the full-time-equivalent federal work force, but they will never reverse the trend. With or without their cooperation, the federal work force is simply not going to grow, not with the promises made for leaner government. Democrats may have made bureaucracy lovable again perhaps, but they have done so at an extraordinary long-term cost. Short of some cataclysmic event—a war or great natural disaster—federal employment will stay down. The shadow of government will surely vary over time as budgets and missions shorten and contracts, grants, and mandates lengthen. But that it will exist should not be in doubt. The question is no longer whether the shadow will exist in the future, but what is happening now that the public service no longer begins and ends inside government.

Conclusion

It is one thing for Congress and the president, Democrats and Republicans, even civil servants to prefer an illusion of smallness, and quite another to make the illusion real. After all, few members of Congress understand the mechanics of public personnel, and fewer still have the patience for legislative hearings and bill drafting. As Representative Patricia Schroeder (D-Colo.) once complained to her Civil Service Committee colleagues, "the civil service is a very difficult concept for most people to know about, and once you get beyond this committee, if you did a test on the House floor about the difference between RIFs and freezes and buyouts and everything, their eyes glaze over, and they stare at you like a deer staring in the headlights."[54]

The question for the next chapter, therefore, is how Congresses and presidents were able to create the illusion of smallness described earlier in this book. Simply asked, what are the tools of smallness and how have they shaped the true size of government? The answers can be found 165 miles to the south of David Pryor's home town of Ouachita, Arkansas, in another small town named Cascilla, Mississippi, where future United States Representative Jamie L. Whitten was born in 1910. If Pryor was unrelenting in his effort to measure the true size of government, Whitten was equally dedicated to making sure the federal civil service never got big. Given a mostly free hand by colleagues who left the specialization to him, and using head count ceilings and freezes to accomplish his goal, Whitten not only assured that Pryor would never get the answer he so desired, but that the federal government would be condemned to an often random process for deciding which jobs would stay in house and which would join the shadow.

CHAPTER FOUR

The Tools for
Staying Small

THE ILLUSION of smallness would have occurred with or without Representative Jamie L. Whitten, Democrat of Mississippi. Congress had already pressed early head count constraints. But very different tools would have been used for keeping government small had Whitten stayed in Cascilla instead of running for Congress in 1940.

Although Whitten came to fame for many reasons during his record-setting fifty-three years in the House, it was his so-called Whitten Amendment of 1951 that did more than any other single act to create the head count pressure that continues to exist today. Simply described, the amendment placed a ceiling on total federal civilian employment, while freezing the creation of new permanent positions. As he later explained, "I had no ax to grind, and have none now, except to do what I can for orderly government. Sometimes I think politically it would be much wiser to get a staff and keep count of Federal employees and release it to the press complaining about the total number now and then. Had I followed that course, I might have gotten an award of merit. . . ."[1]

Whitten chose a more direct approach later in 1951, however. His brief amendment to the 1951 Supplemental Appropriation Act merely asked the Civil Service Commission to make full use of its authority to make temporary appointments "in order to prevent increases in the number of permanent personnel." It was mostly an exhortation that would have had virtually no effect but for a freeze on new appointments that was contained in the second clause: "all reinstatements, transfers or promotions to positions in the Federal civil service shall be temporary." Having only been in Congress for nine years, he had already learned that exhortation without sanction would have no effect. Even with the freeze, the first Whitten Amendment would not have mattered but for two other events.

The first occurred six months later. With the Korean War in full bloom, President Harry Truman interpreted the Whitten Amendment in the strictest terms, issuing Executive Order 10180, which ordered that "all appointments in the executive branch of the Government shall be made on a non-permanent basis except those of Presidential appointees and postmasters in all classes of post offices."[2] The freeze was to last through the state of emergency surrounding the Korean conflict, which, as it turned out, lasted until Congress ended the emergency in 1976.

The second event occurred six months later still. Notwithstanding Truman's order, Whitten attached a stronger and longer version of his amendment to the Third Supplemental Appropriation Act of 1952. As before, the federal government would be required to make all new appointments on a temporary or indefinite basis. This time, however, there would be a ceiling on total permanent employment equal to the total number existing on September 1, 1950, and no promotions for any civil servant who had not served for at least one year in the next lower grade. At least until the Korean War emergency was over, every department and agency would have to conduct annual reviews of all positions to assure that none were overgraded.

The amendment had an immediate effect. Between June 1950 and June 1953 the number of permanent civil servants fell from 1.5 million to 1.15 million, while the number of temporary employees soared to nearly 1 million. Promotions were frozen, recruitment of scientists and engineers suffered, and agencies began pushing for repeal. Whitten's strongest critics were not outside Congress, however, nor on his own committee. They were on the Senate Committee on Post Office and Civil Service, which had never been consulted about the amendment. In March 1953 the Committee's Subcommittee on Federal Manpower Policies issued a scathing report, concluding in what were unusually harsh terms toward a colleague, that the amendment was "ill-advised" and poorly drafted: "The subcommittee believes that detailed legislation spelling out personnel practices such as the Whitten amendment hamstrings good administration. This type of detailed legislation prevents the executive departments' administrators from exercising sufficient latitude in carrying out the will of Congress." After noting that "the Whitten amendment has overrestricted personnel administration," the subcommittee urged that the amendment be repealed.[3] It would not get its wish for a quarter of a century. By then, every last member of the manpower subcommittee had retired.

Whitten was just hitting stride by 1976. It would be three years before he would be named chairman of the full Appropriations Committee and fifteen before he would surpass Carl Vinson's record as the longest serving member of Congress. That his amendment stood for so long has less to do with Whitten's physical endurance than with his iron grip on the appropriations process. Notwithstanding his concerns about the growth of government, he was the master of pork barrel legislation. The father of the Tennessee-Tombigbee waterway and hundreds of smaller pork barrel projects on behalf of his district, Whitten kept his amendment alive against increasingly vitriolic attack, particularly from postal service advocates, by time and again invoking his folksy attack on big government. Although he later protested that his amendment was not a one-man show, his amendment would have been repealed years, even decades earlier had he not survived as what many called the "permanent secretary of agriculture," doling out help to allies and denying aid to adversaries.

Even Whitten could not have held his ceiling down, however, unless a succession of Congresses and presidents had agreed that head counts should count. Despite numerous efforts to thaw the Whitten freeze and lift its ceiling, members rarely put themselves on the record in favor of big government. They may have wanted more flexibility for departments, as the House Subcommittee on Federal Manpower Policy urged in 1954, but they never questioned the need to control the size of the federal work force. Nor did they worry that contractors might still produce the goods. Congress and the president established the Atomic Energy Commission in 1946, knowing that it would rely on private contractors for much of the work in harnessing the atom, and created the National Aeronautics and Space Administration in 1958 knowing full well that the agency would become a "surge tank" filled with contractors. Better the jobs be in the private sector than in a bloated federal bureaucracy.

By the 1950s, as Donald Kettl notes, government was buying everything from nuclear research to laundry services. Worries over an expanding federal work force, coupled with Whitten's head count pressures, led the Eisenhower administration to order departments and agencies to purchase as much as possible from the private sector, forbidding the federal government from starting or conducting "any commercial activity to provide a service or product for its own use if such product or service can be procured from private enterprise through ordinary business channels."[4] That order led in turn to a 1967 budget circular, A-76, establishing a review process for balancing government and private production of federal goods. Frustrations with ambiguities in the original circular led to top-to-bottom revision in 1983, as the Reagan administration embraced privatization as one of several weapons in its war on waste.

What Congress and the president could not know in the 1950s is that the head count pressure would work its own will in driving federal jobs outward and downward over time. Having topped out at 3.4 million at the end of World War II, federal civilian employment (excluding postal workers) fell to 1.4 million by 1950, rose again to 2.1 million during the Korean conflict, and fell to 1.8 million by 1960. But for a few hundred thousand employees here and there, the head count constraints worked. Meanwhile, even as they cut, capped, and constrained the federal work force, Congresses and presidents added one new program on top of another, forcing agencies to choose between nonimplementation and a shadow work force. Even had Whitten known that his 1950 amendment would eventually spark the creation of a shadow work force of 8 million contract and grant workers, he likely would not have objected. Nor would his colleagues.

Before turning to the history of how head counts came to count, it is important to note that not all the shadow creating was accidental. As noted above, there is considerable value in the surge-tank model of federal production, not the least of which is the ability to move quickly on highly specialized projects. It makes no sense, for example, to address the federal government's Y2K (year 2000) computer problem by training a whole new generation of specialists in an antiquated computer language, when agencies can easily purchase the COBOL expertise from retired IBM employees on short-term contracts. What goes up can come down more quickly if federal civil servants are not delivering the goods.

But even when the surge-tank makes logical sense, as in the creation of agencies such as NASA, head counts are never far from consideration. As we shall see, NASA turned to a surge-tank in part because it could not get the personnel slots needed to build a new agency with more traditional federal civil servants. In 1962, the year after President John F. Kennedy committed the nation to a lunar landing, NASA's total work force consisted of 3,500 contractor employees and 23,000 civil servants; two years later, with the Apollo program in full swing, it had grown to 10,000 service contractors, performing basic administrative tasks; 69,000 contractor scientists and engineers doing basic research and development, and 32,000 civil servants.

These are not estimates, but hard head counts that NASA kept as a way to track the thousands of employees who showed up for work each morning at its facilities. No one knows how many more contractors worked in NASA's shadow work force, building rockets and space vehicles under what were then 1,700 separate contracts.[5]

Sometimes it was impossible to tell who worked for whom. Beset by head count pressure, NASA contracted with AT&T to create a subsidiary, called Bellcomm, as an umbrella engineering directorate. "Bellcomm manufactured nothing," writes NASA historian Arnold Levine. Rather, it coordinated all engineering activities, from preparing specifications for the NASA's Apollo program office to evaluating manned spaceflight experiments and defining the scientific objectives for lunar missions. Although NASA made all the familiar arguments about the need for a private contractor, an internal memorandum suggested otherwise. "We originally planned to carry this effort out primarily within NASA as part of the Apollo Office," Associate Administrator Robert Seamans later wrote. "When we had difficulty recruiting the caliber of people we wanted and obtaining sufficient manpower slots from the Office of Management and Budget (sic), we went to AT&T and asked them to set up a dedicated organization, which became Bellcomm."[6]

When the NASA budget collapsed after the moon landing, so did contractor employment, a perfect case study in the value of the surge tank philosophy. In the year before the first moon landing, the number of contractor scientists and engineers fell to 51,000, while NASA's own work force dropped by less than 800. Bellcomm went out of business in 1972, and with it, much of the institutional memory associated with the lunar landing.

NASA's downsizing confirmed a central rule of federal shadow making: almost every effort to control the size of government has been designed to make sure that no federal employees get hurt. When government downsizes, it usually does so through attrition and buyouts, not through reductions in force. Employees who get their jobs first are almost always protected.

A History of Head Counts

It is not particularly difficult to constrain federal employment once the decision to do so has been made. Over the decades, Congress and the president have invented three simple approaches to the task: ceilings on total employment, freezes on hiring, and occasional downsizings in total employment. Each will be considered below.

Ceilings

Ceilings have been the most frequently used tool for holding government employment constant since size became an issue after World War II. A ceiling is nothing more than a fixed total for setting maximum federal employment. A ceiling can be built cathedral style over the entire government or applied as a lean-to over specific agencies. Government-wide ceilings give the president the greatest flexibility in shifting job slots from one agency to another, while agency-specific ceilings give Congress the greatest control in actually determining the shape of a given department such as Defense. Ceilings are easily enforced through the budget process. The Office of Management and Budget (OMB) simply allocates a head count to each agency that must be met at the beginning of a fiscal year.

Despite this ease of administration, ceilings have prompted intense opposition from personnel experts and the General Accounting Office (GAO). Anecdotal evidence suggests that ceilings rarely produce greater efficiency on their own. To the contrary, they can generate a number of games for evading the totals, not the least of which is the kind of shadow casting discussed in this book. They can also weaken performance. Writing in the wake of Jimmy Carter's 1977 ceiling, GAO offered the following inventory of effects: services to the public and other agencies are reduced, essential work is deferred or canceled and work backlogs are increased, imbalances between clerical and professional staff and shortages in certain skills occur, and managers become more concerned with the number of persons actually employed on a particular day than with getting essential work accomplished through the most effective, efficient, and economical use of people.

Presaging the language of future Pryor letters, GAO also noted that agencies can also move work downward and outward, thereby obscuring "the reality that the Government incurs the cost of all manpower resources devoted to Federal programs even though many of the people are not on the Federal payroll." GAO minced few words in its conclusion: "Although employment ceilings may be a tool to assure that concerns about the total number of Federal employees are met, ceilings are at best an inferior substitute for effective management. Management at all levels needs to aggressively seek ways to improve productivity."[7]

It was hardly the first time GAO had complained about the substitution of ceilings for hard choices about where to add and subtract head count. Reading back through the archives of reports, the criticism comes up again and again, as GAO continues to tilt against the head count mentality. The agency was not without its occasional victories, however. In 1982 the federal government switched from a simple count of all permanent employees, whether full- or part-time, to a full-time-equivalent (FTE) system that established ceilings on the basis of the number of work years required to achieve an agency's overall mission. In theory, the FTE system would require agencies to allocate head counts more thoughtfully. As GAO argued, the FTE approach "has the potential to improve Federal agencies' work force planning if the work-year ceiling levels are established on the basis of agencies' workload rather than arbitrary levels which the administration considers politically acceptable."[8] As if to confirm its Don Quixote reputation, GAO also recommended a tracking system that would provide a full accounting of all employees, public or private, needed to make government work.

Fifteen years and ten reports later, GAO reiterated its recommendation in assessing the buyouts used in implementing the Federal Workforce Restructuring Act. After first noting that the provisions of the act designed to guard against a shift of jobs to service contractors were unclear, GAO argued that the unintended consequences of the downsizing "could have been mitigated had agencies done adequate strategic and workforce planning. Such planning would have helped agencies to clearly define the agency's mission and identify the workforce mix needed to successfully accomplish that mission."[9]

Freezes

Despite their disadvantages, ceilings offer considerable flexibility when compared to freezes. A freeze is simply a complete ban on hiring. Because the federal government is constantly losing employees through attrition, freezes can have an immediate effect on total employment. The Whitten Amendment contained just such a prohibition on hiring any new permanent employees, but it did not reduce government employment. As noted earlier, the freeze was only on permanent employees, leaving temporary employment the only option.

Symbolically, freezes offer much greater political benefit over ceilings. They allow Congress or the president to claim complete and total victory over the hegemonic tendencies of big government. However, past research by GAO suggests that they have negligible effect on long-term employment. Because freezes (and government shutdowns) are generally applied government-wide rather than on specific agencies, and because they tend to take their toll on the front lines, where the turnover rates are highest, freezes are almost always of short duration. Notwithstanding the willingness of House Republicans to take the heat, if only for a moment, in the government shutdowns of late 1995, most Congresses and presidents would rather not face the public outcry as key jobs go unfilled.

As a result, it is not clear that freezes actually work in either saving money or reducing employment. According to GAO's assessments, the four hiring freezes in the Carter and early Reagan administrations provided an "illusion" of control, but no lasting effect. "Because they ignored individual agencies' missions, workload, and staffing requirements, these freezes disrupted agency operations, and in some cases, increased costs to the Government. . . . Publicity surrounding the hiring freezes has helped create an impression that they substantially reduce the size and cost of Government. However, the recent Government-wide hiring freezes have been ineffective."[10] Some agencies compensated for the freeze by hiring temporary employees who were then converted to permanent status once the freeze was over; others compensated by increasing overtime and using service contractors; still others simply ignored the freeze, knowing that OMB had no quick-time capacity to monitor compliance.

Part of the problem with this freezer burn, so to speak, is that the federal government's work force planning systems were and still are woefully inadequate. OMB's currency is dollars, not positions, yet it has always had the primary responsibility for overseeing ceilings and freezes. And while the Office of Personnel Management (OPM) deals in head counts, it does not have the budgetary leverage to enforce the ceilings and freezes. OMB has always played the enforcer, and OPM almost always has played the friend.

Because OMB has no capacity and little interest in monitoring head counts, and because freezes are often short-lived, agency compliance is minimal to begin with and is almost impossible to monitor, given the lack of any oversight capacity. Despite its primary role in the four Carter and Reagan freezes, OMB never bothered to develop a methodology that might show whether the freezes did, in fact, save the money claimed. In claiming an $11 million savings from the 1981 Reagan freeze, for example, OMB did not account for the $222 million in lost revenue caused by the freeze in Internal Revenue Service hiring, which sharply reduced audit and tax collection activity. Moreover, OMB did not balance the savings in full-time permanent positions against the increases in temporary, part-time, and intermittent positions. In the 1977 Carter freeze, for example, full-time-permanent employment fell by nearly 10,000 jobs, but employment rose by over 67,000 in temporary, part-time, intermittent slots.

Downsizing

However they are structured, ceilings and freezes are relatively passive instruments for reshaping government. They exert downward pressure through accident. In theory, downsizing should be a much more deliberate act. Departments and agencies would determine the appropriate number of employees for each agency mission, then set targets for reductions. Painful though the results might be for at-risk employees, Congress and the president would authorize an array of downsizing devices designed to drive employees out in specific positions and would reallocate the savings to "core competencies," as some experts describe the central personnel needs of agencies. In reality, of course, downsizing is hardly any more deliberate than other government reshaping efforts. Looking back over the past fifty years, downsizing has been an essentially random act that has mostly relied on attrition to achieve its goals.

Downsizing through attrition is easily the least painful approach for organizations. No one but the exiting employee has to make a decision about who stays and goes. Organizations can easily convince themselves that attrition is also the fairest way to spread the downsizing pain. If the job is not good enough to hold an employee, perhaps it is not important enough to defend. Unfortunately, vacancies do not occur evenly. Because quit rates are much higher at the bottom of most organizations than at the top, the decision to use attrition-based downsizing is essentially a decision to attack the front lines.

Private firms have hardly been particularly focused either. Facing downsizing pressures, private firms use the same tactics for reducing head count that the federal government uses. According to a recent survey of 531 firms that have been through recent downsizings, 91 percent used employee attrition, 72 percent used involuntary separation, 44 percent used early retirement incentives, and 43 percent used voluntary separations. As the numbers suggest, few firms use one device alone.[11]

What may make the federal government different from private firms is its unwillingness to track the realities. No one knows who's coming or going. The federal head count may look relatively stable on the surface, rarely moving more than a few thousand from year to year, but underneath, it is constantly changing. In fiscal year 1997 alone, the federal government hired over 280,000 employees and separated more than 330,000. Of those separations, roughly two-third involved retirements and one-third were quits.[12]

There is more than enough attrition, therefore, to fashion a more deliberative downsizing plan. Yet most of the movement in and out of government is random. During the early 1980s, for example, the Department of Labor used attrition to cut its work force by 6,000 positions, even as it hired 8,000 new employees. It was a lost opportunity, however. According to the National Academy of Public Administration, "neither the hiring activity nor the attrition activity was monitored or managed effectively, resulting in an organization that was older, less diverse, with a higher supervisory ratio to employees supervised, and with skill imbalances, professionals doing clerical work, and significant unmet training needs."[13]

The explanation is hardly surprising. Departments and agencies would have to define their core competencies. Imagine the difficulties involved. Someone would have to establish clear mission priorities for agencies, which in turn would have to make clear connections between those priorities and organizational capacity. Someone would have to sort through the responsibilities to determine which ones are inherently governmental and which could be contracted, granted, or mandated outward. Someone would also have to assess the relative skills needed to cover the core competencies. Someone would need to move those core competencies from one unit to another as priorities rise and fall. And someone would have to forecast future needs in time to both recruit new capacity and sever the old. Those someones simply do not exist, nor does the data to track the ebb and flow of capacity across units and time.

This lack of attention to detail raises particular concerns about the other tactics used in federal downsizing: buyouts and reductions in force. These two tactics are diametrically opposed in important ways. Buyouts are entirely voluntary and tend to attract higher-paid employees into leaving, while reductions in force are coercive and tend to push lower-paid employees out. As a result, buyouts tend to produce more dollar savings. According to GAO's analysis of the voluntary separation incentive payments used early in the Workforce Restructuring Act downsizing, federal employees who accepted the buyouts as a step into early or already-planned retirement averaged $48,000 a year in annual salary, while those who took the buyout as part of a simple resignation averaged $35,000. In contrast, employees who left government under reductions in force averaged just under $30,000. The difference involves "bumping and retreating," a practice in which more senior employees use their seniority to displace more junior employees. Although buyouts cost money and reductions in force do not, GAO estimates that buyouts can generate as much as $60,000 per position more than reductions in force over a five-year period.[14] (Such shortsightedness is hardly exclusive to government, of course. Private sector downsizings tend to follow the same pattern.)

Notwithstanding the potential savings, Congress did not enact its first buyout bill until 1993. Congress simply could not bear to pay federal employees to leave. Once Congress decided to act, however, it placed few limits on the buyouts. As a result, the Workforce Restructuring Act buyouts worked their will, luring approximately 175,000 federal employees to leave over the first five years of the downsizing, while allowing agencies to meet their downsizing targets well ahead of the year-by-year schedule set by the act. The only problem is that no one knows whether the employees who took the buyouts would have retired within five years anyway. Nor does anyone know how many of the 175,000 employees who left were immediately replaced with new employees, but the best guess is that the buyouts may have produced only 60,000 real departures.

More important, there is little evidence that the buyouts separated the "right" employees, particularly if right means the so-called "control" employees that the Gore reinventors targeted for a 50 percent cut. "The federal government spends an estimated $35 billion annually for salaries, benefits, and the administrative costs of its management control functions," the Gore streamlining task force explained in 1993. "Roughly, one in three federal employees is involved. The job of many of these people is to create and enforce rules. Without dramatically reducing the influence of these people on line managers and workers, reinvention and culture change cannot succeed. As a result, streamlining headquarters and regional offices where most of these control functions are located is essential, and additionally will save money without cutting services."[15]

The problem was that the reinventors had no way of clearly identifying the targets. The best they could do was focus the downsizing on department and agency headquarters and hope that control jobs would be caught in the collateral damage. At least during the first two years, however, the downsizing was indiscriminate. As table 4-1 shows, the ratio of control to noncontrol personnel remained mostly unchanged.[16]

It is not clear that the Gore reinventors would have targeted their cuts even if they had the needed tracking system, however. Targeting would have meant inflicting real pain on real people, something even the most diehard reinventor may find difficult to do. "An aggressive attack on the management control structure must not become an attack on the civil servants employed in these structures," the streamlining task force cautioned.

> They have been doing the jobs they were asked to do. They deserve an opportunity to redirect their careers, to be retrained and perhaps relocated, and to directly provide services rather than controlling the people who do.

Table 4-1. *Downsizing in Control and Noncontrol Positions, 1992 and 1995*
Percent

Management control position	Fiscal year 1992 work force	Fiscal year 1995 work force[a]
Defense agencies		
Personnel	1.5	1.6
Budget	1.2	1.3
Accounting and auditing	2.4	2.6
Acquisition	4.9	4.9
Headquarters staff	6.6	7.4
Supervisors	12.7	11.9
Non-Defense agencies		
Personnel	1.7	1.6
Budget	0.4	0.4
Accounting and auditing	2.4	2.5
Acquisition	2.0	2.0
Headquarters staff	14.6	14.2
Supervisors	12.5	11.6

Source: General Accounting Office, *Federal Downsizing: Better Workforce and Strategic Planning Could Have Made Buyouts More Effective* (August, 1996).
a. Data are from the first half of fiscal year 1995 only.

If an employee whose job is eliminated cannot retire through an early retirement program, and does not elect to take a cash incentive to leave government service, then every effort will be made to find another job offer, either within the government or in the private sector.[17]

No work force planning system meant no targeting, of course. Despite all the rhetoric to the contrary, the downsizing produced an entirely unexpected effect at Defense. Control positions actually increased as a proportion of total department employment during the downsizing, confirming a longstanding organizational hypothesis on the asymmetries of downsizing.

According to the theory, control personnel can be expected to increase during downsizing, both because more control is needed to manage the transitions and because control personnel are, well, good at controlling their own destiny. "The buyout authority gave agencies a powerful tool to manage their downsizing by directing personnel cuts where they were needed most," GAO concluded. "However, it appears that many agencies used buyouts to meet workforce reduction goals without restructuring their agencies' workforces."[18] Ever was it thus in GAO's eyes. Better work force planning could have produced a much better result. If only someone had noticed.

Some would argue that reductions in force (RIFs) gave the government downsizers an even more powerful tool for reshaping the hierarchy. After all, RIFs are compulsory and cannot be avoided. That is why involuntary separation is a tactic in nearly three-quarters of all private sector downsizings. What makes government different is that RIFs interact with civil service rules to create a toxic poison for morale. As already noted, such reductions can create extraordinary disruption, as employees spend countless hours trying to figure out the bumping routine for their departments. According to the National Academy of Public Administration, the RIF system has never changed with the times. "It was established at a time when seniority was a key factor in many [human resource management] systems. Retention, removal, and related RIF decisions are based on seniority, employment status, veterans preference, and past performance. As a result, RIF decisions are historically-based rather than based on the ability of employees to meet an agency's current and future needs."[19]

Moreover, it is nearly impossible to use RIFs to target poor performers or weak units. The bumping and retreating rights are simply too powerful. Although several federal agencies did use RIFs to meet the Workforce Restructuring Act targets, the total numbers were painfully small compared to the voluntary and attrition-based separations. In all, only 7,500 federal employees were RIFed in the 1994 to1995 period, of which a third came at the Philadelphia, Portsmouth, and Norfolk naval shipyards.

Although neither buyouts nor reductions in force were used to target poor performers, several agencies did protect their core work force through deliberate means. For example, scientists and engineers at the Army Material Command were ineligible for the agency's buyout program. By restricting access to the buyouts, the agency assured that its core competency remained mostly intact as it dropped from 110,000 employees to 60,000. Similarly, the Office of Personnel Management targeted nonessential activities for an aggressive privatization program. By reducing its head count through privatization of its investigations service and training programs, OPM was able to maintain its core competency as its overall work force fell by almost half. Denying buyouts to certain staffs or targeting specific units for elimination was hardly the most popular approach to managing the downsizing, of course. It would have been much easier to let attrition and random retirements take their course. But the Army Material Command and OPM both felt obliged to make the hard choices. Would that other agencies had that kind of courage.

The Big Chill

Given the political cost of RIFs and the financial cost of buyouts, it should not be surprising that Congresses and presidents have returned time and again to ceilings and freezes as the dominant tools for managing head count. From the end of World War II to the present, politicians have usually taken the easy route, holding government to one ceiling after the other and occasionally imposing a freeze just for good measure. As appendix C shows, there have been at least thirty-five different efforts to reshape the body of government over the past half-century, ten of which involved thaws or roof raisings and twenty-five that put government back in the freezer again. The emphasis is on the words "at least," for there is no easily accessible government inventory of head count policy. The best that can be done is to collect the events one by one by digging down through history year by year, statute by statute.[20]

A Cooling Trend

Before turning to the history in more detail, it is useful to note three trends from the history. The first trend can be spotted toward the left margin of appendix C, in the "tool" column. There, the tools used to constrain government growth clearly change over time, as Congresses and presidents invented new ways of keeping government small. It would have been inconceivable in the 1950s for Congress to create a buyout program to move civil services off the payroll, just as it would have been inconceivable for a private firm to do so. By the 1990s, however, Congress and the American public had accepted the wisdom of paying employees to leave.

The second trend can be found in the "goal" column. There, the declining support for thaws can easily be spotted. The days when a House committee might publicly criticize downsizing as ill-conceived, as the House Manpower Subcommittee did in attacking the Whitten Amendment, are long gone. So are the thaws. Once the postal service was moved off the head count budget in 1970, Congress felt no need to provide urgent exemptions to the Whitten ceilings. Half of the eight thaws had been put in force to put more mail carriers on the streets.

This is not to argue that Congress ignored the impacts of the recent downsizings, as evidenced by reading back through the manifest of GAO reports and Pryor letters. However, when committees convened to hold hearings, the questioning tended to focus on how to make sure the downsizing worked, not on how to protect inherently governmental functions. Even as Congresses and presidents assert that they would never knowingly allow the private sector to co-opt sovereign functions, the restrictions are so vague and the definition of "inherently government" so poorly understood that it is a promise without force.

The legislative hearings on the Workforce Restructuring Act, both pre- and postpassage are a case in point. In the Senate, for example, the purpose of the first hearing on S. 1535 was designed to sharpen the tools, not blunt the attack. "The purpose of this bill," said Senate Governmental Affairs Committee Chairman John Glenn (D-Ohio) in calling the hearing to order, "is to provide agency heads with downsizing tools and employee retraining initiatives to cut the fat and build the muscle of the work force." More specifically, Glenn wondered whether buyouts might be the more effective device for removing middle managers: "while at the lower levels of employment, the lower GS levels, attrition can probably do the job for us with no incentives, at the middle-mangers areas, the 13's, 14's, and 15's, which is where we have some of this over-employment, if you will, the question is: Can we change these ratios with this legislation?"[21]

His committee colleagues followed suit, demanding action to prevent "backfilling" of empty posts by contract employees and how to target the right employees. Only Pryor engaged the issue of how deep to cut.

> The concern that I have had, Mr. Chairman, all along with the development of this bill—is that we may reach that point, when finally the managers and the agency directors say, wait a minute, we have cut our workforce back so deeply, that now we have to go out and hire contractors and consultants to do this work to replace them. I hope that we are not going to fall into that trap. This is a practice that has become all too much a part of the modus operandi of our Federal workforce, and even our State workforces out there. There is a great trend now throughout the whole public sector to let public employees go and to replace them with private contractors who are basically unresponsive.[22]

Although the final act prohibited such job shifting, the provision was unenforceable. Lacking a system for tracking movement from government to contractors, all Congress could do was make a symbolic gesture. If it cannot be defined, let alone tracked, it cannot be prevented.

The third trend in the history can be found in the "origin" column of appendix C. The first twelve efforts to control government employment originated in Congress, while nine of the last ten came from the executive branch. It is fair to argue that reshaping the body of government was a congressional responsibility from early in World War II all the way through the Civil Service Reform Act of 1978. Presidents may have had the constitutional responsibility to faithfully execute the laws, but Congress had absolute authority over the head counts.

The explanation can be found in the congressional backlash to Franklin Roosevelt's New Deal expansion. It is a backlash that was already apparent in late 1937, when Roosevelt asked Congress for the reorganization authority needed to implement the Brownlow Committee report. Although most of the Brownlow plan had passed through the House, reorganization authority stalled in the wake of Roosevelt's effort to pack the Supreme Court. According to James Morone, the firestorm eventually spread to the Brownlow plan, prompting some 330,000 telegrams to Congress against blanket reorganization authority. The backlash was so intense that Roosevelt actually felt obligated to issue the following statement:

A. I have no inclination to be a dictator.
B. I have none of the qualifications that would make me a successful dictator.
C. I have too much historical background . . . to make me desire any form of dictatorship . . . in the United States of America.[23]

Although Roosevelt eventually won the authority needed to create an Executive Office of the President, he lost whatever trust he still had with Congress. Congress began pressing almost immediately for passage of the Administrative Procedure Act in 1939, igniting a battle over executive discretion. The president's allies were led by Attorney General Francis Biddle, who argued passionately against any weakening of presidential authority, while his adversaries were led by former Harvard Law School dean Roscoe Pound, who created a caricature of public servants as fundamentally unqualified to make administrative rules. Roosevelt may have won the administrative procedure battle by postponing final action until after World War II, but he clearly lost the war over the size of government. Congress established its Joint Committee on Reduction of Nonessential Federal Expenditures in 1942, which almost immediately recommended a 300,000-person cut in federal employment.

Roosevelt's great adversary in this fight was not a former law school dean, but the powerful senior senator from Virginia, Democrat Harry Byrd Sr. As both the joint committee's first chairman and a member of the standing Civil Service Committee, Byrd authored the first statute recorded in appendix C, the Byrd-Langer Amendment, which allowed departments and agencies to continue paying overtime to certain classes of employees, provided that departments and agencies justify the number of employees on the payroll. As a first cut at congressional control of head counts, the amendment still deferred to the president through the director of the Bureau of the Budget. The enforcement mechanism was tepid at best:

> If any such department or agency fails to present such information or if, in the opinion of the Director, the information so presented fails to disclose that the number of such employees in any department or agency is necessary to the proper and efficient exercise of its functions, the personnel of such department or agency shall be reduced, upon the order of the Director, by such number as the Director finds to be in excess of the minimum requirements of such departments or agency.[24]

Byrd also authored the second statute recorded in appendix C. This statute extended overtime pay again and ordered the budget director to both provide quarterly estimates of the number of employees needed for the "proper and efficient exercise of the functions of their respective departments and agencies" and release any excess personnel.

The fact that the director never released anyone eventually led to the first personnel ceiling in modern times, courtesy of Byrd. Ironically, the ceiling was linked to the first pay increase in years. The proposed 20 percent increase was championed by the Senate Civil Service Committee as essential for addressing the federal government's "pitiful wage scale." As the committee completed its work, Senator Byrd intervened with another amendment. "Certainly, if Congress is requested to increase salaries," he wrote the Civil Service Committee, "the question of reducing the bloated personnel of the Government bureaus is in direct and pertinent issue, especially in view of the fact that this personnel is being reduced very slowly."[25] Having been denied a vote in his own committee, Byrd prevailed on the floor and in conference with the House: the budget director would be required to establish agency-by-agency ceilings based on estimates of the personnel needed for "proper and efficient exercise of the authorized functions" and to reduce head count accordingly.

Once again, however, Byrd was frustrated. "Even this authority did not produce the desired results," Byrd's Joint Committee on Reduction of Non-essential Federal Expenditures concluded. In view of "this deplorable situation" and "harking back to the warning . . . made" in recommending the 300,000-person cut in 1943, the committee added the first numerical head count ceiling to the Employees Pay Act of 1946. Under the ceiling, the aggregate number of non-Defense Department civilian employees would be set at no more than 447,363 after June 30, 1947. As the joint committee explained its action, "it is at last expected that the executive branch will be forced to reduce personnel to a level somewhere near what is actually required to carry on its functions efficiently and economically, thereby abolishing the 'deadwood' and overload of personnel which has been accruing since 1933."[26] It is a classic statement of the anti-New Deal origins of the ceiling approach.

Despite the joint committee's self-congratulatory statement, the new ceiling did not work. At the urging of the Bureau of the Budget and secretary of the Treasury, Congress immediately gave the bureau waiver authority to be used if a planned reduction would be "inimical to the public interest," and repealed the head counts entirely in 1950.[27]

It would be up to Jamie Whitten to devise the perfect ceiling. Instead of having Congress set a fixed head count target, Whitten adopted a much simpler formula, merely tying the total number of permanent positions to a date in time, thereby leaving enforcement to the executive branch, which Truman immediately embraced in Executive Order 10810.

The question is how presidents eventually won back the authority to set head count policy. Despite the temptation to argue that time heals all wounds, the fact is that presidents simply became tougher. Congress ceded control to Reagan because he promised a war on waste. Carter had started the pendulum moving with three freezes of his own, the first coming as part of his declaration of war on the national energy crisis in March 1977. Dressed in a cardigan sweater when he spoke to the American public, Carter used the talk as a kind of informal State of the Union address, moving from energy to the economy and onto government reorganization during the hour long conversation. He promised to cut the White House staff by a third (a promise achieved through a shadow staff of detailees from other agencies), eliminate needless regulation, rid government of unnecessary luxuries "such as door-to-door limousine service," and put a ceiling on total federal employment. He issued the freeze order on March 2, 1977, only six weeks after his inauguration.

Reagan was even faster, issuing his freeze as his very first act on his first day in office as president. As he explained the freeze, "This is an order that I am signing, an immediate freeze on the hiring of civilian employees in the executive branch. I pledged last July that this would be a first step toward controlling the growth and the size of Government and reducing the drain on the economy for the public sector. And beyond the symbolic value of this, which is my first official act, the freeze will eventually lead to a significant reduction in the size of the Federal workforce."[28] The fact that he signed the order in the Capitol building is not without symbolic reference. Congress had initiated its last head count ceiling. Although it would produce the Base Closure and Realignment Act in 1988, it was finally willing to give presidents authority over downsizing. They had proven themselves just as tough as Congress.

Of Battles Waged and Lost

The most important information in appendix C involves impacts. Alongside the dramatic impact of the Whitten amendment, there is an impressive assortment of failures to slim the midlevels of the federal hierarchy. When coupled with the overall effort to constrain total employment, this failure forced government to push more and more work outward and downward through the shadow work force. Given the chance to protect its middle and senior levels against downsizing pressure, the federal hierarchy was more than willing to saw off its bottom.

What the appendix cannot show is the steady expansion of the federal mission over the decades. By ignoring the question of what government does, reinventors of both parties have focused almost entirely on the question of how government operates. Facing unrelenting pressure to do more with less, federal departments and agencies did what comes naturally through enlightened self-interest: they amended the handy saying to read "doing more with fewer federal workers," which inevitably lengthens the shadow of government. Because Congress and the president have absolutely no work force planning process and no way of tracking the shadow, departments and agencies could follow their instincts without fear. Indeed, they could find ample encouragement for shadow casting in everything from Nixon's new federalism to the A-76 process, all of which clearly order departments and agencies to push increasing amounts of their work outward and downward. Granted, little of the pushing has involved midlevel jobs, but at least departments and agencies are honoring the general intent. Again, given a choice between creating shadows or not implementing the law, the federal government has done the right thing. They are, in fact, doing more with less.

Thus there are two important lessons in the history of head counts. The first involves the generally failed efforts of departments and agencies to break through their ceilings, and the second involves the generally failed efforts to target the midlevels of government for targeted downsizing. Together, the failures have created enormous pressure to make shadows, which most departments and agencies have obliged.

MAINTAINING THE CEILING. As noted earlier, the first head count ceiling was honored mostly in the exception. The politics of head counts had not quite hardened into a national inevitability. Byrd's efforts were easily dismissed as little more than southern griping about the New Deal, while the Whitten Amendment was often belittled as bad policy. Once the Joint Committee on Reduction of Nonessential Federal Expenditures was abolished in the mid-1950s, Byrd moved onto other issues, not the least of which was the fight against civil rights. After Byrd retired in 1965, Whitten was left to defend his ceilings over what was to be a very long career.

As also noted earlier, Whitten was on the defensive from almost the moment his ceiling passed in 1951. As noted above, his legislative draftsmanship took a beating from the House Manpower Subcommittee in 1953 and he became a pariah within the good government community. Nevertheless, he had what appeared to be an unassailable position in making the case for smaller government. Invited to defend his handiwork before the full House Committee on Post Office and Civil Service in 1954, he presented himself as but a simple man in search of a simple solution to government excess. He also presented his work as but one member's modest effort to do the right thing:

> I know you gentlemen are just as sincere as I could possibly be and believe as much as I could possibly believe in good government. But I have tried in whatever way I knew how to gain by experience and to get the best folks I knew to help write something that I thought was badly needed. If you run into some place where some relief is required, I would be the first to meet with you to work it out. If you can figure out some way to get the [Civil Service] Commission to do what it can do under the rider, I think all the headaches will be ended. Apparently they do not want to use that unless you will in turn pay the price of giving up all regulation.[29]

Whitten's argument was simple: the federal government already had authority to breach his amendment under special cases. The Civil Service Commission just was not using it to force Congress to repeal his amendment. "There is precious little reward in public office for doing a hard job and trying to do it right," he argued. "Most of it comes in satisfaction. Unfortunately, sometimes you seem to get more votes by big promises and forgetting the consequences. . . . I have no ax to grind in this thing. I believe in it and I am going to scrap for what I believe."[30] Any thoughts that the committee might have had about repealing the amendment were gone by the end of the hearing. The best the committee could do in defending its turf was to raise the Whitten targets by 10 percent of the number of permanent employees on September 1, 1950.

That the Whitten Amendment survived this early assault is testament to the power of head counts as a way to describe the size of government. That the first major exemptions to the ceiling involved the postal service is testament to the power of the mails as a tool of congressional influence back home. No member of Congress wants to jeopardize this central resource of incumbency. Having tried and failed to exempt the Post Office from the Whitten restrictions in 1954, the Civil Service Committee resigned itself to taking nearly annual inventories of the damage done to postal service.

Consider the 1965 hearings that led to freedom for the Post Office Department. After starting the hearing by promising that the exemption would only apply to the postal field service, and not to its headquarters or any other federal entities, the House Subcommittee on Postal Operations allowed witnesses to whale away at Whitten and his amendment. The subcommittee was dutifully respectful in its analysis of how the Whitten Amendment had altered postal operations, calling attention to the creation of an entirely new shadow employment category, which was called "temporary substitutes" and which was occupied by 57,000 persons, none of whom had career status or civil service pensions. The subcommittee was also understandably irritated at the continued interference of the Appropriations Committee in postal operations. "I am one who feels that the Appropriations Committee should not interfere with the work of this committee," one member said with a degree of false bravado. "It is none of their business."[31]

What makes the hearing unusual perhaps is the degree to which the subcommittee invited its witnesses to attack the Whitten Amendment. The president of the United Federation of Postal Clerks characterized the amendment as a straitjacket and a restraint on fair labor practices. "The Whitten amendment has accomplished something that neither snow, nor rain, nor sleet, nor gloom of night has ever been able to do—namely 'staying these couriers,' that is, our clerks and carriers, 'from the swift completion of their appointed rounds.'" The president of the National Federation of Federal Employees argued that personnel administration was "a job which no legislative body is competent to undertake." The president of the American Federation of Government Employees called the Whitten Amendment "an anachronism that has hampered far more than it has assisted the Federal service." "If the Whitten amendment ever had any applicability to the Post Office Department—and this is dubious originally—it certainly has none now," the president of the National Postal Union added. "It has introduced a vicious cycle of instability and waste and has created mass resentment on the part of the employees." The testimony was repeated almost word for word in the Senate, where the Subcommittee on Postal Affairs held parallel hearings before exempting the postal field service from any further torture from the Whitten Amendment. The bill passed by voice votes in both chambers and became law on August 6, 1965. If Whitten had any objections to the change, he did not make them known.

Emboldened by their success, opponents of the Whitten Amendment moved forward with full repeal in 1967. The House Manpower Subcommittee took the lead this time, building its case in much more respectful tones as it pushed repeal upward to the full Post Office and Civil Service Committee. The Whitten Amendment had served a useful purpose as a "temporary measure to forestall a rapid buildup of the permanent Federal work force as a result of the Korean emergency," the full committee noted in its legislative report, but the amendment had eventually "forced management officials in the departments and agencies to resort to the use of combat-trained military and/or contractor personnel to perform work historically and successfully done by civil service employees."[32]

The committee also noted its commitment to keeping government small. "In recommending this change, the committee does not consider the removal of the ceiling as a lack of interest on their part in controlling or limiting civilian employment but a recognition of the need to consider the total labor costs to get the job done. . . . If conditions again warrant a ceiling the committee will initiate legislation to that end." More to the point of this book, it was not the ceiling that caused the problems so much as the freeze on permanent appointments. Keeping government small could be handled through the budget and appropriations process, but making it temporary or permanent was up to the Post Office and Civil Service Committees to decide. The ceilings and freezes, but not the restrictions on rapid promotions, were repealed on October 11, 1967.

Before turning to Whitten's revenge, it is important to emphasize that Congress was clearly aware even in 1967 of the shadow-making effects of head count ceilings. "Actually, the statutory ceiling has stood in the way of economy and efficiency," the head of the Civil Service Commission, John W. Macy, Jr., wrote the House. "It has forced Federal agencies to consider an unrelated factor in meeting their manpower needs. In so doing, it has encouraged the use of temporary personnel in work which should have been performed by permanent personnel."[33]

Within a year, Whitten's Amendment, or at least its ghost, was back in force. This time, it came through the *Revenue and Expenditure Control Act of 1968*, which contained a 10 percent surtax on federal income taxes to pay for the Vietnam War. With the war going badly and the economy starting to sour, President Johnson had petitioned Congress for the money to prevent a budget deficit. Congress obliged, but not without also imposing a new version of the Whitten Amendment. Congress could hardly impose a tax increase on the American public without taking a cut on government.

Under the final language, federal full-time civilian employment would be capped at the number of such employees on June 30, 1966, while the number of temporary, part-time, and seasonal employees would be capped at the number of such employees in the corresponding month of 1967. The amendment, which had emerged from the House Appropriations Committee, made no exemptions for postal servants. It passed into law on June 28, 1968.

The fact that the cap on full-time employment went back to June 1966 was no small irony. The House Postal Operations Subcommittee had finished its work two months after that date. The subcommittee responded to the new Whitten ceiling with another repeal, joining with its Senate counterpart in a remarkably harsh attack in a conference report titled *Postal Assaults and Personnel Ceilings*:

> In the judgment of the conferees, to leave the postal service to the mercy of the employment ceiling would be the ultimate in false economy.
>
> It would irreparably damage the postal service.
>
> It would severely hamper business and industry, and tend to undermine the economy at a time when vibrant economic growth is imperative to support the Government's fiscal reforms.
>
> It would virtually hamstring postal management and enforce drastic curtailment of postal services.

It would relegate the American public to second-class situations in terms of availability and usefulness of their chief means of communication.

The results would be disastrous in the face of ever-rising and uncontrollable mail volume.

The chaos in the Postal Establishment would be equaled only by the indignation of an outraged public.[34]

The postal service exemption passed on voice votes again and was followed the next summer by repeal of the overall ceiling. Perhaps it was because Nixon sounded so tough on executive employment or perhaps it was just the exhaustion of Vietnam, but Congress took a five-year breather from the personnel ceiling and freeze business. Nixon had ordered a 5 percent cut in federal employment as part of his wage and price freeze of 1971. Although there is no historical record on just how the Nixon administration tried to achieve the cuts, federal employment did fall by 60,000 jobs (3 percent) from 1971 to 1973.

As appendix C shows, Congress reentered the ceiling-building, freeze-making business in 1974, focusing its energies on the Department of Defense. This time, the Armed Services Committees were directing the effort. Instead of a time-specific ceiling, they established a specific head count target of 1,025,527. The number rounded up to 1,058,000 in 1975, then fell to 1,031,000 in 1976. The fact that the committees began rounding was a small victory for the executive branch, it can be supposed, but the return to directed head counts was a clear defeat. Congress had reverted to a head count approach not seen since the Federal Employees Pay Act of 1946. Although Congress did repeal the remaining elements of the Whitten Amendment in 1976, if a bit by accident when it ended the state of emergency that had been proclaimed at the start of the Korean War, Carter quickly imposed his own freeze and Congress returned to ceiling making by adding another Whittenesque restriction to the massive Civil Service Reform Act. This new four-year ceiling, which held full-time employment to September 1977 levels, came from Representative James Leach (R-Iowa). The idea had originated in the Senate, however, with Senator John Heinz (R-Pa.), who had been rebuffed by his colleagues on a voice vote. As Heinz explained his reasoning in "additional views" to the final legislative report, "The Committee may have overlooked what should be one of the most fundamental principles of any substantive reform and what is one of the chief causes of citizen concern and complaint about government. That problem, simply, is size, and the principle—equally simple—is that a responsible reform designed to stream-line the bureaucracy and make it more efficient should necessarily make it smaller."[35] As noted earlier, it was the last time that Congress would initiate a ceiling, not because ceilings fell from grace, but because presidents had finally proven their toughness in setting ceilings of their own.

TARGETING THE MIDDLE. Despite all the promises, ceilings have long proven to be a poor device for actually reducing the true size of government. De-partments and agencies long ago discovered how to use temporary employ-ees, contractors, grantees, and mandates to produce goods and services under head count constraints. All ceilings do is limit the number of card-carrying federal employees. Lacking a tracking system that might track the total work force, be it federal, nonprofit, private, state or local, Congress and the presi-dent have little control over the eventual shape of the hierarchy.

That is why they occasionally turn to more deliberate shaping tools such as RIFs and restricted buyouts. That such tools have never fully succeeded is the second part of the shadow-making dynamic. Restricted by nearly invio-lable ceilings and mostly immune to targeted downsizing at the midlevels, departments and agencies throw their first shadows at the bottom. It is only natural to protect the middle. Consider two recent examples of targeted ef-forts to slim the midlevels of government.

The first campaign was launched in 1983 and involved a four-year battle against the midlevel bulge. Called the "bulge project," the campaign began with the Grace Commission's call for a war on waste. Although the commis-sion did endorse federal pay increases, particularly for senior executives, it also concluded that there were too many white-collar workers in high-level positions. According to the commission's final report, which was published under the title *War on Waste,* "Only 26% of private sector middle and upper management personnel are employed at a level comparable to GS-11 and above, compared to 72% in the Federal Government—i.e., a Government concentration 2.8 times as great as that in the private sector."

After blaming low entry-level pay as the central motivation for promot-ing employees ever upward, the commission also attacked the federal classi-fication system for creating the "inverted pyramid" distribution of senior and midlevel executives, noting that federal personnel policies caused "in-ordinate use of overtime; creation of thousands of unnecessary, temporary positions; assignment of inappropriate spans of control to managers; con-tracting of jobs to the private sector at a higher cost than could be accomplished internally . . . ; and excessive layering of management, including excessive use of deputies and assistants, duplicate organizational frameworks, and over-graded positions."[36]

Although the Grace Commission can take some credit for opening the battle of the bulge, GAO had long been arguing for a campaign against "grade creep." Alongside its long list of reports on work force planning, GAO had produced two massive reports on overgrading, the first in 1975 that dealt with all of government and the second in 1981 that dealt just with the Defense Department. Both reports reached the same general conclusion: average federal grade, which is a measure of the relative height of a given job within the work force hierarchy, was going up too fast. Some of the grade creep resulted from changing jobs—fewer clerks and more scientists; fewer messengers and more analysts—but much more resulted from a lack of attention. "Maintaining the integrity of the classification system is management's direct responsibility," GAO wrote in 1975. "But some managers want to upgrade as a means of rewarding and recruiting employees—the major resource for accomplishing Government programs."[37]

At least for GAO, the solution was not to wage war against the bulge. It was to pay attention to work force planning. "Mechanisms such as average grade controls or high grade reductions do not distinguish between justified and unwarranted grade escalation," GAO wrote in 1981. "Further, they tend to cause other problems such as staffing imbalances, reduced employee morale, high turnover, and reduced services. Position management, on the other hand, directly attacks unwarranted grade increases. Position management—a system approach for determining the number of positions needed, the skill and knowledge requirements, and the grouping and assignment of duties and responsibilities among positions—has as prime objectives personnel cost control and grade level conservations."[38]

As if to prove GAO's point, Reagan's battle of the bulge was an unmitigated failure. Designed to cut 40,000 midlevel positions, the effort could not prevent a 10,000 increase. Unlike the Gore effort discussed below, the four-year battle plan did not target any particular group of employees or agencies. Nor did it carry any force of law or executive order. Although OPM did compute agency-by-agency statistics on the bulge, there is no evidence that the president or his central management agencies cared about the program. As table 4-2 shows, the federal government was no thinner at the end of the battle in 1987 than it was at the beginning. According to OPM's own "bulge indices," which were designed to track gains and losses in the middle, every employment category went up during the Reagan battle, as did every ratio

Table 4-2. *The Battle of the Federal Employment Bulge, 1983–97*

Number of FTE employees, unless otherwise specified

Measure	1983	1987	1989	1992	1997
Total employment	2,009,428	2,040,080	2,078,892	2,106,026	1,777,840
GS 1–10 employees	782,747	797,166	799,469	766,699	594,126
GS 11–15 employees	486,722	531,229	578,441	645,032	638,427
GS 11–15 managers and supervisors	125,209	136,996	149,608	160,891	126,267
Average grade GS 1–10	8.42	8.57	8.74	9.07	9.54
Average Grade GS 11–15	12.27	12.26	12.26	12.30	12.33
Ratio total GS 11–15 to GS 1–10 employees	1:1.6	1:1.5	1:1.4	1:1.2	1:0.93
Ratio GS 11–15 managers and supervisors to GS 1–10 employees	1:6.3	1:5.8	1:5.3	1:4.8	1:4.7
Ratio GS 11–15 managers and supervisors to GS 11–15 nonmanagers and nonsupervisors	1:2.9	1:2.9	1:2.9	1:3.0	1:4.1
Ratio GS 11–15 managers and supervisors to GS 1–15 nonmanagers and nonsupervisors	1:9.1	1:8.7	1:8.2	1:7.8	1:10.8

Source: Analysis of data provided through the Central Personnel Data File, U.S. Office of Personnel Management.

of managers to nonmanagers. Average grade increased, as did spans of control between supervisors and subordinates. No matter how the data is cut, Reagan's battle of the bulge was lost.

As the table also shows, the second battle of the bulge, led by Vice President Al Gore, was much more effective. There were almost 35,000 fewer middle-level managers as the battle came to an end in 1997, while spans of control had grown dramatically. Whereas there were eight nonmanagers for every one manager in 1992, there were eleven by 1997. Moreover, the midlevel cuts came across government, not just at the Defense Department. Although almost 18,000 of the total cut came from air force (down 1,800), army (down 8,300), navy (6,400), and other Pentagon units (1,450), every department and agency but Justice (up 2,000) and State (up 18) lost midlevel managers. Interior and Treasury both lost roughly a sixth of their managers, Agriculture, Commerce, Labor, and Transportation each lost almost a fifth of their managers, Education and General Services lost over a third, EPA and HUD lost almost two-fifths, Energy and NASA lost more than a half, and OPM lost more than two-thirds.[39]

There are four reasons for Gore's much greater success. First, he had a huge federal downsizing on his side. Building upon the administration's February 1993 executive order mandating a 100,000-position cut in total employment, the Federal Workforce Restructuring Act set clear annual targets for reducing total federal employment, which, in turn, created clear pressure within departments. Employees could read the statute if they had any doubts about the vice president's mandate. It is much easier to cut midlevel positions when total employment is falling than to reallocate midlevel positions when total employment is rising.

Second, Gore had the $25,000 buyouts as incentives. There is no question that the buyouts allowed some modest targeting of retirement-eligible midlevel managers. Of the 83,000 buyouts made between 1993 and the first half of 1995, for example, almost three-quarters involved recipients who were eligible for either early or regular retirement. Whether those employees would have left of their own accord sooner or later is in some dispute, but the fact remains that they did leave, vacating at least some of the midlevel management positions.[40]

Third, Gore had the unrelenting focus of his president. Unlike Reagan's battle of the bulge, which was launched by an OPM memorandum as more a guerrilla war than a full-scale attack, the Gore effort carried the presidential seal. The campaign began with a presidential order on September 11, 1993, ordering each federal department and agency to develop a streamlining plan to address "the means by which it will reduce the ratio of managers and supervisors to other personnel, with a goal of reducing the percentage who are supervisors or managers in halving the current ratio within 5 years."[41] Although it is not clear that the streamlining plans were ever reviewed, the fact that the president made the order was an important signal that Gore held the ultimate trump card.

Finally, Gore had Gore. Although there is much to criticize in the reinventing government campaign, including the general reluctance to attack the upper reaches of the hierarchy, there is no doubt that Gore gave the effort his full attention. He endured endless meetings on some of the most boring topics known to management science and emerged energized. Nor is there any doubt that he changed the national dialogue about the public service, moving attention away from power-hungry bureaucrats to creativity-stifling bureaucracy. As the last chapter argued, the semantic shift allowed the Clinton administration simultaneously to claim victory in the war on bureaucracy and to liberate the bureaucrats from a host of needless rules.

Gore's campaign was not an unqualified success, however. According to GAO's assessment, most agencies met the midlevel management targets in part by reclassifying supervisors as nonsupervisors and team leaders. At the NASA Marshall Space Flight Center in Alabama, for example, 41 percent of the manager-to-nonmanager shift involved reclassification. At the Bureau of Land Management, the number was 40 percent; at the Federal Aviation Administration, it was 35 percent. The question, of course, is whether a manager by any other name supervises just as much. There are more team leaders today in government than in all of Little League, Pop Warner football, and peewee soccer combined, but there may have been no real reduction in the number of layers between the top and bottom of agencies.

Nevertheless, credit must be given where credit is due. Gore did something that a succession of presidents could not do. His campaign actually reduced the number of midlevel managers, whereas Nixon, Ford, and Reagan had all tried and failed. Whether the managers ended up as team leaders may not matter. They certainly learned that someone was paying attention to work force management.

THE CIRCLE IN THE PYRAMID. The problem is that Gore could not stop the flooding of the midlevel ranks more generally. Whereas GS 11-15 employment (row 3 in table 4-2) fell 7,000 positions during the 1992–97 period, GS 1-10 employment (row 2) dropped by more than 170,000 positions. Put the second number together with the more than 100,000-position decline in blue-collar, or federal wage system jobs, and the conclusion is clear: the bottom of government is thinning rapidly. The evidence is in the numbers (row 2) and the average grade (row 6). The fact that the total number of GS 1-10 jobs plummeted, while the average GS 1-10 grade actually increased by its largest margin in a decade can only mean that the bottommost jobs were taking the brunt of the cuts. As the federal work force sloughed off its lowest graded jobs in what was largely an attrition-based downsizing, the rest of the GS 1-10 category rose in grade. (Again, this kind of erosion is not exclusive to government downsizings. The front line is generally the first to go in the private sector, too.)

The midlevels simply did not suffer as much. Not only did the total number of midlevel employees move up during the downsizing, but also the loss of 35,000 managers did not affect average grade. Indeed, average grade for the GS 11-15 ranks (row 6) actually increased, despite the loss of nearly one-quarter of what should have been the more highly graded managerial posts.

The relative stability in the GS 11-15 ranks could mean one or both of two things. First, it could be that managers who were reclassified into non-managerial positions were left at the same grade. This is hardly a surprising possibility given the fundamental principle of downsizing noted at the start of this chapter, that no current federal employees get hurt. Second, it could be that most of the vacated positions were "backfilled," meaning that the occupant left, but the job and grade, sans managerial responsibilities, were occupied by the next in line. Although the Workforce Reduction Act specifically prohibited any backfilling of federal jobs by private contractors, it did not require that more highly graded jobs be forever abolished upon the incumbent's departure. Neither did any of the Clinton missives to the departments and agencies. The hierarchy most certainly lost weight in the total number of employees, but it did not lose a pound in average grade. Nor did it lose any of the senior-most layers of management that constitute the thickening of government. To the contrary, the federal government actually got taller, if not wider, during the downsizing. That may be a diet that any overweight American would gladly follow, but it is not necessarily healthy for assuring government accountability.

It is not exactly clear where the bottom-level jobs went. Some no doubt disappeared forever; others ended up in service contracts, still others must have gone down to the states. Lacking careful tracking data, there can only be suspicions. Although OMB specifically requested that agencies keep information on any shift of jobs from in-house to contractors, OMB has not had the personnel to follow through on the request. OMB had to trust agencies to do the right thing, even though the incentives appear to be with contracting out. "Unless agencies are specifically authorized to hire or keep needed Federal employees in circumstances where a meaningful cost comparison indicates that in-house performance is the desirable alternative," GAO testified in 1994, "agencies could well be in the position of having to contract for services regardless of the study's results, and this obviously diminishes the incentive to do the kind of hard analytical work that is required to make a good decision."[42] The path to such permission was so tortured and difficult that agencies were well advised to simply cut the job and contract out, even if such action violated the Workforce Restructuring Act. Again, however, there could only be suspicions. As American Federation of Government Employees President John Sturdivant warned, "I would just hope that that contract with America does not provide for more contracting out of America. . . . Downsizing Federal employees while upsizing contract employees will only wrongsize the Federal Government's overall work force."[43]

Whatever the reasons, whether an intentional shell game, an accident of incentives, or the by-product of a legitimate desire to protect those already on board, the federal hierarchy became more circular under Gore. Some of the change most certainly resulted from the changing job mix needed to do the government's work. The bottom of government has been slimming for decades, with the advent of new technologies. Between 1954 and 1961, for example, the federal government hired 1,800 new lawyers, 45,000 engineers, 16,000 accountants, 12,000 scientists, 4,000 social scientists, and 20,000 transportation experts, while cutting 2,000 messengers, 14,000 typists, and 10,000 general secretaries. Although the shift toward more complex jobs has been under way since the 1940s, it stretches credulity to argue that over a quarter of a million GS 1-10 and blue-collar jobs could become suddenly obsolete in just four years. The fact is that the federal government mostly got rid of the jobs that were the easiest to get rid of, meaning the ones with the highest attrition and the least political muscle.

The rest of the pyramid still exists, of course. It just resides outside of the federal head count, among the millions of people who work for contractors, grantees, and state and local governments. As a result, it is best to view the federal hierarchy as well on its way to becoming a circle within a much larger pyramid. The federal government will always deliver services on behalf of Congress, the presidency, and the federal courts. It is just no longer clear who will actually do the delivering. Sometimes it will be card-carrying federal employees, other times contractors and grantees and their subcontractors and subgrantees, and still other times state and local employees. As long as the federal work force must operate under fixed and declining ceilings, the faithful execution of the laws will rely more on writing careful contracts, grants, and mandates than on the traditional chain of command between elected representatives and the career work force below. That is neither liberal nor conservative. It simply is the way government must operate given the politics of head count.

The Consequence of Counting Heads

Congresses and presidents have long known that ceilings and freezes might create shadows. The rise of a largely unregulated temporary work force was one of the well-understood consequences of the Whitten Amendment, as was the increasing use of contracts and grants to create hidden capacity. Consider the congressional investigations that followed the three most visible ceilings described in appendix C: the Whitten Amendment, the Civil Service Reform Act of 1978, and the Federal Workforce Restructuring Act of 1994.

The Whitten Amendment

Congress quickly figured out that the Whitten Amendment was changing the shape of government. The first hearing on the use of private labor to produce public goods was conducted in 1953 by the Senate Federal Manpower Subcommittee. Although Congress had long worried about waste in government, the Whitten Amendment forced Congress to confront the shadow work force.

According to the subcommittee, the post–World War II period had witnessed a vast expansion in the number of Americans working for the federal government under contracts and grants. By the government's own admittedly fuzzy estimate, the federal shadow work force "may well double the approximately 2,500,000 people indirectly employed by the Government." Having found that nearly every department and agency employed contract labor in "some form or other," the subcommittee concentrated on the ten government agencies that appeared to be the heaviest consumers. Although the subcommittee concluded that contracting was almost always the only way possible to procure the services required, it bemoaned the lack of an "overall policy as to what should be done by contract and what should be done by the Government itself." More to the point of this book, it also found that much of the contracting was driven more by political exigency than by wisdom.[44]

Consider its investigation of the link between the Whitten ceiling and contracting out at the Defense Department. During World War II, the Department of the Army operated its Tennessee munitions loading arsenal under a cost-plus-fixed-fee contract with the Proctor and Gamble Defense Corporation. Once the war was over, the army returned the plant to its civil service employees, many of whom had been fighting the war abroad. With the Whitten Amendment in place, the army shifted back to a contract with Proctor and Gamble in mid-1951, prompting the subcommittee to ask about the need for a cost-plus-fee contract when civil servants could have done the work for cost only. The subcommittee found similar job shifting in the navy's Bureau of Ships, creating what it saw as needless delays and cost over-runs, including over a million hours of overtime in fiscal year 1952. "The manpower ceiling is one of the primary reasons for the existence of many Defense Department contracts," the subcommittee concluded. "Congress may have effected a deceptive economy by imposing manpower ceilings which have actually promoted greater expenditure of public funds by forc-ing the agencies to circumvent manpower ceilings through the use of pri-vate contracts."[45]

The subcommittee also found inappropriate shadow casting in the fed-eral government's own red tape. Faced with the delays inherent in hiring civil servants through the normal classification and recruitment process, departments and agencies have long had ample incentives to use contracts as a back door to fill jobs. Even in 1951 Congress could see the conflict be-tween honoring the search for merit and the need for speed. The only way to reduce the contract-created jobs would be to undertake a "streamlining of civil-service hiring procedures."[46]

Despite the subcommittee's suggestion, neither branch ever promul-gated a policy for sorting through appropriate and inappropriate shadow casting. It was not for a lack of occasional interest, however. Congress inves-tigated the shadow from time to time, presidents prohibited contracting out of inherently governmental activities now and again, and the General Ac-counting Office has never stopped calling for some semblance of a federal work force policy.

The 1978 Civil Service Reform Act

Congress also understood the effect of personnel ceilings when it passed the 1978 Civil Service Reform Act. The debate was surprisingly hot for a subject that usually draws a collective House yawn. Having been denied at the markup stage of the bill, proponents of a ceiling brought their case to the floor in an amendment authored by Jim Leach (R-Iowa). Future Vice Presi-dent Dan Quayle (R-Ind.), gave the most impassioned speech on behalf of the ceiling. "In order to confront the problem of the bureaucracy we must deal with the bureaucrats themselves, who seem to multiply regardless of our reform or reorganizational efforts. Every President since Herbert Hoover has pledged to reduce the size of the Federal bureaucracy, but to no avail. . . . There have been promises of reform and Government reorganization since before I was born. I would hope that we who stand here today would finally begin to act to develop genuine civil service reform."[47]

Leach followed suit by noting that

Not only should direct Federal employment be capped, but indirect employment also should be more carefully constrained. Frightening statistics
recently presented by HEW Secretary Califano to the Senate Appropriations
Committee indicate that at the same time the U.S. Government is paying
salaries to 144,000 regular HEW employees, HEW is indirectly paying the
salaries of another 980,000 who work for private think tanks, universities,
State and local government, and related programs. Thus the equivalent payroll for this one Federal Department alone exceeds 1 million.[48]

The amendment was not without its opponents, however, including
future presidential contender Mo Udall (D-Ariz.), who raised procedural
and substantive concerns. "Everybody has got a lot of good ideas about civil
service. I expect that before midnight we are going to hear most of them at
the rate we are going. I had a Member back here with the bright idea that
every Member of Congress should have the right annually to fire one bureaucrat without any cause or argument." After reminding his colleagues
that the amendment had already failed in committee on a 13 to 8 vote, Udall
urged caution. "Sure, we ought to look into this overall problem of excessive
Federal employment, but I do not think there are many of us here tonight
who have the information we need to say that we are going to put a rigid
ceiling on Federal employment."[49]

Udall was joined by another future presidential contender, Patricia
Schroeder (D-Colo.), who warned her colleagues about the "shell game" of
contracting out, while asking her colleagues just how many people worked
in the shadow of government. Although Leach did acknowledge that the
number of contract-created jobs had increased substantially faster than the
civil service itself, he could not answer the question. The best he could do
was note that his amendment prohibited a shift of jobs from the federal
service to contractors, a provision that was, and still is, virtually unenforceable without firm numbers against which to measure gains and losses. The
amendment was not to be denied, however. It passed 251 to 96, with 85
members not voting, gaining enough locomotive velocity to assure passage
into law later that fall.

As would be the case with passage of the Workforce Restructuring Act
fifteen years later, the House held its first hearing on job shifting within the
year. "We have determined that lowering of personnel ceilings does not result in less Federal spending," chairman Herbert Harris (D-Va.) declared at

the opening of his Human Resources Subcommittee hearing. "When faced with a lowered personnel ceiling, but no reduction in budget, agencies merely contract out functions, even when it would be more cost effective to perform the work in-house."[50] Driven by the early Carter freezes and the Civil Service Reform Act, the number of permanent federal employees held steady at roughly 2.35 million from 1977 to 1978, confirming once again that ceilings do constrain permanent employment.

At the same time, however, the number of temporary employees had grown from 366,000 in 1977 to 1.4 million in 1978. No one knew, of course, whether the number of contractor employees had gone up, too. As one witness argued, "There is no wonder to me why over the past several decades we have been unable to develop more specific labor data on Government contractors and consultants. The reason [is that] the various administrations have not wanted to see the data. So long as there has been little or no information, then the public has no basis to know or thus to question."[51]

The hearing, and this book for that matter, turned on a simple fact: personnel slots had become more precious than dollars. They were harder to get and harder to spend. Since contract and grant dollars would flow regardless, it was easier for departments and agencies to push the jobs downward and outward than to fight for the personnel slots.

The hearing also turned on a simple political reality: Congress and the president were not about to require truth in job creating. Harris's 1979 bill requiring departments and agencies to estimate the number of federal employees who would be required to perform the functions being contracted out under all service contracts went exactly nowhere. Neither did Schroeder's 1981 bill requiring the federal government to establish a work force planning system that would count all heads working for government regardless of the source of funds. Much as Schroeder wanted to weigh what she described as the "32-ton marshmallow" called the federal work force, her colleagues were simply not interested in the numbers. But for the occasional grandstanding associated with capping or freezing federal employment, most members of Congress simply did not care about the size of the work force.

That Schroeder's work force planning bill did not pass is hardly surprising. Its failure reflects the accumulated incentives that make the shadow so easy to ignore. As we have already seen, Congresses, presidents, political parties, and civil servants themselves (at least the ones with the good jobs) have ample reason not to worry about shadows. It allows them to claim that the era of big government is over, even as the federal government pushes more and more jobs downward and outward. Even as Congresses and presidents pay heed to the job shifting issue by passing minor amendments and issuing executive orders prohibiting the steady leakage of institutional memory outward, the pronouncements are mostly symbolic gestures to federal employee unions. If Congress and the president truly cared about the shadow, they would lay a tape measure against it as frequently as they measure other things that matter.

The Federal Workforce Restructuring Act

Congress began holding hearings on the Federal Workforce Restructuring Act almost immediately after its passage in 1994. The ink on the parchment was barely dry when House Compensation and Employee Benefits Chairwoman Eleanor Holmes Norton (D-D.C.) began taking testimony on legislation to prohibit contracting out in the wake of the planned 272,900 work force cut. Granted, section 5(g) of the act had prohibited any such backfilling. But Holmes Norton was not convinced. "Far more likely than that abuse," she argued, "would be the substitution of contract employees for bought-out employees. . . . The broad authority of buyouts could become an open invitation to agencies to use an unregulated shadow government of contract employees to replace civil servants."[52]

For starters, OMB was relying on the agencies to police themselves. "We asked agencies if they have used service contracts to perform the work of employees who left because of buyouts," General Accounting Office Director of Federal Human Resource Management Issues Nancy R. Kingsbury reported on OMB implementation of the act at a Compensation and Employee Benefits Subcommittee hearing on September 22. "Twenty-nine of the 30 agencies responding said they had not, while the remaining agency was unsure. We also asked agencies if they had any requests for contract proposals pending to perform the work of employees who left with a buyout in fiscal year 1994. Of the 29 agencies responding, 26 reported that they did not have such requests and the 3 remaining agencies were unsure."[53] It was hardly the kind of systematic oversight that might reassure a congressional subcommittee of faithful execution, particularly a subcommittee charged with defending the civil service. Any agency willing to answer such a survey truthfully is too dumb to be an agency.

The fact, however, is that OMB had absolutely no way to check on section 5(g) compliance. By 1994 OMB was already well into its own restructuring, finally eliminating whatever remained of its once-proud Division of Administration Management. The division had once been a major player in providing central oversight of government management, but it had been slowly downsized with each presidential promise to cut White House staff. Forced to choose between budget and management analysts, OMB invariably protected the budget staff. By 1992 there was barely enough left of the *M* in OMB to bother with. Its staff was down to barely a dozen, most of whom were clustered around the deputy director for management, whose position had been created as a presidential appointment under the 1990 Chief Financial Officers Act. With the *B* preoccupied by budget cutting and the *M* virtually nonexistent, there was no one available to monitor implementation of any prohibition against contracting out, particularly a provisional one that had been written by a certain pesky senator from Arkansas.

Nevertheless, someone had to keep pressing the obvious. Holmes Norton asked her questions whenever she could, including at a Civil Service Subcommittee hearing chaired by her colleague, Frank McCloskey (D-Ind.). Caught between a firm number (federal head counts) and an unfirm number (contracting dollars), agencies had ample room to make shadows, a point hammered home by Holmes Norton in another exchange with OMB's Koskinen.

MS. NORTON: Well, there have already been—there have already been allegations that even now, even early, there is contracting out of bought-out employees' work. Given what you have just said, that the point was to do permanent downsizing and to increase efficiency, surely you would have no objection to a restriction saying that you can't do with contracting out money what you couldn't do with straight-out money for civil servants. I mean, what could be the possible objection to that, given your own statement of objective?

MR. KOSKINEN: Well . . . that is an arbitrary way of dealing with it and another restriction on limitation in trying to allow the agencies flexibility on doing their work. Because in some cases . . . you are eliminating work in one area and moving it to another area, and you are moving people around. And if you now say, well, the minute you have a buyout or you eliminate a person in one area you cannot contract that out, you in fact eliminate the flexibility of an agency to restructure its work force.

MS. NORTON: Wait a minute. You said that you certainly can't get another civil servant to do it, and now you are saying, however, maybe you could get a bought-out employee to do it? You have already said . . . the downsizing on that side is permanent. The 272,000, that is it. But you are saying that maybe a bought-out—an employee from somewhere else should be doing that work.

MR. KOSKINEN: What I am just saying is . . . I think the more arbitrary restrictions we put on this, the more we will limit the flexibility of the agencies to, in fact, try to refine their mission and the way they accomplish it, and I think that would be a mistake. . . .

MS. NORTON: I would just note for the record, because I disagree profoundly with Mr. Koskinen, that anybody sat down in these agencies, figured out the work to be done and then matched it with employees.[54]

Koskinen would later leave his OMB post, take a few months off, then return to shepherd the government's effort to reprogram its computers in time to prevent the year 2000 disaster. Battling the impending Y2K computer shutdown by hiring a legion of out-of-work COBOL programmers must have seemed like an imminently more rational process than defending the shadows created under the Workforce Restructuring Act. The problem for Koskinen was and still is that no one quite knows just where to draw the bright line between appropriate and inappropriate shadow casting. Is a shadow created by a ceiling somehow less appropriate than a shadow created by an earmarked appropriation to a college or university? Is a shadow created to defend the private sector from government more appropriate than one created because federal agencies cannot compete for the best and brightest scientists? These questions form the basis for the next chapter.

Conclusion

It is impossible to know just how big the full-time permanent work force would have become had Whitten and his successors not been so successful in creating head count ceilings. The number of federal employees would most certainly be much larger than 1.9 million. A sizable number of mandate-created jobs would have stayed at the federal level, while many service contracts would have never been let. Add the state and local mandate employees, the service contractors, and postal service workers together, and the likely "on-budget" full-time-equivalent federal work force would top well over 10 million. Recall that only a tenth (1.6 million) of the shadow work force actually worked delivering products to government in the prototypical contractor relationship.

The politics of smallness would not allow the federal government to carry these hidden workers on budget, of course. Nor is there any reason to imagine that the federal government would be particularly effective at managing a production line. NASA may need to build a satellite from time to time to be an effective buyer of high technology, for example, but it has no capacity to build rocket motors and space shuttles. That is not its comparative advantage in a democratic state.

The more interesting question is just how big the federal work force would be if scholars and politicians could actually agree on what constitutes an inherently governmental function. Is writing legislation inherently governmental? Enforcing laws? Guarding prisoners? Teaching citizenship? Flying the space shuttle? Fighting wars? All are areas where contractors have gained at least a toehold. Fourteen hundred contractors went to Bosnia as part of the U.S. peacekeeping force in 1997, while 9,200 contractors went to the Gulf War theater in 1990. Although such an exercise would produce far more grays than blacks and whites, it might force Congress and the president to develop a list of core competencies that should always reside inside government. It might also lead them to a more rational discussion of the total work force needed to deliver the goods on behalf of the federal government. As it takes place now, who delivers government services is more a function of accident than intent. Agencies are far more likely to ask how close they are to their ceilings than whether a given task is inherently or even remotely governmental. It is all part of the head count charade. Such charades are essential, however, when government uses head counts as a tool of smallness.

CHAPTER FIVE

The Tools for Sorting Out

Ceilings, freezes, and downsizings are hardly shining examples of finely tuned administrative policy. Without exception, such constraints have been designed to assure that the government meets its target, nothing more. If the government meets its target through careful work force planning, so be it; if it meets its target through attrition or voluntary buyouts, so be it, too. Ceilings, freezes, and downsizings are very blunt management tools, indeed.

The bluntness is unmistakable in the head counts themselves. Except for the Defense Department, Congress and the president have studiously avoided setting agency-specific targets when they impose a head count ceiling or freeze. Despite its substantial expertise for setting such targets through its authorizing and appropriating committees, Congress has generally delegated the agency-by-agency application to the president. Having discovered that such targets were nearly impossible to track and enforce, Congress quickly adopted the single government-wide head count approach chronicled in appendix C. But for the Defense Department reductions following the Vietnam War, the occasional Postal Department thaws, and the more recent military base closures, the president has been responsible for deciding when and where the cuts fall.

When head count constraints are applied deliberately, they can strengthen government performance and help agencies shed bureaucratic weight. That is certainly how the military base closing effort worked. Given a broad mandate from Congress and the president to winnow the nation's military bases at the end of the cold war, the Base Closure and Realignment Commission eventually closed 243 bases and cut over 100,000 civilian jobs before it closed itself in 1995. But when head count constraints are applied without targeting, they can eviscerate government capacity as attrition and age become the key determinants of who stays and goes.

Ceilings, freezes, and downsizings are not the only ways that Congress and the president control the mix of federal employees, however. The federal work force is also constrained by two mechanisms for sorting jobs between government and the private sector, one which requires all inherently governmental jobs to remain inside the traditional federal work force, and the other which requires that all commercial activities be open to competition from outside. In theory, these sorting mechanisms would work hand-in-hand with a head count constraint to assure that the appropriate jobs stay or go. In reality, the two mechanisms have never been closely linked to the head count constraints, in large measure because of the definitional tangle surrounding just what the words inherently governmental and commercial activities mean. Lacking useable definitions, departments and agencies let the head count constraints work their will in a mostly random fashion.

Before turning to these sorting mechanisms in more detail, it is first important to ask how presidents have used their head count discretion in the past. The history does not bode well for giving presidents continued discretion in the future.

How Presidents Manage Head Counts

Despite their new-found aggressiveness in pursuing head count constraints, recent presidents have hardly been more sophisticated about controlling the mix and match of federal employees than Congress. Lacking the tracking systems to target their cuts, they have left the downsizing to a mostly informal, often random process at the Office of Management and Budget (OMB).

Just how OMB actually assigns head count during ceilings and freezes has never been completely transparent to those either inside or outside of government.[1] There is no evidence that the agency has a sophisticated methodology, or any methodology at all for that matter, for allocating head count gains and losses. Nor is there any evidence that agencies bargain with each other or OMB for extra slots, or that personnel slots can be traded back and forth like scarce commodities in an informal market. Having operated for decades under head count constraints, OMB generally assumes that individual departments and agencies will get smaller unless they can provide a compelling justification and the dollars for each new slot. It is an assumption that hardly demands sophisticated allocation methodologies, particularly given the discretionary spending caps enacted under the Bush and Clinton budget agreements. Either a department or agency has the dollars and mission to warrant an increase (for example, Justice) or not (for example, Housing and Urban Development).[2]

The central problem at OMB appears to be a disconnection between the agency's own experts on federal personnel policy, who are housed in the Personnel, Postal, and Executive Office of the President Branch, and the budget officers who make the head count allocations. Although the personnel branch has considerable expertise on agency-by-agency capacity, it has never been actively involved in allocating head count, not in its current incarnation as part of a branch or in its earlier life as a separate office within the General Management Division. With just five full-time-equivalent staff members throughout most of the history covered by this book, the unit's main concerns have been the budgetary effects of pay and benefit increases and the more general oversight of the federal government's personnel agencies, most notably the Office of Personnel Management, the Merit Systems Protection Board, and the Federal Labor Relations Authority. As a result, the individual budget units have been responsible for the implementation and oversight of federal head count constraints.

Ironically, the personnel branch actually prospered in the wake of the Clinton administration's sweeping reorganization of OMB. Under the reorganization, almost everyone in the General Management Division was reassigned to the five new Resource Management Offices (RMOs) that replaced the five old budget program review offices. Having been reorganized repeatedly during the 1980s, there were only thirty-three employees left in the division by 1994 anyway, down from 224 in 1970, when the old Bureau of the Budget was given its new name and a renewed emphasis on management.[3] After the reorganization, there were none. By 1995 the *M* in OMB consisted of just three statutory offices: the Office of Federal Financial Management, which fell from forty-one full-time-equivalent staff members in 1993 to twenty by mid-1994; the Office of Federal Procurement Policy, which fell from thirty to twenty; and the Office of Information and Regulatory Affairs, which fell from fifty-six to fifty-two.[4] Although the old Office of Federal Personnel Policy gained a measure of stability as one of the two divisions in the new Health and Personnel RMO, it lost four staff members in the reorganization.

In theory, the 1994 reorganization was designed to enhance the kind of comprehensive thinking that might allow the executive branch to translate the blunt force of a head count constraint into a systematic reshaping of the federal work force. As OMB Director Alice Rivlin explained in announcing the plan,

> The basic premise of the new course we have chosen for OMB is that, to be successful in improving Executive branch operations, OMB's oversight role must better integrate our budget analysis, management review and policy development roles. . . . Critics of these recommendations may say that efforts to "integrate" management and budget will end in merely bigger budget divisions, whose management responsibilities will be driven out by daily fire-fighting on budget issues. We believe this criticism is based on a false premise that "management" and "budget" issues can be thought about separately. In fact, the changes are intended to improve OMB's ability to oversee agency programs and policies to ensure their efficiency and effectiveness.[5]

Also in theory, the RMOs would determine the appropriate head count for each agency based on a general assessment of workload, productivity, and mission. That is most certainly what OMB intended in designing the job descriptions for the new "program examiner" positions that subsumed the old budget examiner title. Not only are program examiners required to conduct studies of financial management and procurement, develop strategies for improving basic management systems, review major reorganization proposals, and improve the procurement of property and services, but they are also responsible for studying personnel management and systems to help develop and initiate long-range plans and goals.[6]

That is also what OMB intended in revising its Circular No. A-11, which instructs agencies on basic budget assumptions. "Agency proposals should result from a comprehensive system that integrates analysis, planning, evaluation, and budgeting, and reflects the policies of the President; consideration of appropriate roles for Federal, State, and local governments, as well as the private sector, in conducting the activities covered; missions, goals, and objectives of the agency. . . ; and implementation of the President's policies on management improvement."[7]

In reality, neither agencies nor program examiners were given much opportunity to think comprehensively about head count. To the contrary, the circular instructs agencies as follows: "Growth in agency workload generally will be assumed to be offset by productivity increases so that related

employment should not increase. Personnel currently funded will be uti-
lized to the maximum extent in staffing new programs and expansions of
existing programs. Reduced personnel levels should be planned where
workload is stable."[8] In explaining these assumptions, OMB reassured agencies that improvements in "skills, organization, procedures, and supervision
will produce a steady increase in productivity," allowing agencies to assign
these underengaged employees to other tasks. At the same time, OMB in-
structed agencies to assume that new information systems should result in
lower personnel requirements in the second year following installation or
upgrading.[9]

This is not the kind of policy workload management that might use
head count constraints as a lever to improve government operations. Rather,
it blends the bluntness of head count constraints with a wishful thinking
that can subtly and surely erode the long-term capacity of government. As
for the hoped-for consolidation of budget and management promised in
the OMB reorganization, the implementation has received mixed results.
Budget officers do have more of an opportunity to link budget with management, but they may have less time to do so. As with the rest of government, OMB assumed that its program examiners, as budget examiners were
renamed, would absorb the added responsibilities of OMB 2000 through
unspecified productivity gains.

Moreover, even though most program examiners felt greater responsibility for management improvement, some told the General Accounting
Office that they simply did not know what to do about it. "They also said
that the reduction of centralized management expertise in the statutory offices and the elimination of the General Management Division left them
with fewer sources of expertise and assistance," GAO reported in late 1995.
"Because program examiners had little time to spend looking for the expertise that was available, they said that certain management issues were not
addressed or received less attention."[10] OMB's reorganization may actually
have made federal head count implementation even less systematic than
before. Well intended though it was, it moved agency decisions even further
from a unified process of sorting out. Given the lack of time and expertise,
the best an individual program examiner might do is convey a general in-
struction to stay small. Anything more sophisticated would be well beyond
OMB's sadly diminished expertise.

The question for the following pages, therefore, is not whether program
examiners will continue to call for smallness—there is no doubt that Congress and the president see the benefits of a government that looks smaller

and delivers at least as much. Rather, the question is what the government might do to make the sorting out more systematic. There are times when using a shadow work force is the perfectly legitimate path to higher performance, other times when it is the product of administrative ignorance, and still other times when it is a failure of leadership. Although the federal government has never made an attempt to separate the shadows that hide weakness from those that add strength, much of the shadow casting profiled in this book appears to be for the wrong reasons.

The place to start sorting the shadows is with two of the most important, yet ambiguous, dividing terms in the government management dictionary: "commercial activities" and "inherently governmental functions." Congress and the president might be much more effective at protecting the core capacity of government if they only knew just what the two terms meant. In fact, like so much in politics, the two terms mean pretty much whatever Congress and the president say they mean at any given point in time.

The Definitional Tangle

As noted throughout this book, Congress and the president have long understood that the federal government could not fulfill its mission without outside help. From the very beginning of its space and nuclear weapons programs, for example, the government has relied on contractors and consultants to conduct the essential research and manage the programs. Sometimes, the only way to tell the difference between federal employees and contractors is the color of the time card. Unfortunately, the search for dividing lines between the traditional civil service and the shadow work force has been a moving target at best. Like so much that happens in the American system of government, politics has been more important to the definitional effort than rational science. As the following pages will suggest, however, the lack of precision is most certainly not for a lack of trying.[11]

The Bell Task Force

With federal contracts expanding rapidly with the creation of NASA in the late 1950s, the Kennedy administration launched the first, and arguably last, major review of the dividing line between public and private. Acting on the president's request, new budget director David Bell convened a senior task force composed of NASA administrator James Webb, White House Science Adviser Jerome Wiesner, Defense Secretary Robert McNamara, and the chairmen of the Atomic Energy Commission, the Civil Service Commission, and the National Science Foundation. The Bell report began with a sweeping assessment of what it called the government's "increasing reliance" on private contractors to do the research and development work of government.

Those contractors were hardly selfless giants, the report argued. They had come to depend for their existence and growth "not on the open competitive market of traditional economic theory, but on sales only to the United States Government. And, moreover, companies in these industries have the strongest incentives to seek contracts for research and development work which will give them both the know-how and the preferred position to seek later follow-on production contracts."[12] Because the profit incentive would lead contractors to expand their markets even to the detriment of agency capacity, the Bell Task Force set two criteria for casting the choice to contract out: "(1) Getting the job done effectively and efficiently, with due regard to the long-term strength of the Nation's scientific and technical resources, and (2) Avoiding assignments of work which would create inherent conflicts of interest."[13]

The Bell Task Force argued that it is "axiomatic that policy decisions respecting the Government's research and development programs—decisions concerning the types of work to be undertaken, when, by whom, and at what cost—must be made by full-time Government officials clearly responsible to the President and to the Congress. These are basic functions of management which cannot be transferred to any contractor if we are to have proper accountability for the performance of public functions and for the use of public funds."

The task force clearly understood that the distinction was easier stated than applied, however. To maintain in-house control, the government would need enough technical capacity in house to know when and if contractors were doing the job. It would also need to be "particularly sensitive to the cumulative effects of contracting out Government work. A series of actions to contract out important activities, each wholly justified when considered on its own merits, may when taken together begin to erode the Government's ability to manage its research and development programs."[14] In short, government could push so much of its work down and out that it would eventually atrophy as a source of control. NASA needs to know how to build satellites, not just how to acquire them; EPA needs to know how to build waste water treatment plants, not just how to grant them; the Department of Energy needs to know how to run a nuclear reactor, not just how to oversee a contractor who knows how to do this.

The task force clearly recognized the trade-offs between the flexibilities promised by contracting out and the potential erosion of government's core capacity to perform its mission. Although it also expressed support for the former, it reserved its strongest warnings for the latter. As the final report warned, "the Government's ability to perform essential management functions has diminished because of an increasing dependence on contractors to determine policies of a technical nature and to exercise the type of management functions which Government itself should perform," that a new generation of nonprofit contractors "are intruding on traditional functions performed by competitive industry," that "universities are undertaking research and development programs of a nature and size which may interfere with their traditional educational functions," and that government itself was "relying so heavily on contractors to perform research and development work as simply a device for circumventing civil service rules and regulations."

Most important, the task force warned that the growing contract work force was eroding the distinction between public and private. Its warning is well worth reading in its whole:

> A number of profound questions affecting the structure of our society are raised by our inability to apply the classical distinctions between what is public and what is private. For example, should a corporation created to provide services to Government and receiving 100 per cent of its financial support from Government be considered a "public" or a "private" agency? In what sense is a business corporation doing nearly 100 percent of its business with the Government engaged in "free enterprise"?[15]

How remarkable that a committee of hard-nosed scientists and budget analysts would raise such basic questions regarding civil society. How equally troubling that it decided not to answer them. "We have not, however, in the course of the present review attempted to treat the fundamental philosophical issues indicated in the preceding paragraph," the task force report noted. "We accept as desirable the present high degree of interdependence and collaboration between Government and private institutions."[16]

Words of Art

The Bell Task Force clearly struggled to find useful applications of what have become two of the most confusing phrases in government: "commercial activities" and "inherently governmental functions." On the surface, each term makes sense. It is in the application that confusion appears to reign.

COMMERCIAL ACTIVITIES. Start with commercial activities, arguably the simpler of the two dividing lines. OMB Circular No. A-76, which governs commercial activities, could not provide a clearer definition: "A commercial activity is the process resulting in a product or service that is or could be obtained from a private sector source." It is a definition that has changed little since 1955, when the Eisenhower administration prohibited federal departments and agencies from starting or carrying on "any commercial activity to provide a service or product for its own use if such product or service can be procured from private enterprise through ordinary business channels."[17] (See box 5-1 for examples of commercial activities provided as an attachment to the 1983 revision of the circular.)

Almost three decades later, the Reagan administration restated the principle in a 1983 revision: "In the process of governing, the Government should not compete with its citizens. The competitive enterprise system, characterized by individual freedom and initiative, is the primary source of national economic strength. In recognition of this principle, it has been and continues to be the general policy of the government to rely on commercial sources to supply the products and services the Government needs."[18] Thirteen years later still, the Clinton administration restated the principle once again, releasing guidelines, A-76 *Revised Supplemental Handbook*, that provided a rather different rationale:

> Americans want to "get their money's worth" and want a Government that is more businesslike and better managed. . . . Circular A-76 is not designed to simply contract out. Rather, it is designed to: (1) balance the interests of the parties to a make or buy cost comparison, (2) provide a level playing field between public and private offerors to a competition, and (3) encourage competition and choice in the management and performance of commercial activities. It is designed to empower Federal managers to make sound and justifiable business decisions.[19]

Despite some agreement on the purpose of A-76, the actual process for testing the respective strength of the two sectors is both cumbersome and confusing. The federal government is allowed to engage in commercial activities for an assortment of reasons, some that are objective—including national defense or intelligence security, patient care, temporary emergen-

Box 5-1. *Examples of Commercial Activities*

Audiovisual products and services
Photography (still, movie, aerial, and
    so on)
Audiovisual facility management and
    operation

Automatic data processing
Programming and systems analysis,
    design, development, and simulation
Equipment installation, operation, and
    maintenance

Food services
Operation of cafeterias, mess halls,
    kitchens, bakeries, dairies, and
    commissaries
Ice and water

Health services
Physical examinations
Dietary services
Veterinary services

Industrial shops and services
Fire protection and prevention services
Custodial and janitorial services
Refuse collection and processing

Maintenance, overhaul, repair, and testing
Maintenance of aircraft and aircraft
    components, motor vehicles, railway
    systems, office furniture and equip-
    ment, and space systems

Management support services
Advertising and public relations
Debt collection

Testing Services
Testing of ordnance, clothing, lumber
    products, optical products, and testing
    equipment

Office and administrative services
Library operations
Translation
Compliance auditing

Other services
Laundry and dry cleaning
Training: academic, technical, vocational,
    and specialized

Real property
Construction, alteration, repair, and
    maintenance of roads and other
    surfaced areas
Landscaping, drainage, mowing and care
    of grounds
Dredging of waterways

Security
Guard and protective services
Forensic laboratories

Special studies and analysis
Cost benefit analyses
Regulatory studies
Management studies
Legal/litigation studies

Transportation
Operation of motor pools
Trucking and hauling

Source: Executive Office of the President, Office of Management and Budget, Circular No. A-76
rev. (1983), pp. 7–10, Attachment A.

cies, and functions for which there is no commercial source available or
those involving ten or fewer employees—and some that are entirely subjective, including the need to maintain core capability, engage in research and
development, or meet or exceed a recognized industry performance or cost
standard.

There are two ways that departments and agencies can deflect the A-76 process. First, they can define a given activity as inherently governmental, thereby earning a complete exemption from further review. Second, they can demonstrate that a given activity, while commercial in nature, can be performed at a lower cost inside government than outside. This defense requires that the agency (1) develop a work statement for the specific commercial activity, (2) complete a management study of the organization, staffing, and operation of the most efficient government organization (MEO) for producing the good or service, and (3) solicitation of private bids to assess the relative cost of delivery by the private sector versus the MEO. A private source can only win the competition with a bid that is at least 10 percent lower than the MEO price. Even if government wins the competition by meeting or beating the private bid, however, it must still build the MEO, meaning that taxpayers should benefit regardless of the outcome.

Taxpayers cannot benefit, of course, unless the A-76 studies occur. Whether because departments and agencies are somehow convinced they have become MEOs through a decade of downsizing, or because they either do not have the staff resources to conduct the studies or believe everything they do is inherently governmental, the number of A-76 studies has declined dramatically since the mid-1980s. According to the General Accounting Office, there were exactly zero non–Defense Department positions studied in 1997, and at least three departments, Education, Housing and Urban Development, and Justice, had not studied a single position since 1988. Table 5-1 shows the level of A-76 activity from 1984 through 1997. Readers should note that A-76 activity is measured in the total number of positions studied, not in dollars.

There are two patterns worth noting in the table. First, administrations vary significantly in their general commitment to A-76. The federal government studied an average of over 16,000 positions a year under Reagan (1983–88), 5,200 per year under Bush (1989–92), and 7,000 under Clinton (1993–97). Second, the Department of Defense plays the same masking role in the A-76 process that it did in the more general shrinking of government discussed in chapter one.[20] Remove Defense from the A-76 totals, and activity tumbles from 4,100 non–Defense Department positions a year under Reagan to fewer than 1,500 under Bush, and exactly 84 under Clinton.

The point here is not to endorse greater A-76 activity. To the contrary, it is to suggest the limited utility of using A-76 as the primary sorting device for managing federal head count. Even with the fullest presidential commitment possible in the mid-1980s, A-76 covered barely 2 percent of the full-

Table 5-1. *Number of Circular No. A-76 Cost Comparisons, 1984–97*
Number of positions

Year	Total positions studied	Defense positions studied	Non-Defense Department positions studied
1984–87	63,636	48,028	15,608
1988	17,249	12,000	5,249
1989	8,469	6,100	2,369
1990	9,547	6,989	2,558
1991	2,026	1,243	783
1992	564	496	68
1993	509	441	68
1994	1,691	1,623	68
1995	2,386	2,128	258
1996	5,267	5,241	26
1997	25,255	25,255	0
1988–97	71,963	61,516	11,447

Sources: for 1984–87, General Accounting Office, *Managing the Government: Revised Approach Could Improve OMB's Effectiveness*, GAO/GGD-89-65 (May 1989), p. 57; for 1988–97, General Accounting Office, *OMB Circular A-76: Oversight and Implementation Issues*, GAO/T-GGD-98-146 (June 4, 1998), p. 4.

time-permanent civil service. The definition of commercial activity may be clear in the abstract, but the utility of the term as a method for shifting jobs from government to the shadow and back is limited at best. Without assaying the value of A-76 as a disciplining tool, it seems reasonable to argue that it can never be more than a minor lever in allocating head count constraints more systematically.

INHERENTLY GOVERNMENTAL FUNCTIONS. As noted above, departments and agencies can exempt themselves from A-76 by declaring a given commercial activity an inherently governmental function. Like commercial activities, the term seems easy to define. According to the Office of Federal Procurement Policy (OFPP), which was created in 1974 to strengthen federal oversight of an increasingly complicated procurement system, the term encompasses "a function that is so intimately related to the public interest as to mandate performance by Government employees." That means activities that "require either the exercise of discretion" or "the casting of value judgments in casting decisions for the Government."[21]

Defined formally in 1992, an inherently governmental function is nothing less than the faithful execution of the laws, which OFPP defines as any action to: "(a) bind the United States to take or not take some action by contract, policy, regulation, authorization, order, or otherwise; (b) determine, protect, and advance its economic, political, territorial, property, or other interests by military or diplomatic action, civil or criminal judicial proceedings, contract management, or otherwise; (c) significantly affect the life, liberty, or property of private persons; (d) commission, appoint, direct, or control officers or employees of the United States; or (e) exert ultimate control over the acquisition, use, or disposition of the property, real or personal, tangible or intangible, of the United States, including the collection, control, or disbursement of appropriated and other Federal funds."

Much as OFPP's effort to define a bright line can be admired, its policy letter mixed in just enough exemption to leave the reader wondering whether such a bright line could ever exist. "While inherently governmental functions necessarily involve the exercise of substantial discretion," page 3 of the letter reads, "not every exercise of discretion is evidence that such a function is involved. Rather, the use of discretion must have the effect of committing the Federal Government to a course of action when two or more alternative courses of action exist." "Determining whether a function is an inherently governmental function often is difficult and depends upon an analysis of the factors of the case," the letter adds on page 4. "Such analysis involves consideration of a number of factors, and the presence or absence of any one is not in itself determinative of the issue. Nor will the same emphasis necessarily be placed on any factor at different times, due to the changing nature of the Government's requirements." As if to acknowledge its own difficulties finding the bright line, OFPP added two appendixes that gave examples of activities likely to be declared inherently or not inherently governmental functions. A sampling is provided in box 5-2.

There are two problems with the list and the letter that produced it. First, as noted above, the policy letter was heavily caveated with "could be" and "might be" legalese. Try as it might to define terms and set boundaries, OFPP left plenty of room for reinterpretation, not the least of which was its statement that "This policy letter is not intended to provide a constitutional or statutory interpretation of any kind, and should not be construed, to create any right or benefit, substantive or procedural, enforceable at law by a party against the United States, its agencies, its officers, or any person."[22] As such, the letter could not be used to create a basis on which to challenge an agency action. Notwithstanding the value of such boilerplate, agencies could rightly conclude that practically anything goes.

Box 5-2. *Distinguishing the Functions of Government*

Inherently governmental functions	Not inherently governmental functions
Direct conduct of a criminal investigation	Services related to budget preparation
Command of military forces	Reorganization and planning activities
Conduct of foreign relations	Analysis to be used in developing policy
Determination of agency policy	Development of regulations
Determination of program priorities or budget requests	Evaluation of another contractor's performance
Direction and control of federal employees	Acquisition planning
Selection of individuals for federal employment	Responses to Freedom of Information Act requests
Counterintelligence operations	Participation in any situation where a contractor might be perceived as an
Approval of agency Freedom of Information Act responses	agency employee or representative
Conduct of administrative hearings	Inspection services
Determination of budget policy, guidance, and strategy	Legal interpretations of regulations and statutes

Source: Office of Federal Procurement Policy, 1992.

Second, the policy letter gave departments and agencies nearly exclusive authority to make the inherently governmental decision. Although it did reserve the right to review a particular decision, agencies had to follow their own interpretation. If the Department of Energy decided that having contractors write congressional testimony for the secretary was not an inherently governmental function, so be it. "The extent of reliance on service contractors is not by itself a cause of concern," OFPP's letter writers argued. "Agencies must, however, have a sufficient number of trained and experienced staff to manage Government programs properly. The greater the degree of reliance on contractors the greater the need for oversight by agencies. What number of Government officials is needed to oversee a particular contract is a management decision to be made after analysis of a number of factors."[23]

The Politics of Sorting

Despite the relative difficulties in defining commercial activities and inherently governmental functions separately, the two terms interact to form separate zones for privatization; contracts, grants; and mandates, and full government involvement. The zones are summarized in figure 5-1. Presum-

Figure 5-1. *Sorting Out Options*

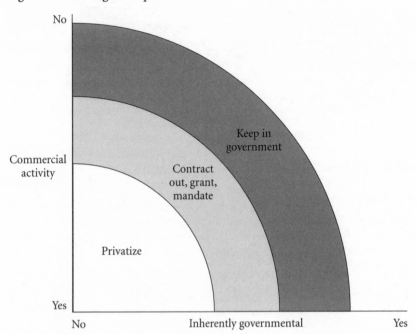

ably, the government should never privatize a noncommercial activity that is an inherently governmental function, and it should never retain a commercial activity that is not an inherently governmental function. It is not enough to examine the two terms separately. The sorter must ask whether an activity is commercial and inherently governmental simultaneously.

The definitional tangle comes from the fact that the answer is rarely definitive. Consider the list of commercial activities in box 5-1. Doing laundry for the navy can be a purely commercial activity in home ports such as Norfolk, Virginia, but may be an inherently governmental function in the Persian Gulf. Weapons testing can be a commercial activity for an M-16 rifle, but may be an inherently governmental function for a missile defense system.

Where the boundaries for each zone are set depends on more than just context, however. It also involves politics. Witness the decision to allow government agencies to bid against private firms to perform commercial activities for other government agencies. The Reagan administration almost certainly would not have allowed the Agriculture Department's National Information Technology Center in Kansas City to best IBM and Computer Sciences Corporation in a competition to build a $250 million Federal Aviation Administration data center, as it did in 1997. Nor would that administration have allowed the Treasury Department to create a Center for Applied Financial Management that would compete with private firms in providing $11 million in administrative support to other government agencies in 1997, or the Interior Department's Administrative Support Center in Denver to win a contract from the Social Security Administration to provide payroll services in fiscal 1998.[24] Not only did the Clinton administration allow all three departments to bid and win, but it also openly encouraged government to take on the private sector through the creation of "franchise funds" that allow departments and agencies to carry over a percentage of retained earnings from year to year. Congress approved a five-year experiment with the franchise funds as part of the Government Management Reform Act of 1994. Thus it is best to view the sorting zones in figure 5-1 as highly flexible, giving departments and agencies enormous discretion in defining commercial activities and inherently governmental functions pretty much as they see fit.

The politics of sorting were undeniable, for example, in the recent debate over the Federal Activities Inventory Reform Act (FAIR) of 1998. The final bill was only meekly based on the original proposal, which was entitled "The Freedom from Government Competition Act." That bill, which was authored by Senator Craig Thomas (R-Wyo.), began with a sweeping indictment of the traditional sorting process: (1) "government competition with the private sector of the economy is at an unacceptably high level, both in scope and in dollar volume" and (2) "current laws and policies have failed to address adequately the problem of government competition." In its initial form, the act would have prohibited agencies from beginning or carrying out "any activity to provide any products or services that can be provided by the private sector," or from obtaining any goods or services from any other governmental entity, meaning the franchise funds described above. It also would have created an OMB entity called the Center for Commercial Activities to promote maximum conversion of government activities to private sector sources.

Facing intense opposition from federal employee unions, supporters of the reform act eventually accepted the much more modest proposal embedded in FAIR. Under the final proposal, which basically codified the A-76 process, federal departments and agencies are required to identify and publish comprehensive lists of all activities deemed not inherently governmental. Once published, every activity on the list is theoretically subject to competition at the department or agency head's discretion. Despite its earlier criticism of the A-76 sorting process, the Freedom from Government Competition Act accepted OFPP's definition of inherently governmental functions word for word as a complete exemption from conversion, as did FAIR as a complete protection against listing.

What distinguished FAIR from A-76 was the annual listing requirement and an entirely new appeals process. Under the act, an interested party can challenge the omission of an activity from the list within thirty days of its publication, to which the agency must respond within twenty-eight days, to which the interested party may file an appeal within ten days, to which the agency must respond a final time within ten days. However, just because an activity is declared not inherently governmental does not guarantee competition. Again, it is up to the agency head to decide what stays and what goes. Because there is no judicial review under the act, all agency decisions are final.[25] (At least one earlier version of FAIR had provided for judicial review by the United States Court of Federal Claims to render judgment on omissions from the inventories.)

Although the act was much less constraining than the original Thomas proposal, it was not without controversy. Dennis Kucinich (D-Ohio) rose in strong opposition to the bill, claiming that its primary purpose was "to force the Federal Government to identify likely targets for privatization or contracting out. The Federal contractors would like the government to help them identify new business opportunities."[26] Kucinich and his fellow Democrat from Minnesota, Bruce Vento, both argued that the government had done enough downsizing through the Workforce Restructuring Act and was contracting out too much already. "The fact is we spend more on the contracting of services, close to $120 billion in fiscal year 1997, than we spend on pay and retirement for the entire civilian work force," Kucinich argued in a perfectly appropriate apples-to-apples comparison. "In fact, some of the more recently created Federal agencies like the Department of Energy, the National Aeronautics and Space Administration, and the EPA have relied from the start on contracting out services rather than performing them directly." Kucinich's zone of privatization and contracting out was small, indeed, as well it would be, given his description of such actions as "a piecemeal dismantling of our republic."

Obviously, supporters of the bill envisioned a much larger zone for private delivery of public services. Noting that the bill was supported by the

Clinton administration and over a hundred organizations, Representative John Duncan, Jr., (R-Tenn.), heralded FAIR as a way to get federal agencies "out of private industry and stick to performing those functions that only government can do well. At the same time it will allow our great private enterprise system to do those things it does best, providing commercial goods and services in a competitive environment." Pete Sessions (R-Tex.) put it more succinctly by cribbing from the original version of A-76: "The government should not be in the business of competition with private business."

According to Stephen Horn (R-Calif.), the debate was "eerily familiar" to the controversy surrounding passage of H.R. 9835 in 1954. That bill, which passed the House only to die in the end of session rush in the Senate, also provoked intense opposition, raising the ire of a junior member named Thomas P. O'Neill Jr, who pleaded on behalf of a navy rope plant in Massachusetts. As Horn summarized the debate, "Others discussed the Federal operations making coffee roasters, dentures, sleeping bags, and even iron and steel plants. Most of these operations are now defunct, and we have contracted with private vendors to make dentures, and the coffee to stain them, with specialized firms that have those functions as their core missions."[27]

It is not yet clear how fair FAIR will be. Congress might use the list of not inherently governmental functions as a basis for statutory privatization. Then again, agencies may continue mostly as is with what appear to be occasional, half-hearted studies of their commercial activities. What is clear, however, is that the sorting tools currently available for translating head count constraints into deliberate sculpting are hardly deliberate themselves.

Sorting the Shadows

Given the definitional discretion embedded in the current sorting systems, it should come as no surprise that the shadow of government might reflect a mix of both good and ill. A department that wishes to insulate a particular activity from the provisions of A-76 can do so, if not with complete impunity, at least with significant delaying power; an agency that wishes to push an inherently governmental function out to a contractor can also do so, arguably with even greater impunity.

But whether the decision is to protect or push, head count constraints assure that the decisions have unintended consequences both within each department or agency and across the rest of government. The decision to protect a unit in Commerce may force contracting out at HUD, the decision to mandate out in Health and Human Services may create capacity for civil service expansion in Justice. Even if OMB never puts the decisions together in any kind of systematic analysis, head count constraints eventually reshape government. Whether the result is a sculpting or demolition depends largely on whether the shadows of government are used to hide weakness or build strength. Box 5-3 offers a sampling of how contracts, grants, and mandates can be used to do either.

When Shadows Hide Weakness

There clearly are times when shadows are used not as a source of strength, but as a way to get a job done in the face of administrative sloth or outright incompetence. Although such shadow casting may make perfect sense in the short run, it eventually weakens government by excusing systemic problems or outright negligence.

EVADING HEAD COUNTS. The first excuses in the box reflect the fear and loathing associated with head count pressures. Given a choice between inflicting pain and contracting out, the federal government will almost always contract out.

This is not to suggest that the government backfills downsized positions through some deliberate process. Much as Senator Pryor can be admired for his longstanding effort to police such behavior, most of the head count shadow casting is much less sophisticated. As at OMB, most departments and agencies do not have the work force planning systems to engage in such deliberate shell games. Although downsized employees occasionally do return to their agencies as contract workers, as National Institutes of Health radiologists did in the late 1980s, most agencies simply cannot play such games. To do so would mean linking an agency's human resource office, which is responsible for downsizing, with its acquisition office, which is responsible for contracting. The two barely talk to each other, let alone know how to work together to exploit administrative loopholes.

The fact is that the federal government simply does not have a work force planning system to shift jobs deliberately. As D.C. Delegate Holmes Norton argued in 1994,

> If you were in General Motors or some place making cars, you would not simply say what I want is 300,000 bodies. You would have to figure out first whether you could make enough cars and sell enough cars with the bodies that were left, and you would be forced by the bottom line to sit down and

Box 5-3. *Evading Weaknesses and Acquiring Strength through Contracts, Grants, or Mandates*

Evading Weaknesses	Acquiring Strength
To relieve head count pressure in a department or agency.	To acquire skills not available inside government.
To spare departments and agencies the "heartbreak" of downsizing.	To augment government capacity during a temporary crisis.
To avoid targeted downsizings.	To create public/private partnerships on projects of national significance.
To evade pay limits on specific positions deemed essential to a department or agency operation.	To allow agencies to more easily expand and contract with mission.
To escape federal administrative rules.	To create a blended work force where appropriate.
To compensate for poorly trained, under-motivated federal civil servants.	To create new recruitment opportunities for hard-to-fill positions.
To evaluate future employees outside the formal hiring process.	To save money on functions that are not inherently governmental.
To generate levels of performance not achievable with a government work force.	To generate market pressure as a device for lowering costs or increasing efficiency.
To make sure the job gets done right.	
To shield the federal government from blame in the event that a risky program fails.	To protect the private sector from government encroachment.
	To protect civil society from government.

figure that out department by department. You have not done that, and it is the greatest fear of this committee that, when all is said and done, we will end up with whatever is left—with overworked Federal employees, with people screaming, screaming at the top of their voices, that they want to do contracting out because they can't do the work that has to be done. All of this stuff is going to loosen up because the preparatory work, agency by agency, the hard work, the grunt work, the brain work of figuring out how many people are necessary to do the unit of work simply has not been done.[28]

Would that the federal government could be so duplicitous as to move jobs back and forth deliberately. That would mean it had the capacity to identify jobs by level or occupation that should stay or go. The reality is that the federal government would rather do anything, including selling its institutional memory, than target specific employees for downsizing.

Much of the explanation is personal. Firing employees is the toughest thing a manager must do in any organization, be it public, private, or non-profit. The trauma of firing employees is real, the demoralizing effects lasting. Targeting buyouts on specific groups of employees is hardly easier. Someone still has to make a painful decision. As Koskinen reported to the Holmes Norton subcommittee in 1994, "for a lot of different reasons and a lot of different agencies, people have offered buyouts across-the-board for matters of equity, for matters of morale, for matters of efficiency."[29] To do otherwise would mean making a deliberate decision.

Consider the buyouts used to implement the Workforce Restructuring Act in 1994. But for a handful of agencies that would not give buyouts to certain employees—for example, the Federal Aviation Administration would not open its buyouts to air traffic controllers—the vast majority of buyouts were on a first come, first served basis. Having been forced to separate employees through a reduction in force, managers may use a shadow work force just to avoid the future pain. "Even if saving money isn't the issue, I think you're going to stay with contractors or anything else that doesn't resemble a permanent work force," said a National Science Foundation executive in a focus group of human resource managers convened in 1998. "Going through a RIF or an adverse action is probably in the back of many managers' minds. . . . It's the depersonalization that occurs when you are hiring temps who are perceived as second class."[30] No one gets fired when the money runs out on a shadow work force. They just fade away when their checks stop coming.

Much as federal managers who have to fire valued employees deserve sympathy, the alternative to such deliberate downsizing is the accidental corrosion of government's core competency. Although the Gore reinventors can be criticized for their unrelenting hostility toward control personnel, a hostility that is based on a narrow view of control personnel as mostly useless naysayers who get in the way of the heroic program staff, at least they were willing to define a target. That took the kind of courage in all too short supply elsewhere at the top and middle of government.

EVADING BUREAUCRACY. Departments and agencies also use contracts, grants, and mandates to evade the antiquated administrative systems that plague the federal government, a case that was effectively articulated by the first Gore reinventing government report.

Gore was hardly the first to make the case against overcontrol, however. Program managers have felt besieged by internal red tape for decades. The National Academy of Public Administration (NAPA), a congressionally chartered research organization, called for reinventing government a full decade before Gore put pen to paper: "What is bitterly ironic is the fact that Federal managers, both political and career, typically regard themselves as captives of a series of cumbersome internal management 'systems' which they do not control." Describing the systems as "so rigid, stultifying, and burdened with red tape" that they undermine government's capacity to serve the public on "a responsive and low-cost basis," NAPA offered an all-too-familiar complaint in its report to Congress and the president:

> Many of the restraints and regulatory requirements which now make it so difficult for Federal managers to function have their origin in commendable efforts to prevent or control waste, abuse of authority, or corruption. . . . Unfortunately, the cumulative impact of an ever increasing number of procedures, findings, appeals, and notifications is to jeopardize the effective execution of [government]. Moreover, regulatory requirements, once adopted, tend to be retained long after they have ceased to make any constructive contribution to program management.[31]

To reinforce its point, NAPA put a drawing of Gulliver bound by the Lilliputians on the cover of its report.

What neither NAPA nor Gore ever wrote about is the role of such constraints in driving managers to create shadows. Much as federal managers might complain publicly about the contracting out of high-impact jobs, many attest privately that they have greater control over the work done as a result. There is no need to go through endless appeals to fire poorly performing employees nor any need to wait to add new staff. "I just completed a search for a Chief Information Officer that took a year and a half," a senior official at the National Institutes of Health reported in the 1998 focus group. "I think that the systems for some of the more common occupations across government are not flexible enough. And there doesn't seem to be anybody in charge, either in the executive branch or the legislative branch, who understands that and who's willing to do something about making mechanisms available to pay the right amount of money so the government can be competitive with the private sector."

Over time, the convenience of contracting can lead even the most dutiful federal manager to take the easy route. They can pay prevailing wages for high-demand positions, while giving their contract employees the breathing room to do their jobs unencumbered by pesky overseers and what they see as needless paperwork. Having been besieged by the Lilliputians despite a half-century of well-intentioned reforms, who can blame them for taking the easy escape? In 1949 Herbert Hoover promised a government that worked better and cost less, as, in later years, did Johnson, Nixon, Carter (a government as good as the people, too), Reagan, and Clinton-Gore. Although the Gore effort appears to have penetrated more deeply than its predecessors, shadow casting may be the only way to make the numbers add up to performance.

EVADING INADEQUACY. Contracts, grants, and mandates can also be used to hide poor performance within the government's own work force. When departments and agencies want the job done right, they sometimes look outside.

There are two ways to prevent such shadow casting. The first is to provide the pay and training to make the government work force evenly effective. "When you look at the problems we see in information technology [IT] units right now, the real issue is effectiveness," a Social Security human resource manager noted in the 1998 focus group. "The fact of the matter is that for certain IT skills the government is just not competitive. So your only solution is to go to a contingent work force or you're not going to get the job done." A Labor Department official echoed the problem. "You want somebody who knows the latest technology because you're trying to advance. You have to go out on contract to get that person because you're not going to be able to rely on having trained staff available. So it's a question of looking ahead and determining whether you are investing in your people, and if not, it's cheaper to go out and get it someplace else." As for investing in training, budget cutting creates a climate in which training is the first to go. "Many of the agencies have deliberately determined that training is not a priority," said a navy human resource executive. "One of the first things that's cut when you downsize is training. . . . If you don't invest in your people, what you wind up doing is changing the nature of your workforce in order to get the work done." Having disinvested in the government work force, shadow casting becomes the only alternative to get the job done right.

The second way to prevent this inappropriate shadow casting is to hold the government accountable for results, not compliance. Unfortunately, even the effort to shift accountability from rules to results can involve a plethora of rules. For all its commitment to focusing on results, and for its admirable rejection of "one-size-fits-all" implementation, the 1993 Government Performance and Results Act carried a high degree of compliance accountability. Agencies are required to develop five-year strategic plans, complete with a comprehensive mission statement, long-term goals, descriptions of just how the agency expects to achieve its goals, a schedule of significant steps and needed resources, and a set of proposed measures against which to assess progress made.

Hence the first strategic plans were to be completed by September 30, 1997, with annual performance plans to follow immediately. The statute was supplemented by a July 1998 revision of Budget Circular A-11 that added thirty-four pages of detailed text providing definitions of terms (general goal, general objective, outcome goal, output goal, performance goal, performance indicator, program activity, program evaluation); timing instructions for submission of initial strategic plans, updated and revised plans, and interim revisions; formatting of documents; transmittal instructions; deadlines, coding rules; principles for choosing program indicators; coverage of each plan; and verification and validation plans. Even with the details, agencies could hardly be faulted for being confused about just what OMB and Congress might have intended. Consider the following definitions of general goals and general objectives as an example:

> General goal: Included in a strategic plan, this goal defines how an agency will carry out its mission over a period of time. The goal is expressed in a manner which allows a future assessment to be made of whether the goal was or is being achieved. The goal may be of a programmatic, policy, or managerial nature. General goals are predominantly outcome-type goals.

> General Objective: Included in a strategic plan, The objective(s) are paired with a general goal, and can be used to help assess whether a general goal was or is being achieved. An objective usually describes a more specific level of achievement than a general goal.

> Outcome goal: A description of the intended result, effect, or consequence that will occur from carrying out a program or activity.

> Output goal: A description of the level of activity or effort that will be produced or provided over a period of time or by a specified date, including a description of the characteristics and attributes (e.g., timeliness) established as standards in the course of conducting the activity or effort.[32]

There is nothing wrong with demanding common formats, detailed plans, and careful evaluation as part of producing higher performance, of course. Nor is there anything troublesome about subjecting those plans to close scrutiny. Toward that end, I have argued that federal Inspectors General (IGs) ought to take a more aggressive role in both designing and validating the measures that departments and agencies use to track their annual performance: "This does not mean that IGs should merely present their own performance plans to their agency heads. Nor does it mean that they should only be involved in evaluating the integrity of the data presented in support of agency plans. I believe that the core statute clearly instructs the IGs to participate in the actual design of the program indicators. They should weigh in on the construction of the measures, validate the data, and credential the final reports to Congress."[33]

At the same time, however, the longing of some program managers for the ease of producing results through a contract is understandable. One of the central tenets of performance accountability is that the principal must be able to control the outcome desired. Given the systems and layering of responsibilities discussed above, managers can hardly be faulted for seeking the surety that comes with the very different language of contracting and grant making—a language of deliverables, actions, reporting authorities, and due dates.

EVADING BLAME. Shadows clearly weaken government when they are used to avoid blame. There are times, although rare, when having a contractor in charge of a dangerous or risky program is the most comfortable position for the government politically. In 1985, for example, just a year or so before the Shuttle Challenger tragedy, NASA asked the National Academy of Public Administration to examine the feasibility of privatizing the entire space shuttle program. Although NASA was appropriately concerned about the long-term burdens of running what it hoped would soon become a relatively routine cargo program, its senior officials also expressed worries about the potential for another "204 incident," a term used to identify the fire that took the lives of three Apollo astronauts in 1967. Privatizing the shuttle would give the agency some protection in the event of another catastrophe by shifting blame to the contractor.

The Challenger investigation obviously proved otherwise. Although the contractor, Morton Thiokol, was harshly criticized for suppressing internal objections to the launch of Flight 51-L, NASA's decision-casting process was clearly identified as the contributing cause of the accident. NASA's middle-level contract managers not only knew that the O-rings used to seal the solid rocket motor joints would be compromised at low temperatures, but they also made no effort to relay the intensely felt Thiokol worries upward on the night before launch. To the contrary, NASA contractor managers clearly pressured Thiokol to reverse what had been its original recommendation not to launch until temperatures went up. "My God, Thiokol," one NASA manager asked, "when do you want me to launch, next April?" It was as if, one Thiokol engineer later testified, the contractor had to prove beyond a shadow of a doubt that it was unsafe to fly instead of proving just the opposite. As the presidential commission appointed to investigate the accident concluded,

> The decision to launch the Challenger was flawed. Those who made that decision were unaware of the recent history of problems concerning the O-rings and the joint and were unaware of the initial written recommendation of the contractor advising against the launch at temperatures below 53 degrees Fahrenheit and the continuing opposition of the engineers at Thiokol after the management reversed its position.... If the decisionmakers had known all of the facts, it is highly unlikely that they would have decided to launch 51-L on January 28, 1986.[34]

When Shadows Add Strength

Shadow casting to get the job done right because government can only do wrong betrays a nearly complete failure of leadership. If government is not properly structured or led to get its appropriate jobs done right, Congress and the president should get to work on creating the conditions needed for success.

Using shadows to evade pay constraints, administrative paralysis, and head counts is equally troublesome. Although hiring a shadow work force may seem like the only path to success at the time, departments and agencies are deceiving themselves for the long term. It may be that government must fail every once in a while to prove that it needs the capacity to succeed.

All shadows are not cast for the wrong reasons, however. There are perfectly appropriate reasons for choosing a shadow work force over a traditional civil service work force, not the least of which are the disciplines imposed by profit lines and market pressures. Box 5-3 offers a sampling of ways in which shadows can strengthen government.

If there is one word to separate the shadows that hide weakness from shadows that build strength, it is "deliberative." Shadows that build strength involve hard choices about where government begins and ends, who should do what work, and how to deliver the goods in time. "It's time to lower the level of rhetoric of outsourcing and contracting out," former OFPP administrator Steven Kelman remarked in 1998, as Congress began debating a stack of bills requiring agencies to hold public versus private competitions for any activities not deemed inherently governmental functions. "It's not a question of big government/small government, nor is it a question of do you or don't you like the federal workforce. It is a good management principle to stick to your core competency."[35]

ACQUIRING SKILLS. Start at the top of the list with the first three ways that shadows strengthen government. Simply stated, the federal government must be able to acquire skills that it cannot develop or maintain on its own civil service work force. Having chosen to run the nation's nuclear weapons plants with contractors, for example, the Department of Energy never developed an internal capacity to clean up nuclear waste. Thus when it came to start closing the facilities at Savannah River, Fernald, or Rocky Flats, the department had little choice but to acquire cleanup specialists from the private sector.

The question is why casting a shadow under such circumstances is any more acceptable than using a contract to evade pay limits on positions already within the civil service. The answer lies in the inability to build the internal capacity at a reasonable cost. If the federal government is not paying enough to recruit the auditors, computer programmers, and program analysts to deliver public goods effectively, Congress and the president should raise the rates or create a special pay system such as the one used by the Federal Reserve Board. But if it has never had the capacity to begin with or has allowed the capacity to slowly leak away through head count cuts, the federal government may eventually have no choice but to use a shadow work force to get the job done. Thus does the inappropriate use of contracts to evade pay ceilings eventually force the appropriate use of contracts to buy back the institutional memory (if it ever existed) from the private firms that now own it.

In a similar vein, the federal government has reasonable cause to use contracts to address crises such as the Y2K computer problem, particularly when the need is clearly limited to the crisis. As noted earlier, it makes no sense to rebuild the federal government's COBOL competencies for a one-time event. Such onetime events hardly need be restricted to a year or two. At NASA in the 1960s, for example, the Apollo program created a surge in contractor involvement that peaked five years into the program, falling back as the program reached its goal in 1969.

ACQUIRING FLEXIBILITY. The next three ways that shadows strengthen government also involve deliberation. NASA remains the premier example. Its work force, both civil service and contract-created, was designed to rise and fall with mission demands from the very beginning. Although there were clearly places where the Whitten Amendment forced the agency to contract out activities that it would have preferred to create and maintain in house, NASA's success depended on acquiring expertise already available on the outside. The surge-tank model also happened to fit NASA's political circumstances. Despite President Kennedy's embrace, it is not clear that NASA's mission was broad enough to assure public support for a massive new bureaucracy. Even with its limited civil service work force, NASA faced more than its share of controversy, as America launched a war on poverty in the midst of a war in Vietnam. As the pressures to do more with less increased with the heating up of both wars, NASA pushed more and more of its work into the shadow, prompting calls for a rebalancing of in-house and out-of-house capacity. Nevertheless, as NASA historian Arnold Levine writes, "The case for service contracts rested on one powerful argument that was never adequately refuted: An agency with such urgent and unique assignments could not have done the job with its in-house staff alone. . . . Faced with ambiguous guidelines, NASA officials believed that resort to the private sector was inevitable and that the question of whether a task was covered in-house or by contract was less important than the knowledge that the capability would be there when needed."[36]

More recently, many federal agencies have been using contracts and temporary appointments to create a blended work force composed of permanent civil servants, more-or-less permanent contractor employees, and outside consultants and easily severable part-timers and temporaries, all theoretically working side by side toward the public good. The only difference is that the permanent employees will stay at the end of the surge, while the temporaries will go. At the Department of Energy, for example, temporaries are carrying an enormous burden in the cleanup of aging nuclear weapons plants. "What we need to be able to do is hire very, very top flight managers to help us close these sites without a promise that we'll be able to keep them on our rolls indefinitely," a senior Energy Department officer explained in the 1998 focus group. "So we need to pay top dollar and we need to be able to provide benefits competitive with the rest of the government and maybe even beyond. Then we need to be able to shake their hand at the end of five or six years and say thank you very much."

Although blending most certainly reflects head count pressure, making a virtue out of stark reality, it also addresses the difficulties the federal government faces in recruiting young Americans to public service. The old notion of spending a lifetime in the civil service is just that, old. Young Americans expect to change jobs much more frequently than their parents did and are much more reluctant to make work the centerpiece of their lives. Blending is a perfectly reasonable way to expose reluctant young people to the public service careers, while harnessing their talent and energy, if only for a moment. It is also a way to test future public servants before casting tenured appointments. The National Institutes of Health does just that in appointing scientist to tenure track positions.

SAVING MONEY. The final four ways that shadows strengthen the government involve dollars and sense. There is absolutely nothing wrong with saving money on tasks that are not inherently governmental, the problem again being how to define the term with enough precision. Democrats and Republicans have long agreed that government should never pay more than it has to in purchasing any good or service. It should be a "smart buyer" at all times, demanding the highest value for the money.

They have also long agreed that government should protect the private sector whenever possible. Although Democrats and Republicans alike believe in the efficiency-producing effects of competition, the question is how best to protect the private and public sectors from each other. Much as the Reagan administration pushed government to conduct A-76 cost comparisons, even to the point of issuing a 1987 executive order requiring individual agencies to review at least 3 percent of all agency jobs annually until all commercial activities had been exposed, there is little evidence that the effort produced more than frustration. In looking back over the nearly thirty years of effort that culminated with the final Reagan push, Kettl offers a dreary conclusion: "the government's program for contracting out commercial activities has been plagued with problems since it was first implemented by the Eisenhower administration in 1955. . . . Nothing troubled A-76 more than the government's difficulty in defining the desired product and then trying to determine if private contractors were delivering satisfactorily."[37]

It is not clear that the longstanding effort to protect the private and nonprofit sectors from government has done the two any favors, however. Being in the shadow of government can create enormous economic dependency, thereby exposing individual organizations to enormous risk during lean times. If the advantage of shadow casting is that no one inside the federal work force gets hurt when the downsizing begins, the clear disadvantage of being in the shadow is that the hurt lands there. Even as the federal government uses the shadow to perform essential tasks, it is under enormous pressure itself to keep costs low, which heightens the tension between those who make the shadows and those who occupy them.

Take the ongoing battle between the nation's research universities and the federal government over indirect cost recovery as an example. The federal government wants to have its cake, in the form of high-quality research, and it wants to eat it too, in the form of not paying the true costs of producing that research. Hence the ongoing battle over just how much to allow universities to charge in overhead on federal research and development grants. Is it permissible to charge for libraries? Student orientations? Faculty leaves? Alumni magazines? A university yacht? Much as the federal government has tried to drive the allowable rate downward, universities have proved steadfast in demanding a fair share of support for keeping body and soul together. In 1991 the average overhead rate among the nation's top research universities was 52.7 percent; in 1997 the average stood at 52.3 percent. That means that every dollar received in 1997 for direct research and development costs required another 52 cents for indirect expenses.

Whether the proportion of indirect expenses is high or low depends on who is doing the talking. Federal officials and university research faculties think the number is much too high. University administrators think it is too low. What is clear is that research universities have never been more dependent and vulnerable to vagaries in federal grant spending. Most could not survive without the federal grant dollar.

At the same time, it is not clear that pushing jobs outward and downward has resulted in the hoped-for savings. As noted in chapter two, state and local governments siphon off a substantial portion of federal grants for their own priorities, a practice that could be sharply curtailed if the federal government tightened its grant instruments. According to GAO, the opposite holds true. "Our analysis suggests that most grants are designed neither to reduce substitution nor to target funding to states with relatively greater programmatic needs and fewer fiscal resources. This is an indication that the federal government may be getting less fiscal impact than it could from the dollars it spends."[38] If Congress wanted the most cost-effective path to state and local impacts, it would target its resources. That it does not suggests that grants are often more about political benefits than efficiencies.

Even the A-76 program, which has no other purpose but to save money through private competition, cannot prove that it has actually achieved its goals. No one knows just how much it actually costs to do the cost estimates required under the act, although one U.S. senator estimated in 1990 that the Defense Department had a staff of 1,700 at a cost of $150-300 million running the A-76 process. Nor does anyone know whether the savings are ever achieved or where the savings go when they are achieved. "Even after the program had been in place for several years," writes Kettl of A-76, "no one— not OMB, not GAO, not any of the federal agencies affected—really knew how well A-76 was working and how much, on balance, it had saved the American taxpayers."[39] Like the downsizing of government, Congresses and presidents seem satisfied to say they are cutting costs, even if they cannot prove it.

Finally and most important, it is not always clear that such protection serves the national interest. The concentration of power in an ever smaller number of Defense Department contractors is only one example. As noted in chapter one, the downsizing of Defense has produced an upsizing of the top four contractors, who have engaged in a feeding frenzy designed to gobble up smaller competitors. Lockheed's purchase of Martin Marietta, and Loral moved it from number three ($7.5 billion) on the Defense contractor list in 1992 to number one ($21 billion) in 1996; Boeing's purchase of a struggling McDonnell Douglas moved it from number four ($5.4 billion) to number two ($15.9 billion); and Raytheon's purchase of Hughes Electronics, then a division of General Motors, moved it from number seven ($4.7 billion) to number three ($12.1 billion). Little United Technologies bought no one and actually fell in total Defense funding, yet moved up from number eight ($4.5 billion) to number four ($3.4) nonetheless.[40]

None of this is to argue that mergers are inherently negative. There is some evidence that the mergers produce the salutary effect of lower labor cost (perhaps at the price of long-term job insecurity and lower benefits) and job cuts through what business experts call cross servicing and shared administrative support. The long-term question is whether such super-combinations will eventually come back to haunt the customer. At some point, a very small number of firms will own the nation's entire defense capacity, at which point traditional oligopoly theory will likely hold. Forced to buy from Lockheed or no one at all, the federal government will either have to break up the firm or pay the going price. No doubt such considerations were at work in the Justice Department's refusal to grant Lockheed's recent request to purchase Northrup Grumman.

In this regard, Dwight Eisenhower's 1961 farewell address is as relevant today as it was almost four decades ago. "This conjunction of an immense military establishment and a large arms industry is new in the American experience," he explained. "The total influence—economic, political, even spiritual—is felt in every city, every State house, every office of the Federal Government. We recognize the imperative need for this development. Yet we must not fail to comprehend its grave implications. Our toil, resources and livelihood are all involved. So is the very structure of our society." Eisenhower's fears were clear. Government could drive out private curiosity, even as large corporations began to control government. His warning is well worth reading:

> Today, the solitary inventor, tinkering in his shop, has been overshadowed by task forces of scientists in laboratories and testing fields. In the same fashion, the free university, historically the fountainhead of free ideas and scientific discovery, has experienced a revolution in the conduct of research. Partly because of the huge costs involved, a government contract becomes virtually a substitute for intellectual curiosity. For every old blackboard there are now hundreds of new electronic computers. The prospect of domination of the nation's scholars by Federal employment, project allocations, and the power of money is ever present—and is gravely to be regarded. Yet, in holding scientific research and discovery in respect, as we should, we must also be alert to the equal and opposite danger that public policy could itself become the captive of a scientific-technological elite.[41]

Lost in all the debate about savings and shadows is Eisenhower's expression of a fundamental fear that the barriers between public and private, government and civil society, would eventually blur to nothingness. Eisenhower was not some Luddite hoping for a return to simpler times. Nor was he an enthusiast of big government. He was an astute observer of human nature who understood the concentration of power. He understood that government and the private sector had to be protected from each other, lest the basic fabric of civil society thin to nothingness.

The question is whether that protection should take the form of shadow casting or of a more durable wall between government and nongovernment. No doubt the federal government will always need to purchase goods and services from the outside. But whether it should purchase as much is far less clear. It is a question to which we will return at the end of this book.

Sorting by Competency

It is impossible to know just how many of the federal government's 16.9 million shadow workers fall into either the strengthening or the weakening categories. The Energy Department, NASA, and EPA could not function without sizable numbers of contractor employees, nor could Defense, Transportation, and the General Services Administration do their jobs without significant numbers of purchased goods. No one can know how big the federal civil service would be if all inherently governmental jobs were pulled back in, or how small it could become if all commercial activities were pushed out.

The question for the moment is not how large or small the civil service should become, but how Congress and the president should sort positions in the future. Given the inevitability of continued head count pressure, what might departments and agencies do to become more deliberate in deciding what stays and what goes?

One as yet untested answer involves an assessment of core competencies. Simply defined, a core competency is a skill required for the successful performance of an organization's mission. Although the term is more traditionally used by human resource professionals to describe the skills needed in a particular job, it can also be applied to broad organizational demands.[42] Instead of asking what individual employees need for superior performance, an organizational competency approach asks what a given unit needs to produce results of one kind or another.

The core competency approach is reminiscent of the zero-based budgeting model adopted by the Carter Administration in the late 1970s. Like zero-based budgeting, a core competency assessment begins with a broad analysis of what a given organization seeks to accomplish, an analysis that is already embedded in the Government Performance and Results Act (GPRA) strategic planning process. With its goals, objectives, indicators, and measures already specified under OMB Circular No. A-11, a government agency could easily move forward with a detailed assessment of the human resource requirements of successful performance.

Indeed, the skeleton for such analysis is already in place under GPRA. Under A-11, the five-year strategic plans already require agencies to identify the general resources needed for success, as well as the mitigating conditions that might undermine results (for example, El Niño, natural disasters, lower-than-expected economic growth), while the annual performance plans demand a "description of the organizational processes, skills, and technology and of the human, capital, information, or other resources that will be needed to meet the performance goals." Although most departments and agencies are still struggling to define their goals and objectives clearly, prompting House majority leader and former college professor Dick Armey (R-Tex.) to give government an F on the first round of plans, the Department of Transportation earned uniform high grades at both ends of Pennsylvania Avenue. It was one of the few departments or agencies to measure goals, using traffic-related deaths and severity of injuries as core indicators of actual performance.

More to the point of this book, Transportation was also one of the few organizations to discuss the role of its work force in assuring results. It was also the only major agency to set a human resource goal: "Foster a diverse, highly skilled workforce capable of meeting or exceeding our strategic goals with efficiency, innovation, and a constant focus on better serving our customers now and into the 21st Century."

Toward that single end, Transportation promised to "conduct workforce planning across the Department to align human capital requirements with strategic goals"; assess "how the Department's culture should be adapted to support a high performing organization characterized by a high degree of employee empowerment in decision making, risk taking, collaboration, and other related aspects of work"; ensure "that the Department's workforce composition reflects the national workforce"; eliminate "any artificial barriers to the advancement and full contribution of all employees, such as glass ceilings, discrimination, and sexual harassment"; "recruit, develop, and deploy a diverse workforce with those 21st Century competencies needed to achieve the DOT's strategic goals"; maintain the "continuity and institutional knowledge needed to provide strong leadership through better succession planning"; create "a continuous learning environment required of all high performing organizations by implementing policies, providing resources and opportunities, which enable all DOT employees to build the job competencies, computer and technology capabilities, work management skills, flexibility, and organizational knowledge required to achieve the Department's strategic goals"; link department "awards and recognition programs to program outcomes, encouraging employees to work toward strategic goals and objectives, including innovation, cost-cutting, and enhanced customer service"; and implement "worklife policies that support both employees in balancing work and personal priorities and the Department in meeting its goals."[43]

Much as the effort to link human resources to the department's more

Figure 5-2. *Sorting by Core Competencies*

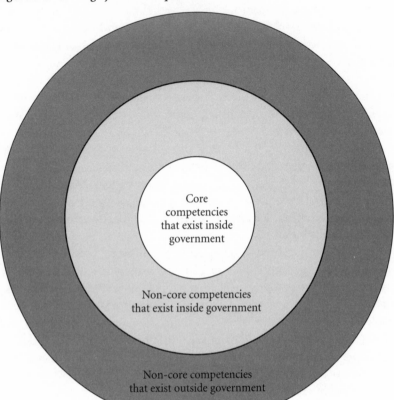

general goals can be admired, the Transportation plan missed one important point. Instead of looking at its work force as a collection of individual
civil service jobs, it also needed to examine the mix of in-house versus out-
of-house capacity. With an estimated contract and grant work force of over
810,000 (see chapter two), the department could have easily justified a
detailed assessment of how its contractors and grantees would make sure
their employees would be empowered, while balancing work and personal
priorities.

    It could also have justified a thorough discussion of the appropriate
mix of workers to achieve higher performance. To what extent, for example,
could customer service be enhanced by bringing certain functions back in
house, or by pushing certain activities out of house? To what extent could

traffic fatalities be reduced by shifting jobs from grants to contracts, or vice versa? To what extent could the severity of injuries be reduced by privatizing certain units? Such questions are hardly beyond the realm of analysis, particularly given the continued head count pressure envisioned in other parts of Circular A-11.

Such an analysis would not start with basic questions about private versus public activities, however. It would start with a systematic assessment of what the agency needs to meet its statutory and performance obligations. Once its core competencies are defined, an agency could proceed to a more traditional commercial activities or inherently governmental review to determine which noncore activities might be pushed out and which should stay in because of lower cost. The result of this analysis would be a multitiered work force built around a relatively small center of civil servants who hold clearly identified core competencies, a larger group of civil servants who perform noncore functions for clearly defined reasons, and a still larger group of employees who were not civil service employees who perform noncore functions on behalf of the federal government under contracts, grants, and mandates. This work force is illustrated in figure 5-2.

Moving to this core competencies model would take more than new analytic capacity, of course. It would take a basic change in how government views its work force. Instead of making civil servants the sole focus of its human resource activities, the federal government would have to adopt a much fuller definition of who constitutes an employee. Not only would such an approach require new data on just who works for government under what instruments, but it would also demand a new bridge between those who hire labor through civil service appointments, those who purchase labor through contracts and grants, and those who create labor through mandates.

Conclusion

Unable to define what should stay in and what can go through deliberate means, the federal government has engaged in fifty years of often random shadow casting. Separate agencies will reach different decisions on keeping certain jobs in house or on driving them outward and downward. The result is extraordinary unevenness across and within agencies, with a given unit's ability to do its job in house largely dependent on the birthdays and quit rates of its employees. Instead of a government that works better and costs less, as Gore would put it, Americans get a government that is highly dependent on a work force that may or may not be accountable to Congress and the president.

Indeed, as the next and final chapter of this book will argue, the illusion of smallness creates a series of secondary illusions that affect the long-range ability of government to fulfill its mission. The illusion of smallness can foster an illusion of merit, as government builds a rule-bound system to assure fairness for its in-house work force while accepting just about any system for its shadow employees; an illusion of accountability, as the government comes to depend on a work force it cannot control; an illusion of capacity, as the government becomes dependent on private and nonprofit agencies for core competencies that no longer reside in house; and an illusion of a unified public service, as some of the very best jobs in the government migrate to the private and nonprofit sector.

CHAPTER SIX

Managing a Government
that Looks Smaller
and Delivers More

CONGRESS AND THE PRESIDENT will
not soon abandon the head count constraints that have done so much to
alter the shape of the government work force over the decades, nor will they
stop searching for ways to reduce the number of civil service employees. To
the contrary, it is highly likely that the first Congress and president of the
new millennium will be pressed to cut the full-time-permanent civil service
by another 272,900 positions or more. The days of a fully self-contained
government work force are long gone, never to return.[1]

Nor could government go back even if Congress and the president
wanted to. The world has changed too much. Much as he worried about the
emerging military-industrial complex, Eisenhower clearly understood the
changes wrought by the cold war. "Our military organization today bears
little relation to that known by any of my predecessors in peacetime, or indeed by the fighting men of World War II or Korea," he argued in his 1961
farewell address. "Until the latest of our world conflicts, the United States
had no armaments industry. American makers of plowshares could, with
time and as required, make swords as well. But now we can no longer risk
emergency improvisation of national defense; we have been compelled to
create a permanent armaments industry of vast proportions."

Forty years later, it is just as easy to warn of an equally imposing policy-
industrial complex, in which a small number of highly specialized consulting firms control the institutional memory at the top of government, while

an equally small number of highly specialized contractors and grantees hold near-monopolies in everything from Superfund community relations to nuclear waste cleanups. There may be perfectly good reasons for creating a policy-industrial complex, not the least of which are the cost savings involved, but there are also risks, including the erosion of the government's own capacity to oversee the complex.

Simply put, the illusion of smallness is here to stay. It is the easiest way that Congress and the presidents can address the prevailing political incentives for a government that looks smaller and delivers at least as much. Short of some cataclysmic event such as a war or natural disaster, federal employment will remain small. Although the size of the contract, grant, and mandate work force will likely ebb and flow over time, depending on the size of the Defense Department budget, there is only one direction possible for the civil service. The question is not whether the federal government will continue to depend on a vast shadow of contractor, grantee, and state and local employees in the future, but what the illusion of smallness might mean for the future of the public service and the overall performance of government. Before asking how the illusion of smallness creates illusion upon illusion, it is first useful to review the major findings of the book.

A Brief Review

This book is based on a very simple question with anything but a simple answer. Estimating the true size of the federal work force involves a series of decisions on where to draw the boundaries between the federal government and its helpers. Using the most expansive definition of just who works for the federal government, the true size of government is close to 17 million people, a number that excludes $30 billion or so in small contracts and foreign purchases.

The estimates are far from perfect, of course, and some readers will disagree with decisions to include this function or that mandate. It is certainly reasonable to ask, for example, whether state and local government employees should be counted as part of the federal work force under grants and mandates, particularly given the available evidence on substitution effects. At the same time, however, it is impossible to imagine the federal government being able to fulfill its mission without encumbering the state and local work force. The Environmental Protection Agency is just as dependent on state and local employees and contractors to do its job as it is on its own full-time-equivalent civil service. To pretend that its total work force is a

mere 17,000 civil servants is to deny the realities of how that agency is organized to operate and to ignore the potential dependencies created when government pushes responsibilities downward and outward.

The interesting question is not whether a government of 16.9 million
workers is large in an absolute sense, although it is roughly nine times larger
than the 1.9 million civil service workers that is used so often to declare the
era of big government over. Rather, the interesting question is how the total
compares with other sectors of the U.S. economy and how that total has
changed over time. At a minimum, four conclusions can be drawn about
the true size of government.

The first conclusion is that the federal government appears to be much
more dependent on a supplemental work force than the private sector is.
Although U.S. corporations have been outsourcing for decades, few approach
a fraction of the dependency on supplemental employees implied in the
estimated true size of government. Even if the dependency calculation is
restricted only to service contractors, the federal government employs two
supplemental workers for every one full-time-equivalent civil servant, making its full-time-equivalent work force roughly a third of its total, a ratio that
is well beyond the most aggressive outsourcing used in the private sector.

The second conclusion is that the true size of the federal government
gives it a remarkable presence in American society as a whole. Indeed, of all
the statistics summarized in this book, the most important may be the number of Americans who depend on the federal government for their income.
According to the Pew Research Center surveys cited in chapters two and
three, roughly four out of ten Americans (or someone in their family) either
works for government (28 percent) or works in its shadow (14 percent). The
statistic raises significant questions for the future of civil society. At what
point, if any, does society become too dependent on government for suste-
nance? At what point, if any, does government become too dependent on
society? What happens if and when a majority of society enters the
government's employ, directly or indirectly? Does the blurring of the boundary between government and private become a threat to the survival of democratic life? Although there are no firm answers to such questions, it may be
time to start asking them.

The third conclusion is that the true size of government has been shrinking for the past fifteen years. In the aggregate, total federal employment,
civilian plus military, had dropped by roughly 900,000 jobs, or 21 percent,
between 1984 and 1996, with a particularly steep drop coming in the wake
of the military base closing effort that began in the late 1980s and the enact-

ment of the Federal Workforce Restructuring Act of 1994. As of December 1998, the civilian head count was 13 percent smaller than it had been at the start of the Clinton administration five years earlier, while the military was down 31 percent. Also in the aggregate, the federal shadow work force dropped by more than 1 million jobs between 1984 and 1996, with the contract work force declining by 17 percent. Although the grant work force increased by 9 percent over the same period, the growth was more than offset by the shrinking contract work force, shrinking the total shadow by roughly 11 percent. Although Clinton was wrong to claim that the era of big government was over, the era was most certainly starting to end.

The fourth conclusion is that the aggregate trends in the true size of government mask enormous variation across departments and agencies. Although it is true, for example, that thirteen of the fourteen departments of government absorbed cuts from 1993 to 1998, the Defense Department accounts for the vast majority of the recent shrinking. Indeed, Defense has been masking the true size of the non-Defense work force for the past forty years. The non-Defense civil service work force grew 53 percent between 1960 and 1996, while the non-Defense shadow, as suggested by the National Income and Product Accounts, grew at a far greater rate. Remove Defense from the 1984–96 trends, and total civilian head count was up ever so slightly at the end of this period, while estimated contract and grant jobs had increased dramatically. Much as the Clinton administration can be credited for slicing domestic civil service head count by more than 100,000 jobs from its recent peak in 1992, the Defense downsizing was responsible for almost all of the good news on the end of the era of big government.

The difference between the advertised size of government and the true size of government in jobs created through contracts, grants, and mandates is easy to explain. It is in the prevailing incentives for policies that allow government to become more efficient without cutting programs. Although there are Americans who believe that the federal government has the wrong priorities and should sharply reduce its programs, a substantial plurality say government has the right programs but should become more efficient. By cutting federal head count even as the program agenda remains steady or expands, American government gives the public exactly what it wants: the cake of perceived efficiency and the benefits of an activist program agenda. It is also one way for America's elected and appointed leaders to claim progress in cutting costs, while reaping significant political benefits.

This is not to argue that the past decade has failed to produce higher productivity. There have been real cuts in both the federal civil service and the shadow work force, and real gains in productivity, service, and efficiency. The Clinton administration's procurement reform has clearly produced faster, cheaper, and smarter acquisitions, and innovation does appear to be on the rise. Thus even as the administration's claim that the era of big government is over can be questioned, there is ample evidence that government is working better today than it did five years ago. Has the federal head count returned to 1960 levels? Only in the most narrow sense. But has it become more effective? The answer is most certainly yes.[2]

The problem lies in the use of head count constraints as the primary tool for keeping government small. Starting with the Whitten Amendment and continuing most recently with the Workforce Restructuring Act, the federal government has relied on personnel ceilings and freezes to keep the work force from growing. Designed for a government work force that was mostly self-contained, the Whitten Amendment and its successors clearly forced departments and agencies to push more and more jobs into the netherworld just outside full-time civil service employment. Even as the head count constraints created the illusion of a small federal work force, departments and agencies were forced to create an increasingly robust shadow work force that could deliver the goods and services to meet growing responsibilities. That is most certainly why mandates began to expand and why service contracts have been growing.

The head count pressure might not create a problem if the federal government had a systematic method for sorting jobs between its full-time, in-house work force and its shadow. As stated throughout this book, not all shadow jobs hide the true size of government or mask weakness. Many contribute significantly to government performance. Unfortunately, it is impossible to know just how many of the federal government's contract, grant, and mandate jobs were created for the right or wrong reasons. The current sorting systems simply do not allow such comparisons. As a result, no one knows whether departments and agencies have the right mix of employees or not. The state of the federal work force in 1999 is anyone's guess, which is precisely not how to run a government that works better, let alone one that costs less.

Illusions upon Illusions

By itself, the illusion of smallness merely represents another example of the politics of administration, albeit one with a fifty-year time line and enormous political incentives. It can hardly be a surprise that Congress and the president would seek to constrain total federal employment as a way to show fealty toward cost cutting, even as they nurture public support for continued federal involvement. That has been the historic pattern in budget politics, too.

What makes the illusion important is its potential effect on the general performance of government. It is quite conceivable that the illusion has no effect at all, that it merely involves a change of venue for the delivery of services, with no reduction in accountability or increase in cost, or that it has actually enhanced performance by introducing market pressure into the production of government goods and services. Good politics does not always mean bad performance.

Nevertheless, there are at least four ways that the illusion of smallness might undermine government performance. Because there is so little information on what is happening in the shadow of government, it is best to think of the potential effects as illusions in their own right. It may be, for example, that the illusion of smallness creates a multitiered government work force in which some federal employees are covered by tight rules on merit, while others are hired and fired with minimal protection. But lacking detailed information on the myriad hiring systems used by federal contractors and grantees, only the illusion of merit created by federal head count constraints can be discussed in writing. Similar challenges emerge on questions of accountability, government capacity, and the state of the public service. Simply put, the federal government can assert that it has a merit system for hiring employees, maintains tight accountability between those who make the policy and those who implement it, retains sufficient in-house capacity to avoid dependency and enforce accountability, and supports a unified public service that can attract the best and brightest to government. But the illusion of smallness renders all four assertions more illusory than real.

The Illusion of Merit

When Congress rebuilt the civil service classification system in 1949, it did so with the complete confidence that its work would govern the public service from cradle to grave, assuring merit in hiring, fairness in promotion, and protection from political whim throughout. Designed to rationalize what had become a patchwork of rules and position descriptions, the statute collapsed the then-existing thirty-one grades into eighteen, while completely restructuring the position descriptions and pay scales within each grade. Although the framework has been reworked over time, most notably by replacing the top three grades with a Senior Executive Service under the Civil Service Reform Act of 1978, the Classification Act has proven a durable, even rocklike, reform. "Even as it erodes slightly with time," I have written, "there are only so many ways to hire and fire employees without abandoning the merit system enacted in 1883."[3]

The problem is that the Classification Act covers only a fraction of the work force that now delivers services on behalf of the federal government. It says nothing about the contract employees who now deliver so much of the goods; offers no guidance on the grantee employees who generate so much of the research and development essential to the federal task; and provides no insights on the state and local employees who labor under federal mandates. Designed to cover the old public service of the 1940s, the Classification Act appears to be completely out of touch with the new public service. Full-time-permanent federal employees are governed by one set of extraordinarily complex rules, while part-timers, contractors, grantees, and state and local employees are governed by a host of separate, often contradictory, rules of their own.

That the Classification Act created its own impenetrable web of rules is not in doubt. "Costs to the taxpayer for this personnel quagmire are enormous," Gore argued of the 54,000 federal employees who administered the system in 1993. "We spend billions of dollars for these staff to classify each employee within a highly complex system of some 459 job series, 15 grades and 10 steps within each grade. Does this elaborate system work? No."[4] Much as Gore's success in abolishing the 10,000 page *Federal Personnel Manual* can be applauded, most of the underlying rules still remain in force in Title 5 of the United States Code of Federal Regulations.

Having fought for the better part of a century to assure that federal employees were covered by a merit-based system, reformers now face a new era in which the millions of workers who produce goods and services on the federal government's behalf are covered by thousands of separate systems, most of which are closed to public scrutiny. The merit system may still hold for the full-time-permanent work force, but the market determines personnel policy throughout much of the shadow. In the short-term that market may produce substantial savings, as government tries to work better and cost less. But those savings will prove ephemeral if they come at the expense of future government obligations. Paying shadow employees lower salaries today may well mean higher entitlement spending tomorrow. Firing shadow employees before they qualify for pensions may make perfect sense in a highly competitive business environment, but it may yet come back to haunt government as those pensionless employees age into Supplemental Security Income for older Americans.

In the meantime, the challenge is to better define the mix of jobs that constitute the federal delivery system. No department or agency has made a more determined effort to do so than the Department of Defense did in rationalizing its blended work force in 1997. Although the department later described its new personnel system as "just a thought," the imagined system was quite precise in describing the nature of what would have been a three-tiered public service. To quote the proposal, at the top would have been a "cadre of permanent, career employees comprised of current employees and 'permanent' employees hired under the 'new' personnel system. This segment of the work force would continue to perform major portions of workload and mission, not subject to surge, sized to represent a 'minimum' or 'constant' workload requirement, and in functions not considered candidates for outsourcing."[5]

The middle would have been built around a much more flexible core of temporary employees "hired for up to five years, immediately eligible for health, life, and [thrift savings program] coverage, but with no immediate government contributions. This segment of the work force would be used to respond to surge, cyclical or otherwise, could be converted to permanent status noncompetitively (and therefore could be used as a 'recruitment pool' for permanent hires), could be released to avoid RIF to permanent work force, and would be much less costly (in average work year costs)." The bottom would have been composed of "contractor employees performing work determined to be non-governmental in nature and more cost effective to outsource or privatize in place."

Much as the proposal reflected a legitimate effort to codify realities, it had serious flaws. "At least for federal employees, the celebrated bridge to the Twenty-First century yet may turn out to be made of Swiss cheese," I wrote at the time. "Some employees will scramble across as the sole survivors of the merit system. Others will be condemned to wait for rare opportunities to move up from contract jobs. Still others will never get beyond a temporary posting, shorn of security and a certain dignity, even as they are asked to work side by side with the protected few. If the temporaries can only advance by the failure of the permanents, so much for teamwork."

Nevertheless, the proposal conveyed an important message about the shadow of government. "Instead of attacking the DoD proposal," I wrote, "advocates of a healthy public service should ask how this agency came to be so radical. The answer is that it is only doing what comes naturally to a government that holds the line on total employees without reducing its obligations. And for that, the Defense Department should be congratulated."[6] Rather than managing to head count as so many agencies do, Defense actually thought ever so briefly about managing to work. Some jobs would involve inherently government functions, others would reflect surge tanking, and still others would be essentially private in character. The trick would have been to develop a reliable system for sorting them all out in a fair and defensible way, for the current classification system would be utterly useless for the task. The system reveals just about everything there is to know about a job—its pay, its level of responsibility, its pecking order—but not whether that job is core or peripheral to a department or agency's mission.

The proposal marks a turning point in thinking about the shadow of government, not because it was necessarily the right policy, but because it confronted the true size of government as an issue to be managed, not ignored. By counting contractor employees as members of the federal work force, not as mere pieces of furniture to be bought and amortized, the proposal imagined a tighter chain between the top of government and the ultimate bottom. By establishing a first and second tier within government, the proposal also acknowledged the reality that public service involves a range of attachments, from weak to strong, between employer and employee. Knowing who to count and how to govern how the various pieces of the shadow might fit together are critical steps toward managing the true size of government.

Congress and the president cannot legislate on the shadow work force without knowing much more about how it interacts with the civil service at all levels. Consider at least three questions that would have to be answered along the way to the kind of civil service reform imagined in the Defense proposal:

Who Works in the Shadow? No one is quite sure who works in the shadow of government. The federal government may know just about everything there is to know about civil servants, from age to race to years of service, but it knows virtually nothing about the contractors who work by the civil servants' sides. Although there is at least some reason to believe the shadow work force is disproportionately composed of women and minorities, there has never been a census of who works in the middle and bottom tiers of the supplemental work force described above.

What Do Shadow Employees Do? Once again, there is little systematic evidence of what contractors, grantees, and state and local mandate employees do that is both similar and different from federal civil servants. The limited available evidence suggests a three-tiered work force, with very highly paid contractors and consultants who perform senior-level policy and management analysis jobs at the top of government, a middle level of service contractors who do everything from computer programming to auditing, training, and evaluation, and a bottom level, also composed of service contractors, who perform menial tasks no longer deemed inherently governmental functions. It is this bottom tier that appears to have the over-representation of women and minorities.

How Are Shadow Employees Managed and Rewarded? Although there are certainly shadow jobs that are very well paid indeed, there is good reason to believe that the vast majority of those in the shadow work force receive lower salaries, fewer benefits, and work in more precarious situations than the career civil service employees do. The limited available evidence suggests, for example, that private firms achieve their cost savings over government by giving more authority to their frontline managers to hire and fire. They also encourage greater turnover, maintain a younger employee base on average, and provide more limited benefits.

Until government knows more about what is happening in the shadow, legislative action is risky at best, fraught with unanticipated consequences at worst. Codifying realities, as the Defense Department proposed, hardly makes sense until the realities are known. And for that, a much deeper tracking system and a commitment to a work force planning methodology that would allow government to better understand its human capital, be it civil service or shadow, would be needed.

Moreover, government must also struggle with where the public service begins and ends. Just because the shadow exists outside the traditional civil service does not mean it can be shorn of an obligation to the public. No matter how long or short the contract, how large or small the grant, and how limited or broad the mandate, anyone who delivers public goods on behalf of the federal government, whether in the biggest profit-making firm or the smallest nonprofit agency, becomes part of the public service, with all that means for protecting the public trust.

The Illusion of Accountability

The shadow of government clearly changes the nature of accountability between government and its agents. In theory, the principal-agent relationship should hold regardless of where the final point of delivery occurs. Principals would give instructions to their agents all the way down the hierarchy, both formal and virtual, thereby assuring faithful execution of the task. In reality, the shadow adds to the mix multiple layers of agents, many of whom have divided loyalties between their government principals (Congress, the president, agency head, program officer, and contract representative) and their organizational principals (the board of directors, chief executive officer, unit head, team leader, and direct supervisor).

One does not have to go too far down the accountability chain to find mixed motives, diffused responsibilities, and general confusion about who is accountable to whom. At the very best, the shadow weakens the accountability chain between government and producer; at the worst, it diffuses accountability beyond repair.[7] "The contractor's job is to act as agent of the government's policy," writes Donald Kettl of state and local social service contracting. "The relationship is fractured, however, if contractors create independent political ties with policymakers and thus outflank their administrative overseers. In such cases contractors are less agents than partners, helping to shape the very design of the program, free of any significant oversight, and beneficiary of state and local governments' dependence on their performance."[8] He could just as easily have written the same assessment of federal contractors.

The problem of multiple agency in which agents act on behalf of multiple, often conflicting principals, is heightened by the bundling of contracts into omnibus packages. Government principals tend to have greater control when contracts and grants are clearly defined and tightly bounded. Although omnibus contracts can certainly save time and money, they create a series of secondary relationships between contractors and subcontractors that may displace government as a voice in directing the production of goods and services.

That the federal government is drifting toward larger and larger contracts is obvious from the agency-by-agency data. Consider the Environmental Protection Agency as an example.[9] As table 6-1 shows, the number of contract awards have declined steadily since 1983, even as the total dollars in play have inched ever upward. For a period, EPA managed the tension by allowing the number of large contracts to rise. But facing cutbacks in its own procurement work force, EPA began to bundle contracts into larger and larger totals. The result is fewer but bigger contracts, many of which involve multiple agents bundled together in towering relationships that may displace EPA as an active principal. Indeed, the very pressures that lead to

Table 6-1. *Obligations and Activity, Environmental Protection Agency,*
Selected Years

Fiscal year	Number of new contracts awarded	Total contract obligations (millions of dollars, not constant)	Number of active contracts over $50 million
1983	564	356	...
1985	419	592	8
1987	418	1,027	25
1989	328	1,139	90
1991	314	1,199	102
1993	270	1,162	109
1997	224	1,394	86
1998 (first half)	58	1,681	64

Source: Derived from the Contract Information System database, Environmental Protection Agency.

bundling may be symptoms of a larger weakening of accountability. As the National Academy of Public Administration notes, "The rapid growth in core contract requirements without corresponding increases in contracting staff forced EPA to move away from the labor-intensive smaller contracts to long-term instruments with broader scopes under which short-notice, individual tasks could be initiated with a less formal ordering instrument."[10]

There are at least two guarantors of accountability when contracts are broadened: (1) the competition needed to discipline contractors, and (2) a procurement work force that has the resources, skills, and motivation to oversee the fine print.

On the first guarantor, competition is not always the likely outcome of government shadow casting.[11] Competition is impossible both when a small number of contractors control the market and when government demand for services exceeds supply. In New York City's foster care program, for example, ten agencies receive roughly half of the $614 million annual contracting budget, and almost all have deep ties to the political system. As the city's demand for services has grown, the principal-agent relationship has been reversed. "The moment the numbers exploded, the message to the city was, you can be assessing people until you're blue in the face—who cares when you're using every bed they have?" said one senior New York official. "You can't regulate anything when the suppliers control the market."[12] As Kettl describes the generic problem, "The result is less a competitive market than a negotiated network. Neither side in the transaction, in fact, *wants* competition. For the contractors dependent on government contracts for a large portion of their income, competition is a threat to be avoided. . . . The desire for continuity promotes a tendency to develop long-term relationships with contractors that social service managers know and trust. Dependence becomes mutual."[13]

Unfortunately, private firms may have little incentive to honor those standards. Public administration scholar H. George Frederickson offers a particularly dim view of private incentives: "If the dominant ethos or collective attitude in a governmental organization is civically inclined, then the emphasis on service, the greater good, the public interest, and effective government will be obvious. Conversely, if the governmental organization is increasingly served by those with private inclinations, who tend toward practices that in business are regarded as either acceptable or appropriate but that in government are considered unethical or corrupt, then corruption will result."[14] Frederickson obviously overdraws the case for effect. Government employees can be just as corrupt as private employees, and private employees can be just as publicly spirited as governmental employees. After all, it was Morton Thiokol employees who initially recommended against the doomed shuttle Challenger launch and NASA middle managers who exploited the firm's financial interest to coerce a reversal.

Nevertheless, Frederickson is quite right to raise questions about the current fascination with businesslike government. Just because a private firm or nonprofit agency delivers a given service, be it weather forecasting, school lunches, or foster care, does not mean it is excused from worries about the broader public good. Historically, however, government has been particularly reluctant to call upon private contractors and grantees to behave in the public's interest. The notion has long been that contract law would assure proper execution of a given obligation. But as the size of contracts and grants has increased and oversight has weakened, prime contractors have take on increasingly public responsibilities, acting in lieu of the government in imposing order on bundles of subcontractors and grantees.

On the second guarantor, a skilled and motivated procurement work force, there appears to be extraordinary unevenness across the federal procurement offices involved in making and monitoring contracts. In 1993, even before the Workforce Restructuring Act took hold, individual contract officers at EPA and the Labor Department each handled 26,000 contract actions a year, which included new contract placements, modifications of existing contracts, and orders of one kind or another, while Treasury officers handled 23,000 contract actions, and National Science Foundation officers handled 22,000 contract actions, NASA officers handled 19,000, and Health and Human Services officers handled 18,000. At the other end of the continuum, Energy officers handled just 9,000 actions a year and Housing and Urban Development officers handled even fewer: 5,000. Even as the number of contracts has gone down at most agencies, the workload has gone up. At EPA, "the decline in the number of new contracts issues should [have meant] a reduced workload. In fact, the opposite was true. The coupling of significantly increased contract dollars with fewer new contract issuances resulted in larger, more complex instruments. . . . While the work involved in contract placement declined, the contract administration requirement became enormous."[15]

If the accountability problem is hard enough to solve with a well-equipped procurement work force, it is nearly impossible without it. If the federal government is to maintain a shadow, it should make the professionalization of its own shadow watchers a top priority. It should also assure that its human resource managers become central partners in the oversight of the contract, grantee, and mandate work force. These managers are too often ignored when it comes time to purchase shadow employees.

The Illusion of Capacity

Lacking a system to measure core competencies, it is impossible to know how the illusion of smallness has affected the core capacity of individual departments and agencies. Some agencies have surely been weakened over the years, while others are doing just fine. Some have used the steady downsizing as a lever for fundamental restructuring, while others are still evading action.

Fortunately, two recent studies by the National Academy of Public Administration (NAPA) suggest a methodology for asking the core capacity question more systematically. In 1990 an academy panel chaired by a former NASA associate administrator for management used surveys of NASA employees and contractors to assess the technical capacity of the agency to manage its mission and contract work force. Both sets of respondents agreed overwhelmingly that the agency's in-house scientific and engineering capability had declined over the ten years before the study. Although roughly half of those in the NASA sample also agreed that the agency had the in-house competencies needed to make responsible program decisions, there was enough doubt among the in-house and contractor respondents to lead

NAPA to issue a set of recommendations that could easily be applied to every department and agency of government, including:

1. Prepare and issue guidance on technical functional areas to be reserved for in-house civil service performance.

2. Convert contracted technical functions essential to in-house capability from support contractors to in-house performance and rebuild strength in specific technical disciplines critical to agency programs and objectives. Ceiling relief should be sought if required.

3. Provide policy guidance to the [NASA field] centers to retain in-house sufficient project, experiment, advance development, and research activities to provide more hands-on technical work by civil service scientists and engineers.

4. Examine the project mix at each center against agency and center goals and objectives. Select those with marginal contributions and/or staffing for cancellation or transfer....

5. Institute an annual critical position review for all technical disciplines, identify the number and professional levels of in-house coverage that are essential to maintaining a reasonable degree of technical expertise in each critical discipline, and adjust recruiting and/or contracting plans accordingly.[16]

The academy panel made particular note of the effect of a decade of downsizing in the 1970s on the agency's core capacity in the 1990s. Missing from the agency's work force was an entire generation of scientists and engineers who would have filled the gap between their more senior managers and a corps of young recruits hired in the wake of the Challenger accident. Core capacity involves more than just the right number of in-house specialists. It also involves the right mix of experience and training.

Three years later NAPA conducted a similar assessment of in-house capacity at the Environmental Protection Agency. As with the NASA study, the academy's EPA panel concluded that the agency had spread its core capacity across an overly broad agenda of research disciplines and locations, weakening its ability to create a critical mass of competency in any one area. In many places, the agency's technical capacity was exactly one person deep. Ironically, Senator Pryor's campaign to protect the agency from contracting out may have actually weakened overall capacity. Pulling jobs or responsibilities in-house under a head count constraint can only spread core capacity further. In theory, EPA's efforts to honor the inherently governmental requirement should have produced greater accountability. In reality, the academy panel concluded, "these efforts have consumed inordinate time, energy, and resources that might be spent more profitably on understanding and resolving fundamental management issues." Once again, NAPA's final recommendations to the agency could be easily applied government-wide. These recommendations include:

1. Clarify its organizational missions by putting them into a framework, initiate goal-setting and planning, and translate goals and objectives into programs, activities, and budgets. Those outcomes in turn should be used to guide internal decisions and operations.

2. Develop a policy concerning what work must always be done in-house, what work will always be contracted, and what work may be contracted, provided EPA possesses enough in-house capability to be a smart buyer and manager of external resources.

3. Institute workforce planning Agency-wide. Planning should take into account the allocation between intramural and extramural resources to ensure a reasonable degree of technical expertise in critical disciplines.[17]

Such deliberateness is impossible, of course, without more systematic research by government itself concerning what constitutes a core capacity agency by agency and unit by unit. Instead of focusing on what constitutes a commercial activity or inherently governmental function, it is time for government to start addressing the core competencies, be they administrative or technical, that must stay in house for departments and agencies to achieve their missions.

The Illusion of a Unified Public Service

Fifty years ago a book about the true size of government would have focused almost entirely on the civil service. Every last person who worked for government worked inside of government. Luther Gulick could write confidently about the president as the one true master of government because the front lines still resided within the formal boundaries of federal departments and agencies. Presidents could reach every last person in the organization because every last person was actually in the organization.

The public service has changed radically in the fifty years since Congress passed the Classification Act of 1949. Substantial numbers of public servants work outside the classification system today, while even the federal personnel system has been privatized and contracted out here and there across government. Almost all federal hiring investigations are now conducted by the employee-owned United States Investigations Service (USIS), a private firm created when the Office of Personnel Management privatized its Office of Federal Investigations. Funded under a five-year sole-source contract with its former agency, USIS kept employee salaries steady, cut vacation and sick leave by a third, eliminated pension matching, but established a bonus program linked to the firm's annual profit. Departments and agencies can also contract with a host of private firms and federal franchise funds to provide core personnel services, including classification analysis, recruitment, training, mediation, outplacement, and employee career counseling.

The result is a new kind of public service, one marked not by long service in the same agency, but one that also contains a nearly infinite variety of careers, some inside government, many outside. Increasing numbers of public servants will serve for but a moment in government, if at all. Foreclosed from reentry by a federal classification system that knows only one way up, meaning a lifetime commitment, they will work for consulting firms, contractors, and state and local governments, changing jobs three, four, or five times over a thirty-year career.

For young people who believe in the public service but who do not want a long-term civil service career, a job in the shadow of government is a perfect option, giving them freedom to move. "They may not be looking for permanency in a job," a senior Social Security Administration official said in the focus group of human resources experts assembled for this book. "The most important thing may be health benefits that you can offer them. They're not hoping to come and have a contract with your agency or the government for 30 years."[18] But even for those young people who want the long-term career, government may no longer be an option. The fewer entry level jobs there are in a circular hierarchy, the fewer opportunities there are to hire fresh recruits. During the 1970s and 1980s, the federal government hired more than 100,000 new employees a year. Today, it hires an average of just 50,000 a year.[19]

The question here is not whether entry-level jobs still exist, for they most certainly do, but whether those jobs are attractive enough to garner interest from the nation's best and brightest candidates. The answer is not clear.

The good news is that nearly 70 percent of the young Americans interviewed by the Pew Research Center for the 1997 trust in government survey cited earlier in this book believe that government is a good place to work. The bad news is that most young people think it's a good place for almost anyone *but* them.

Table 6-2. *Why Young Americans Will and Will Not Serve, 1997*

Percent

Question	Total	Age 15–16	17–18	19–22	23–24	25–29
Would you say that government is a good place for someone like you to work?						
Yes	41	32	42	43	48	41
No	55	65	52	54	50	54
Why do you say government is a good place for someone like you to work?						
Good pay	13	14	12	18	11	11
Good benefits	18	7	6	23	27	19
Opportunities for advancement	13	4	17	18	18	9
Challenging work	13	15	21	9	13	12
Chance to work on important problems	16	20	18	16	15	13
Job security	11	6	0	11	14	15
Public respect	3	8	1	4	2	2
Work for my community/country	3	3	4	3	6	1
Have good ideas	13	13	17	8	10	17
Government has a good reputation	3	0	11	0	0	5
Interested in government	4	9	5	7	0	3
Already work for government	5	0	2	0	10	9
Why do you say government is not a good place for someone like you to work?						
Low pay	4	3	2	4	4	6
Poor benefits	1	0	1	0	3	0
Lack of opportunity for advancement	3	0	1	4	2	4
Not very challenging work	5	4	8	6	4	3
Little chance to work on important problems	1	0	1	0	1	2
No job security	1	0	1	2	0	2
Lack of public respect	6	5	2	9	8	5
Don't trust government	26	20	32	26	29	27
Just not interested	20	34	18	24	16	10
Can't have a mind of your own	4	2	3	3	8	6
Government is inefficient	4	2	4	5	4	6
Lack the skills to do the work	9	14	12	6	6	9
Don't know much about government	6	8	8	2	0	8
Have different career goals	7	4	4	7	7	9
Which level of government would be the best place for someone like you to work?						
Federal	22	15	19	27	25	23
State	17	9	17	19	19	18
Local	54	71	56	48	45	50

Source: The Pew Research Center for The People & The Press, secondary analysis of data released in *Deconstructing Distrust: How Americans View Government* (Washington, D.C.: The Pew Research Center for The People & The Press, 1998), N = 998.

Asked whether they preferred government or the private sector as an employer, only 27 percent of Pew's respondents between the ages of eighteen and twenty-nine said government. Seventy percent of those who responded to the Pew survey may have thought government was a good place to work for others, but barely 40 percent in a slightly later Princeton Survey Research Associates survey of those between the ages of fourteen and twenty-nine thought it was a good place for them. As table 6-2 suggests, nearly half of those who wanted to serve offered the more noble reasons, meaning challenging work, a chance to work on important problems, having their own good ideas, and working for their community and country. However, nearly as many pointed to government as a place for good pay, security, and the opportunity to advance. Many, though most certainly not all, of the young people who appear to be most enthusiastic about working for government are not necessarily the people government should want working for it.

Together, the various surveys suggest that America's best and brightest will go where they see the best and brightest opportunities. To the extent government creates those opportunities through recruitment programs such as the Presidential Management Internship, all to the good. To the extent those opportunities increasing reside in the shadow, so be it. There is nothing to be gained by shaming those who choose the consulting industry or contractor community for their first jobs. If that is where the exciting jobs are, that is where the exciting students will want to go.

The challenge, therefore, is not to convince those students that they are making a mistake or to shame them for taking the higher paying jobs. Rather, it is to design a federal personnel system that might someday lure them for a stop, however long or short, along their career. "Instead of saying that we want to keep someone for thirty years," a senior Treasury Department personnel officer noted in the focus group, "let's say that it's okay to only have them for five years, and let's set up an employment arrangement that fits." Although the Treasury Department can never compete for tax attorneys on salary alone, it does have a comparative advantage in offering shorter stays. "When they leave, they can command salaries five times higher than they had with us, but in the meantime, we have had their services. If we could recruit people right out of college, telling them that they're only going to stay with us for four years while we provide them with X, Y, Z experience, which is going to make them fabulously valuable on the outside, we might get better people." The best and brightest do not suddenly become less so because they work in a profit-making firm. Nor do public servants become less committed to the public good because they take the more challenging work wherever it may reside.

Managing the New Public Service

As noted at several points in this book, a considerable, though unmeasurable portion of the shadow of government was created by accident. Most departments and agencies let the downsizings, freezes, and ceilings manage them, not vice versa. It is not as if they had much choice, however. Despite constant urging from the General Accounting Office, the federal government has never developed a work force planning system that might allow departments and agencies to be more deliberative in restricting buyouts and reductions in force to less essential, or off-core, activities. They could not have targeted their cuts had they wanted to, which they most certainly did not. Nor could they have targeted their hiring to assure a stable core of essential capacity.

The federal government will never be able to adopt a core competency sorting methodology if it continues to disinvest in its own human resources staff. Unfortunately, the HR function, as it often is abbreviated, has been steadily weakened over the years. Targeted for downsizing and disparaged as the source of endless naysaying, the HR function has been allowed to decay at the very moment it is needed to take a stronger role in sorting out the shadow. According to NAPA, the federal HR profession may even be stagnating. There has been little new hiring over the past decade, the average length of career has been increasing, and the educational level of the relatively few new hires has been dropping.[20]

Fewer in number and under unrelenting pressure, the federal HR profession desperately needs renewal. Having been forced for decades to administer a cumbersome, antiquated classification system, HR employees remain unsure about just where they fit in a highly decentralized, rules-be-damned system. They will continue to drift until they realize that the federal work force extends well beyond the edges of the traditional bureaucracy. If that means they must fight the procurement function to win oversight of the shadow, they should prepare for the battle. And if that means they have to design a new system to replace a classification system that is hopelessly out of date, they should start drafting. "We must focus less on simply promoting people and more on offering them opportunities to move out, or to move in, or to move someplace else," a Labor Department human resource specialist admitted in the focus group. "You really have to try to change the social employment contract to one of personal development, which requires commitment on the part of the agencies." Unfortunately, today's classification system knows only one way in—at the bottom—and one way out—at the end of a career.

Many HR managers seem ready to accept the challenge. As a senior HR manager at the Treasury Department argued, "I really think that it is our job to help people in our organizations understand and be more conscious of the staffing decisions that they are making. We've been able to do the 'no brainers' for years—how to get somebody hired that somebody wanted. We got pretty smart at working the angles. But I think what we're going to be talking about [in the future] are real staffing strategies that are related to what is our work, what do our demographics look like, what does the labor market look like, what kind of benefit packages do we have to offer. . . . I think that really is going to make our jobs more strategic, and that's going to require that we have a lot of information and are pretty artful in using it."

That artful work will not be found in administering the old classification system, however. It is likely to be found in making policy for a new public service that already exists in fact, if not quite yet in law. It is a service that contains a much richer blend of employees, obligations, and skills than any public service in administrative history. At some not-too-distant point, Congress and the president will admit the obvious: the classification system was built for a work force that no longer exists.

The new public service most certainly embraces a broad mix of employees, benefit packages, pay rates, expertise, principal-agent relationships, and personal motivations. It is not at all uncommon to find permanent civil servants working side by side in the same facility with quasi-permanent contractor employees and highly contingent consulting personnel. Much as it is hoped that the various types of employees will be equally comfortable with their status, the reality is often something less. "The interesting thing that I see with contingent workers is that you come up against values that people have about what is good, or what is a model," a senior Treasury Department human resource officer said in the focus group. "I hear things like 'I think it's unethical of us to have people working for us and not paying benefits' or "I think it looks like we are using people up and throwing them away.' I mean those are very flamboyant and emotional kinds of terms, but they have to do with traditional views of federal employment. What does it mean to be a federal employee? What does it mean to treat someone with respect?" The only way to answer such questions is to monitor the shadow of government more closely, which means developing a tracking system capable of comparing apples to apples.

Conclusion

The first step in managing the shadow of government is to simply acknowledge that it exists. Created in part for the right reasons and in part for the wrong reasons, the shadow was designed to make the federal government seem smaller even as its mission grew. It allowed Congresses and presidents to claim victories in whatever war they were waging at the time on government mismanagement, while creating a remarkably complicated web of relationships that diffuses accountability and may erode the traditional barrier between government and the rest of society.

The second step is to stop creating it by accident. It is time to abandon head count constraints as a tool of government work force management. Period. Departments and agencies should be given the dollars to do their jobs and the freedom to allocate those dollars to the work force that best suits their mission. If research and development agencies such as NASA want to pay those in their hard-to-recruit professions high salaries, thereby reducing total head count, let them do so. If operating agencies such as the Social Security Administration want to put their resources on the telephone lines and intake posts, thereby increasing total head count, let them do so, too. Given that there is no one way to staff an agency of government today, the goal of federal work force policy should be to give departments and agencies authority to recruit the right mix of employees.

If Congress and the president want to continue counting heads, they should only do so if they are willing to count all the heads. That means establishing a federal work force budget that shows every last person in what has become a very large true size of government. Perhaps by counting everyone, Congress and the president could get out of the conundrum they have created by promising a government that looks smaller and delivers at least as much. A little dose of reality on just what it takes to run the government is long overdue.

Appendixes

Appendix A. Estimated Gains and Losses in the Shadows of Government, 1984–96

Estimated number of FTE jobs created, unless otherwise specified

Agency	1984					1996					1984–96		
	Civil Service jobs	Contract jobs[a] (est.)	Grant jobs[a] (est.)	Ratio Civil Service/ contract	Ratio Civil Service/ grant	Civil Service jobs	Contract jobs[a] (est.)	Grant jobs[a] (est.)	Ratio Civil Service/ contract	Ratio Civil Service/ grant	Shift in Civil Service jobs (percent)	Shift in contract jobs (percent)	Shift in grant jobs (percent)
Agriculture	108,600	76,000	44,000	1:0.7	1:0.4	100,700	82,000	42,000	1:0.8	1:0.4	–7	+8	–5
Commerce	32,300	12,500	4,000	1:0.4	1:0.1	33,800	26,500	10,300	1:0.8	1:0.6	+5	+112	+158
Defense	1,040,213	5,243,000	5,400	1:5.0	1:0.0	778,900	3,634,000	53,000	1:4.7	1:0.1	–25	–31	+882
Education	5,000	7,000	517,700	1:1.4	1:102.2	4,700	16,000	761,700	1:3.4	1:162.1	–6	+129	+47
Energy	16,700	708,000	8,400	1:42.4	1:0.5	19,100	633,000	40,200	1:33.1	1:2.1	+14	–11	+379
HHS[b]	57,400	51,600	336,000	1:0.9	1:5.9	57,200	102,400	395,100	1:1.8	1:6.8	–0.3	+98	+15
HUD	12,400	2,900	0	1:0.2	1:0.0	11,400	9,400	22,700	1:0.8	1:2.0	–8	+224	0
Interior	73,200	58,800	19,500	1:0.8	1:0.3	66,700	29,700	4,000	1:0.4	1:0.1	–9	–50	–80
Justice	58,200	13,800	700	1:02	1:0.0	103,800	80,000	2,000	1:0.8	1:0.0	+78	+480	+186
Labor	18,600	29,600	358,900	1:1.6	1:19.3	16,000	33,900	165,800	1:2.1	1:10.3	–14	+15	–57

Transportation	61,100	75,500	644,800	1:1.2	1:10.6	62,400	179,900	642,000	1:2.9	1:10.3	+2	+138	-0.4
Treasury	123,200	11,600	0	1:0.1	1:0.0	151,100	52,700	0	1:0.3	1:0.0	+23	+354	0
State	24,100	7,600	0	1:0.3	1:0.0	22,900	16,000	0	1:0.7	1:0.0	-5	+111	0
Veterans	218,500	85,900	0	1:0.4	1:0.0	221,900	72,000	0	1:0.3	1:0.0	+2	-16	0
AID	5,100	9,500	0	1:1.9	1:1.0	3,400	15,300	0	1:4.5	1:0.0	-33	+61	0
EPA	11,400	30,800	206,900	1:2.7	1:18.2	17,200	43,000	143,400	1:2.5	1:8.3	+51	+40	-31
GSA	25,600	102,600	0	1:4	1:0.0	15,700	150,400	0	1:9.6	1:0.0	-39	+47	0
NASA	22,100	171,000	7,700	1:7.7	1:0.3	20,100	350,600	26,900	1:17.4	1:1.3	-9	+105	+249
OPM	5,700	20,200	0	1:3.5	1:0.0	3,400	2,400	0	1:0.7	1:0.0	-40	-88	0
SSA	79,600	5,000	0	1:0.1	1:0.0	64,000	15,700	0	1:0.2	1:0.0	-20	+214	0
TVA	32,000	37,600	0	1:1.2	1:0.0	16,000	63,600	0	1:4.0	1:0.0	-50	+69	0
USIA	8,200	1,700	0	1:0.2	1:0.0	7,000	2,500	3,200	1:0.4	1:0.5	-15	+47	0
Total including Defense	2,083,000	6,790,000	2,208,000	1:3.2	1:1.1	1,892,000	5,635,000	2,000,000	1:3.0	1:1.3	-9.8	-17	+9
Total excluding Defense	1,056,000	1,547,000	2,202,000	1:15	1:2	1,113,000	2,413,000	2,360,000	1:1.8	1:2.1	+5.3	+29.3	+7

Source: Actual figures for the number of civil service jobs come from "Total Executive Branch Full-Time Equivalent (FTE) Employees: 1981–1999," *Historical Tables, Budget of the United States Government* (Government Printing Office, 1997), table 17.3, p. 269.

a. Contract and grant job columns do not equal totals because some agencies were not included.

b. HHS 1984 figures do not include the Social Security Administration.

Appendix B. *Public Opinion toward Government Reform*

Percent

	Reduce government		Maintain government	
	Devolvers	Downsizers	Realigners	Reinventors
Political/social attitudes				
Trust the government in Washington to do what is right just about always or most of the time	15	27	46	54
Impression of federal government has been most influenced by personal experiences	23	19	20	22
Feeling about the federal government				
Basically content	14	10	25	43
Frustrated	61	62	62	48
Angry	29	15	15	7
Federal government is doing only a fair or poor job	88	78	85	61
Government often does a better job than it is given credit for	15	29	28	46
Federal government needs very major reform	60	39	43	22
Agree federal government is too powerful	82	57	68	53
Agree federal government controls too much of daily lives	76	51	59	47
Know number of people employed by federal government decreased	45	32	39	31
Have little or no confidence in federal government handling of domestic problems	66	41	39	29
Have little or no confidence in federal government handling of international problems	36	25	26	16
Have great deal or fair amount of confidence in state government handling of state problems	81	78	78	84
Have great deal or fair amount of confidence in local government handling of local problems	77	68	80	81
Would be very upset if heard someone had claimed government benefits that they were not entitled to	69	53	66	67

	Reduce government		Maintain government	
	Devolvers	Downsizers	Realigners	Reinventors
Political/social attitudes				
Would not care if heard someone had gotten out of jury duty	46	40	42	41
Would be very upset if heard someone had not paid all the income taxes they owed	33	27	32	33
Federal government should be primarily responsible for				
Setting academic standards for public schools	13	28	20	25
Conserving the country's natural resources	35	58	57	56
Ensuring every American has access to affordable health care	41	63	59	65
Providing a decent standard of living for the elderly	39	50	39	54
Promoting greater honesty and stronger morals among people	13	21	17	17
Ensuring that every American can afford to send children to college	27	37	31	40
Ensuring that food and medicines are safe	59	75	79	74
Reducing juvenile delinquency	3	11	6	9
Reducing poverty	23	41	29	39
Managing the economy to prevent a recession	60	67	68	72
Favorable opinion of				
Federal Bureau of Investigation	59	67	66	75
Environmental Protection Agency	43	77	66	81
Postal Service	89	87	92	88
Social Security Administration	47	56	59	72
Internal Revenue Service	20	35	37	46
Department of Education	50	61	59	71
Food and Drug Administration	72	78	75	80
Defense Department	72	76	78	80
Favorable opinion of				
Business corporations	63	61	69	71
News media	35	49	45	60

	Reduce government		Maintain government	
	Devolvers	Downsizers	Realigners	Reinventors
Political/social attitudes				
Military	77	77	77	83
Federal government in Washington	18	34	31	52
Respondent's state government	61	63	64	72
Respondent's local government	69	65	63	73
Favorable opinion of elected federal officials	37	55	52	67
Favorable opinion of Congress	39	49	49	65
Favorable opinion of federal departments and agencies	35	59	54	73
Favorable opinion of Bill Clinton	32	62	57	77
Favorable opinion of government workers	52	72	63	78
Favorable opinion of public employees	74	68	68	79
Favorable opinion of state and local government officials	64	72	65	74
When something is run by the government, it is usually wasteful and inefficient	77	66	60	54
Think federal government should give a very high priority to				
Setting academic standards for public schools	26	33	26	40
Conserving the country's natural resources	24	39	39	35
Ensuring every American has access to affordable health care	30	40	37	42
Providing a decent standard of living for the elderly	23	25	29	31
Ensuring that every American can afford to send children to college	20	29	22	20
Ensuring that food and medicines are safe	50	56	48	51
Reducing juvenile delinquency	20	30	27	29
Reducing poverty	24	29	25	24
Think federal government should do more about				
Setting academic standards for public schools	53	65	57	71

	Reduce government		Maintain government	
	Devolvers	Downsizers	Realigners	Reinventors
Political/social attitudes				
Conserving the country's natural resources	53	65	57	71
Ensuring every American has access to affordable health care	63	74	62	75
Providing a decent standard of living for the elderly	63	78	78	78
Ensuring that every American can afford to send children to college	61	70	67	73
Ensuring that food and medicines are safe	52	65	57	62
Reducing juvenile delinquency	65	68	61	58
Reducing poverty	65	78	59	66
Who is trusted to do right thing: politicians or civil service employees				
Politicians	14	14	14	19
Civil service employees	68	74	68	68
Think the federal government has done an excellent or good job of				
Setting academic standards for public schools	10	21	21	31
Conserving the country's natural resources	27	32	33	38
Ensuring every American has access to affordable health care	13	14	14	24
Providing a decent standard of living for the elderly	18	21	26	27
Ensuring that every American can afford to send children to college	12	18	20	19
Ensuring that food and medicines are safe	57	48	58	65
Reducing juvenile delinquency	10	7	8	16
Reducing poverty	14	11	13	16

	Reduce government		Maintain government	
	Devolvers	Downsizers	Realigners	Reinventors
Political/social attitudes				
For those who think the federal government is doing only a fair or poor job, number who said poor performance was government's fault				
Setting academic standards for public schools	50	54	49	47
Conserving the country's natural resources	65	48	55	43
Ensuring every American has access to affordable health care	54	57	36	42
Providing a decent standard of living for the elderly	61	53	46	45
Ensuring that every American can afford to send children to college	41	51	34	32
Ensuring that food and medicines are safe	50	52	46	38
Reducing juvenile delinquency	29	28	24	24
Reducing poverty	43	35	32	30
Agree that most elected officials are trustworthy	26	40	40	56
Agree that public officials do not care what people like me think	74	58	61	58
Agree that government should see that no one is without food, clothing, or shelter	53	79	67	82
Agree that federal government should do away with poverty	62	76	67	81
Federal government is bound to be inefficient no matter what	12	8	7	5
People will mistrust the government no matter what	22	24	24	22
Rate ethical and moral practices as excellent or good				
Federal government officials	16	24	24	41
State and local government officials	37	38	40	47
Leaders of business corporations	28	28	27	42
Journalists	22	29	32	39
People like yourself	70	65	70	70

	Reduce government		Maintain government	
	Devolvers	Downsizers	Realigners	Reinventors
Political/social attitudes				
Which view is closest to own				
Federal government today has too much power	59	31	39	21
Federal government is using about the right amount of power	17	33	28	39
Federal government should use its powers even more vigorously	23	34	33	39
Respondent believes paying more than fair share of taxes	64	54	57	46
Have a great or good deal of confidence in American people	59	58	61	71
Would prefer government to private sector as employer	17	24	21	26
Want son or daughter to go into politics as a life's work	29	27	22	19
Recommend that young people start their careers in politics or government	28	39	37	45
Think government is a good place to work	59	74	69	75
Party identification (three-way)				
Republican	41	25	36	24
Democrat	19	36	25	41
Independent	33	29	34	31
Party identification (two-way)				
Republicans/Republican leaners	63	38	50	33
Democrats/Democratic leaners	27	50	34	57
Demographic measure				
Sex				
Male	58	43	49	42
Female	42	58	51	58
Race				
White	88	82	88	81
Non-white	11	18	11	19
Hispanic	3	6	2	6
African-American	8	14	8	14

Demographic measure	Reduce government		Maintain government	
	Devolvers	Downsizers	Realigners	Reinventors
Age				
Under 30	24	29	20	22
30–49	45	43	45	44
50–64	20	14	19	18
65+	10	14	15	15
Education				
College graduate	29	21	22	20
Some college	25	25	27	23
High school graduate	35	41	37	39
Less than high school graduate	11	13	15	17
Family income				
$75,000 plus	16	9	13	11
$50,000–$74,999	17	10	16	14
$30,000–$49,999	26	30	28	26
$20,000–$29,999	15	19	15	15
Less than $20,000	18	25	21	26
Region				
East	15	20	27	24
Midwest	26	20	26	26
South	39	41	36	32
West	21	19	21	19
Race/religion/ethnicity				
Total White Protestant	58	47	50	44
White Protestant evangelical	31	27	24	21
White Protestant nonevangelical	25	19	25	22
White Catholic	16	20	21	23
Respondents where anyone in household has ever received				
Federal financial aid for college	32	29	20	30
Food stamps	16	22	16	24
Social Security	32	34	30	32
Welfare	13	17	15	21
Medicare	20	22	29	33
Veterans benefits	13	21	17	17
Self or anyone in household works for federal, state, or local government	23	30	26	29
Self or anyone in household works for nongovernment employer that receives government funds for the work it does	14	15	12	15

Source: The Pew Research Center for The People & The Press, secondary analysis of data released in *Deconstructing Distrust: How Americans View Government* (Washington, D.C.: The Pew Research Center for The People & The Press, 1998), N = 1,762.

Appendix C. *Head Count Ceilings, Freezes, and Thaws, 1940–97*

Measure	Tool	Goal	Origin	Time horizon	Impact
1. Byrd-Langer Joint Resolution of 1942	Disclosure	Urged executive attention	Congress	Wartime	None
2. War Overtime Pay Act of 1943	Disclosure	Required periodic accounting	Congress	Wartime	None
3. Federal Employees Pay Act of 1945	Ceiling	Required executive establishment and monitoring of ceilings	Congress	Five years	Minimal
4. Federal Employees Pay Act of 1946	Ceiling	Set fixed numerical targets	Congress	Five years	Minimal
5. Third Deficiency Appropriation Act of 1946	Thaw	Created exemptions to no. 4	Congress	Five years	Minimal
6. Budget and Accounting Procedures Act of 1950	Thaw	Repealed no. 4 outright	Congress	Indefinite	Minimal (see no. 7)
7. Supplemental Appropriation Act of 1951 (Whitten Amendment)	Ceiling/ freeze	Set fixed numerical targets/ prohibited hirings and promotions	Congress	Indefinite	Major
8. Executive Order 10180 (1951)	Freeze	Prohibited hirings and promotions	Executive	Indefinite	Minimal (duplicated nos. 7 and 9)
9. Supplemental Appropriation Act of 1952 (amendments to the original Whitten Amendment)	Freeze	Limited promotions to higher grades	Congress	Indefinite	Minimal (duplicated no. 7)
10. Third Supplemental Appropriation Act of 1952	Ceiling/ freeze	Clarified provisions of no. 9	Congress	Indefinite	Minimal
11. Classification Act Amendments of 1954	Thaw	Raised Whitten targets by 10 percent for Postal Service only	Congress	Indefinite	Major
12. Postal Service and Federal Employee Salary Act of 1962	Thaw	Raised Whitten targets by 10 percent government-wide	Congress	Indefinite	Major

Measure	Tool	Goal	Origin	Time horizon	Impact
13. Executive Order 11187 (1964)	Thaw	Provided exemptions to Whitten	Executive	Indefinite	Minimal
14. 1965 Amendments to the Supplemental Appropriation Act of 1950	Thaw	Provided exemptions to Whitten for Postal Service only	Congress	Indefinite	Major
15. 1967 Amendments to the Supplemental Appropriation Act of 1950	Thaw	Repealed all ceilings and freezes in Whitten, but not the restrictions on rapid promotion	Congress	Indefinite	Minimal (see no. 16)
16. Revenue and Expenditure Control Act of 1968	Ceilings	Set new numerical targets	Congress	Indefinite	Minimal (see no. 17)
17. Postal Exemptions	Thaw	Repealed no. 16 outright	Congress	Indefinite	Minimal (see no. 19)
18. Second Supplemental Appropriations Act of 1969	Thaw	Repealed no. 16 outright	Congress	Indefinite	Minimal (see no. 19)
19. Reductions in Civilian Employment (1971)	Reductions	Set new numerical targets	Executive (device unclear)	One year	Minimal
20. Department of Defense Authorization Act of 1974	Ceilings/reductions in force	Set fixed numerical targets	Congress	One year	Minimal
21. Department of Defense Authorization Act of 1975	Ceilings/reductions in force	Set fixed numerical targets	Congress	One year	Minimal
22. Fiscal Year Adjustment Act of 1976	Ceilings	Refreshed remaining Whitten restrictions	Congress	Indefinite	Minimal
23. Department of Defense Authorization Act of 1976	Ceilings/reductions in force	Set fixed numerical targets	Congress	One year	Minimal
24. National Emergencies Act of 1976	Thaw	Repealed remaining elements of Whitten	Congress	Indefinite	Minimal (see no. 26)

Action	Type	Description	Authority	Duration	Impact
25. Limitation on Hiring of 1977	Freeze	Prohibited hiring	Executive (memorandum)	Three months	Minimal
26. Civil Service Reform Act of 1978	Ceiling	Set fixed numerical targets	Congress	Three years	Major
27. Limitation on Hiring of 1978	Freeze	Prohibited hiring	Executive (memorandum)	Three months	Minimal
28. Limitation on Hiring of 1980	Freeze	Prohibited hiring	Executive (memorandum)	Nine months	Minimal
29. Federal Employee Hiring Freeze, January 20, 1981	Freeze	Prohibited hiring	Executive (memorandum)	Two months	Minimal
30. Budget Targets for Fiscal Years 1982 and 1983	Reductions in force	Set fixed numerical targets	Executive (budget process)	Two years	Minimal
31. Program to Reduce Grade 11–15 Positions ("Bulge Project"), 1984	Reductions in force	Set fixed numerical targets	Executive (personnel project)	Two years	Minimal
32. Base Closure and Realignment Act of 1988	Reductions in force	Established decision method	Congress	Five years	Major (see no. 35)
33. Reduction of 100,000 positions	Attrition/ early outs	Set fixed numerical targets	Executive Order 12839	Three years	Major (see no. 35)
34. Streamlining the Bureaucracy Initiative, 1993	Unclear	Set general goal	Executive (memorandum)	Short term	Minimal
35. Federal Workforce Restructuring Act of 1994	Ceilings/ buyouts	Set fixed numerical targets	Executive through Congress	Five years	Major

Notes

Chapter One

1. Joseph S. Nye, Jr., "The Leadership Brain Drain," *New York Times*, (April 5, 1998), p. 46.

2. See William C. Adams and others, *Student Attitudes toward Careers in Public Service*, slide presentation, June 1998.

3. John D. Donahue, *The Privatization Decision: Public Ends, Private Means* (Basic Books Inc., 1989), p. 39.

4. Donahue, *The Privatization Decision*, p. 37.

5. Donald F. Kettl writes about this "fuzzy boundary" problem in his September 1998 report, *Reinventing Government: A Fifth-Year Report Card* (Brookings, 1998).

Chapter Two

1. *Examination of the Use of Consultants by the Environmental Protection Agency*, Hearings before the Senate Committee on Governmental Affairs Subcommittee on Federal Services, Post Office, and Civil Service, S. Hrg. 101-18, 101 Cong. 1 sess. (Government Printing Office, February 3, 1989), p. 1.

2. *Examination of the Use of Consultants by the Environmental Protection Agency*, Hearings, p. 3, 31, 32, and 37-39.

3. *Use of Consultants and Contractors by the Environmental Protection Agency and the Department of Energy*, Hearings before the Senate Committee on Governmental Affairs Subcommittee on Federal Services, Post Office, and Civil Service, S. Hrg. 101-554, 101 Cong. 1 sess. (GPO, November 6, 1989), p. 57.

4. Letter from David Pryor to Leon Panetta, February 23, 1993, p. 1.

5. Letter from David Pryor to Leon Panetta, August 30, 1993, p. 1.

6. Letter to David Pryor from Leon Panetta, November 19, 1993, p. 1.

7. Letter to David Pryor from Alice Rivlin, August 19, 1994, pp. 1–2.

8. Information on the Federal Procurement Data System can be found on their website at <http://fpds.gsa.gov/>.

9. Paul Murphy, president of EagleEye Publishers, conducted the data analysis for this work. He never wavered in his commitment to rigor and worked tirelessly to make sure that every possible error was scrubbed out of the analysis. He took what was an interesting question and turned it into a systematic methodology for estimating jobs created, and has my lasting appreciation and respect.

10. Letter to Representative Dennis Kucinich from G. Edward DeSeve, December 7, 1998, attachment, p. 4.

11. Letter to the General Accounting Office from Representatives Stephen Horn and Dennis Kucinich, September 24, 1998.

12. Jeff Gerth, "As Payroll Shrinks, Government's Costs for Contracts Rise," *New York Times*, March 18, 1996, p. A1.

13. "Downsized Workers Are Not Being Replaced by Contractors," fact sheet released by the office of Vice President Al Gore on April 22, 1996.

14. For an introduction to the model, see U.S. Department of Commerce, *RIMS II: A Brief Description of Regional Multipliers from the Regional Input-Output Modeling System* (Bureau of Economic Analysis, 1997); the complete handbook for using the input-output accounts to estimate job creation can be found at the Bureau of Economic Analysis website at <http://www.bea.doc.gov>.

15. Because the contracts database used a different classification system before 1989, EagleEye Publishers, which performed the basic analysis on the author's behalf, converted each category in that classification system into an SIC code by hand.

16. Readers are warned that the same 1994 job multipliers were applied to all four years estimated (1984, 1990, 1993, and 1996), meaning that the model assumed that labor costs did not change per SIC code over the period. The lack of year-specific multipliers introduces an obvious source of unknown error into the model, but is impossible to remedy. Readers are warned again, therefore, that these data are best viewed as reasonably firm estimates, but not absolute counts.

17. General Accounting Office, *Federal Downsizing: Agency Officials' Views on Maintaining Performance during Downsizing at Selected Agencies*, GAO/GGD-98-46 (March 1998).

18. General Accounting Office, *Federally Funded R & D Centers: Information on the Size and Scope of DOD-Sponsored Centers*, GAO/NSIAD-96-54 (April 24, 1996); General Accounting Office, *Federal Research: Information on Fees for Selected Federally Funded Research and Development Centers*, GAO/RCED-96-31FS (December 1995).

19. Information on the Federal Assistance Awards Data System can be found on their website at <http://www.census.gov/govs/www/faads.html>.

20. General Accounting Office, *Federal Grants, Design Improvements Could Help Federal Resources Go Further*, GAO/AIMD-97-7 (December 1996), p. 17.

21. Martha Derthick, "New Players: The Governors and Welfare Reform," *Brookings Review* (Spring 1996), pp. 44–45.

22. U.S. Advisory Commission on Intergovernmental Relations preliminary report, *The Role of Federal Mandates in Intergovernmental Relations* (January, 1996), p. B3.

23. National Association of Counties and Price Waterhouse, *The Burden of Unfunded Mandates: A Survey of the Impact of Unfunded Mandates on America's Counties* (Washington, D.C., October 26, 1993); the United States Conference of Mayors and Price Waterhouse, *Impact of Unfunded Federal Mandates on U.S. Cities: A 314-City Survey* (Washington, D.C., October 26, 1993).

24. Senate Committee on Environment and Public Works, *Analysis of the Unfunded Mandates Surveys Conducted by the U.S. Conference of Mayors and the National Association of Counties* (June 14, 1994), pp. 18–19.

25. Congressional Budget Office, *CBO Papers: The Experience of the Congressional Budget Office during the First Years of the Unfunded Mandate Reform Act* (Washington, D.C., January 1997).

26. "Government Employment and Population: 1962–1996," *Historical Tables, Budget of the United States Government, Fiscal Year 1998*, Table 17.5 (Government Printing Office, 1997), p. 271.

27. These figures come from Virginia Ann Hodgkinson and others, *The Nonprofit Almanac: 1996-1997: Dimensions of the Independent Sector* (San Francisco: Jossey-Bass, 1997); see also Lester M. Salamon, *America's Nonprofit Sector: A Primer* (Washington, D.C.: The Foundation Center, 1992), for an introduction to the numbers, and Gabriel Rudney, "The Scope and Dimensions of Nonprofit Activity," in Walter W. Powell, ed., *The Nonprofit Sector: A Research Handbook* (Yale University Press, 1987), for a broad introduction to the sector and the number of employees respectively.

28. Organization for Economic Cooperation and Development, *Measuring Public Employment in OECD Countries: Sources, Methods, and Results* (Paris: OECD, 1997). My appreciation to Elena Michaels for digging out these data.

29. Jonathan Walters, "Hiring Spree," *Governing*, vol. 11 (February 1988), p. 17; see also Richard P. Nathan, "The 'Nonprofitization Movement' as a Form of Devolution," in D. Burlingame and others, *Capacity for Change? The Nonprofit World in the Age of Devolution* (Indiana University Center on Philanthropy, 1996).

30. These surveys are reviewed in National Academy of Public Administration, Center for Human Resources Management, *New Options, New Talent: The Government Guide to the Flexible Workforce* (Washington, D.C., August 1998), pp. 21–24.

31. For a summary of how the BEA records government transactions, see Bureau of Economic Analysis, "Government Transactions," *Methodology Papers: U.S. National Income and Product Accounts*, (Department of Commerce, 1988).

32. Donald F. Kettl, "After the Reforms," *Government Executive* (April 1998), p. 38.

33. *Use of Consultants and Contractors By the Environmental Protection Agency and*

the Department of Energy, Hearings before Senate Committee on Governmental Affairs Subcommittee on Federal Services, Post Office, and Civil Service, S. Hrg. 101-554, 101 Cong. 1 Sess. (GPO, November 6, 1989), pp. 3–4.

Chapter Three

1. "The World Economy Survey: Spend, Spend, Spend," *Economist* (September 20–26, 1997), pp. 7-8.

2. Karl Zinmeister, "Shrink Government to Save Liberty, Not Money," *American Enterprise* (November/December 1997), pp. 4-5.

3. Jonathan Walters, "Did Somebody Say Downsizing?" *Governing,* vol. 11 (February 1998), p. 17.

4. The Pew Research Center for The People & The Press, *Deconstructing Distrust: How Americans View Government,* (Washington, D.C.: Pew Research Center, March 1998); for a compelling analysis of public support for bureaucracy, see Charles T. Goodsell, *The Case for Bureaucracy: A Public Administration Polemic,* 3d ed. (Chatham, N.J.: Chatham House Publishers, 1994); the Pew survey results are easily accessible on the Internet at www.people-press.org.

5. The Pew Research Center, *Deconstructing Distrust,* p. 33.

6. The Pew Research Center for The People & The Press, *The Internet News Audience Goes Ordinary* (Washington, D.C.: Pew Research Center, March 1999).

7. These data were collected by Lake Research under a contract from the Pew Charitable Trusts and were presented to the trusts in a report entitled "The Show Me Nation: Restoring Trust in Government," September-October 1995. The report was unpublished and involved a survey of 910 randomly selected Americans.

8. Goodsell, *The Case for Bureaucracy: A Public Administration Polemic,* pp. 77–78.

9. I am particularly grateful to the Pew Research Center team for helping me ferret out this typology, including Andy Kohut, who suggested several promising variables that might illustrate the public's ambivalence, Kim Parker, who suggested several more and helped construct the analysis, Greg Flemming, who added his own time to further analysis, and Mary McIntosh, the senior analyst at Princeton Survey Research Associates, who has long been a sounding board for my musings on these issues and who also produced the reanalysis of the leader survey cited later in this section.

10. Whether a typology is valid depends on its ability to explain a given phenomenon independent of other variables. A typology cannot just be another way that some other variable such as political party, race, or gender works its will. One way to check for such effects is to examine the impact of demographic and political variables on the two main anchors of the government reform typology presented in this chapter. As the following regression summary shows, gender, education, age, race, and party identification account for only 11 percent of the variance in whether respondents were likely to be devolvers or reinventors, which means either that 89 percent of the variance is explained by other variables or that the typology is a meaningful description of real public differences.

Independent variable	Unstandardized coefficient	Standard error	Standardized coefficient
Gender (male =1)	0.10	0.03	0.11**
Education (low = 1)	–0.00	0.01	–0.08*
Age (young = 1)	0.00	0.00	0.03
Race (white = 1)	0.00	0.04	0.02
Political orientation (Republican = 1)	0.25	0.03	0.27***
Constant	1.21	0.10	
Adjusted R^2	0.11		

$N = 839$; $*p < 0.05$, $**p < 0.01$, $***p < 0.001$

Further analysis with an expanded list of political variables fails to shake the impact of the typology in describing public attitudes toward government reform. Adding five variables measuring lack of confidence in government's ability to handle domestic affairs (low = 1), concern that government controls too much of our daily life (agree = 1), low ratings of the ethical standards of national political leaders (low = 1) and of government agencies (low = 1), and lack of participation in voting (seldom or never vote = 1) drives the adjusted R^2 to 33 percent of the variance, leaving 67 percent of the variance to the typology and other nonspecified variables.

11. Elizabeth Drew, *On the Edge: The Clinton Presidency* (New York: Simon & Schuster, 1994), p. 229.

12. Ann Devroy and Stephen Barr, "Gore Heads Latest Government Evaluation; Clinton Orders 'National Performance Review' to Identify What Works and What Doesn't," *Washington Post*, March 4, 1993, p. A23.

13. Drew, *On the Edge*, p. 294–95.

14. The link between reinventing government and the health-care release was confirmed in interviews with several of the key pollsters involved in the effort.

15. Jeffrey H. Birnbaum and Timothy Noah, "Another Try: Latest Plan to Make Government Work Just Might Work—Clinton Proposal, Due Today, Gains Clout Because He Is a Democratic President—But Many Past Efforts Failed," *Wall Street Journal*, September 7, 1993, p. A1.

16. For a discussion of how Americans have learned to live with "leviathan," see Linda L. M. Bennett and Stephen Earl Bennett, *Living With Leviathan: Americans Coming to Terms with Big Government* (University of Kansas, 1990).

17. Terry M. Moe, "The Politics of Structural Choice: Toward a Theory of Public Bureaucracy," in Oliver E. Williamson, ed., *Organization Theory: From Chester Barnard to the Present and Beyond* (New York: Oxford University Press, 1990), p. 141.

18. Moe, "Toward a Theory of Public Bureaucracy," p. 141.

19. Moe, "Toward a Theory of Public Bureaucracy," pp. 140–41.

20. Paul C. Light, *The Tides of Reform: Making Government Work, 1945-1995* (New Haven, Conn.: Yale University Press, 1997).

21. James L. Sundquist, *The Decline and Resurgence of Congress* (Brookings, 1981), pp. 315–16.

22. Light, *The Tides of Reform*, pp. 101–2. The new statutes for the *Tides of Reform* database are summarized below:

Scientific Management

 Federal Financial Management Improvement Act of 1996

 Informational Technology Management Reform Act of 1996 (Clinger-Cohen Act)

War on Waste

 District of Columbia Financial Responsibility and Management Assistance Act of 1995

 Paperwork Reduction Act of 1995

Watchful Eye

 Lobbying Disclosure Act of 1995

 Office of Government Ethics Authorization Act of 1996

 Electronic Freedom of Information Act Amendment of 1996

 Presidential and Executive Office Accountability Act of 1996

Liberation Management

 Unfunded Mandates Reform Act of 1995

 Federal Reports Elimination and Sunset Act of 1995

 Administrative Dispute Resolution Act of 1996

23. Light, *The Tides of Reform*, p. 177.

24. Moe, "Toward a Theory of Public Bureaucracy," p. 142.

25. Gore, *From Red Tape to Results*, p. 3.

26. Moe, "Toward a Theory of Public Bureaucracy," p. 137.

27. Al Gore, *From Red Tape to Results: Creating A Government That Works Better & Costs Less*, Report of the National Performance Review (Government Printing Office, 1993).

28. Moe, "Toward a Theory of Public Bureaucracy," p. 148.

29. Gore, *From Red Tape to Results*, p. 89.

30. B. Dan Wood and Richard W. Waterman, "The Dynamics of Political Control of the Bureaucracy," *American Political Science Review*, vol. 85 (September 1991), pp. 806, 822.

31. General Accounting Office, *Federal Downsizing: Better Workforce and Strategic Planning Could Have Made Buyouts More Effective*, GAO/GGD-96-62 (August 1996), p. 2.

32. Byrd is quoted in Kirk Victor, "Executive Branch End Run," *National Journal*, May 16, 1998, p. 1114.

33. Quoted in Bill McAllister, "Critical Jobs Still Unfilled by Clinton; Holdovers or Deputies Occupy Many Slots as Key Appointments Lag," *Washington Post*, August 29, 1997, p. A1.

34. These new data supplement the materials collected in Paul C. Light, *Thickening Government: Federal Hierarchy and the Diffusion of Accountability* (Brookings, 1995); I am grateful to Shannon Swangstue Love for her work in preparing the 1998 material.

35. Moe, "Toward a Theory of Public Bureaucracy," pp. 139–40.

36. Moe, "Toward a Theory of Public Bureaucracy," p. 137.

37. Moe, "Toward a Theory of Public Bureaucracy," p. 138.

38. Morris P. Fiorina, *Congress: Keystone of the Washington Establishment*, 2d ed. (Yale University Press, 1989), p. 40.

39. *Congressional Record*, April 1, 1998, p. H1886-H1887.

40. Alan K. Ota, "Shuster Prepares for Onslaught Against Members' Projects," *CQ Weely Report*, vol. 56 (March 21, 1998), p. 737.

41. *Congressional Record*, April 1, 1998, p. H1893.

42. Secondary analysis of data provided by Center for Responsive Politics; see <http://www.crp.org/lobbyists/database.htm>.

43. Pew Research Center for The People & The Press, "*When Washington Works, Incumbents Prosper.* At <http://www.people-press.org/aug97que.htm> in March 1999.

44. The survey, *Democratic Congressional Chances Helped by Clinton Ratings*, was found at <http://www.people-press.org/mar98que.htm> in March 1999.

45. Goodsell, *The Case for Bureaucracy*, p. 12.

46. I am particularly grateful to Kathleen Hall Jamieson, dean of the Annenberg School, for making these data available to me, and to Elaine Casey, program associate at the Pew Charitable Trusts, for helping assemble them into a meaningful analysis. Unless otherwise cited, all campaign quotes provided in the following pages are drawn from the database.

47. See Light, *The Tides of Reform*, p. 38, for a comparison of Nixon's rhetoric and Gore's.

48. Moe, "Toward a Theory of Public Bureaucracy," pp. 144–45.

49. *The Changing Federal Workplace: Employee Perspectives*, Report by the U.S. Merit Systems Protection Board.

50. Press release from the American Postal Workers Union, Philadelphia Local, May 26, 1998.

51. *Title XIIII of the Government Reform and Savings Act of 1993*, Rept. 103-366, part 3 (GPO, November 15, 1993), p. 9.

52. *The Federal Workforce Restructuring Act of 1993*, Hearings before House Subcommittee on Compensation and Employee Benefits of the Committee on Post Office and Civil Service, H. Hrg., 103 Cong. 1 sess. (GPO, October 13, 1993), p. 79.

53. *The Federal Workforce Restructuring Act of 1993*, Hearings, pp. 82–83; for a confirmation of the quid pro quo, see Mike Mills, "Clinton and Gore Hit the Road to Build a Better Bureaucracy," *CQ Weekly Report*, vol. 51 (September 11, 1993), pp. 2381–84.

54. *Restructuring of the Federal Government*, Hearings before House Committee on Post Office and Civil Service, 103 Cong. 2 sess. (GPO, February 1, 1994), p. 30.

Chapter Four

1. *Federal Salaries and Classifications*, Hearings before the House Committee on Post Office and Civil Service, 83 Cong. 2 sess. (Government Printing Office, June 10, 1954), p. 1129.

2. Executive Order 10180, November 13, 1950.

3. *Analysis of the Whitten Amendment*, S. Rept 35, 83 Cong. 1 sess. (GPO, March 18, 1953).

4. Donald F. Kettl, *Sharing Power: Public Governance and Private Markets*, (Brookings, 1993), p. 41.

5. These statistics can be found in Arnold S. Levine, *Managing NASA in the Apollo Era* (National Aeronautics and Space Administration, 1982), pp. 79, 93, 116.

6. Quoted in Levine, *Managing NASA in the Apollo Era*, p. 89.

7. General Accounting Office, *Personnel Ceilings—A Barrier to Effective Manpower Management*, FPCD-76-88 (June 2, 1977), pp. ii–iii.

8. General Accounting Office, *Improving the Credibility and Management of the Federal Work Force through Better Planning and Budgetary Controls*, FPCD-81-54 (July 17, 1981), p. 10.

9. General Accounting Office, *Federal Downsizing: Better Workforce and Strategic Planning Could Have Made Buyouts More Effective*, GAO/GGD-96-62 (August 1996), p. 5.

10. General Accounting Office, *Recent Government-Wide Hiring Freezes Prove Ineffective in Managing Federal Employment*, FPCD-82-21 (March 10, 1982), pp. i–ii.

11. National Academy of Public Administration, *Effective Downsizing: A Compendium of Lessons Learned for Government Organizations* (Washington, D.C., August 1995), p. 17.

12. Figures from the Office of Personnel Management Fact Book can be found on OPM's website at <opm.gov/feddata/98factbk.pdf>.

13. National Academy of Public Administration, *Effective Downsizing*, p. 21.

14. General Accounting Office, *Federal Downsizing: The Costs and Savings of Buyout Versus Reductions-in-Force*, GAO/GGD-96-63 (May 1996).

15. National Performance Review, *Transforming Organizational Structure* (Washington, D.C., 1993), p. 4.

16. General Accounting Office, *Federal Downsizing: Better Workforce and Strategic Planning Could Have Made Buyouts More Effective*, p. 26.

17. National Performance Review, *Transforming Organizational Structure*, p. 4.

18. General Accounting Office, *Federal Downsizing: Better Workforce*, p. 33.

19. National Academy of Public Administration, *Downsizing the Federal Workforce: Effects and Alternatives* (Washington, D.C., April 1997), p. 52.

20. Lisa Zellmer, my friend and former student from the University of Minnesota, was the key geologist on this dig.

21. *The Federal Workforce Restructuring Act of 1993*, Hearings before the Senate Committee on Governmental Affairs, S. Hrg. 103-683, 103 Cong. 1 sess. (GPO, October 19, 1993), pp. 1–3.

22. *The Federal Workforce Restructuring Act of 1993*, Hearings, p. 46.

23. James A. Morone, *The Democratic Wish: Popular Participation and the Limits of American Government*, (Basic Books, 1990), pp. 138–39.

24. P. L. 77-821, Section 2.

25. Letter from Senator Harry Byrd Sr. to the Hon. Sheridan Downey, chairman, Senate Civil Service Committee, November 15, 1945, in Senate Report No. 742, p. 1187–88.

26. *Reduction of Nonessential Federal Expenditures*, S. Doc. 262, additional report of the Joint Committee on Reduction of Nonessential Expenditures, 79 Cong. 2 sess. (GPO, August 2, 1946), p. 15–16.

27. P. L. 521, Third Deficiency Appropriation Act of 1946, July 23, 1946.

28. *Public Papers of the Presidents of the United States: Ronald Reagan* (GPO, 1982), January 20, 1981, p. 4.

29. *Federal Salaries and Classifications*, Hearings, p. 1145.

30. *Federal Salaries and Classifications*, Hearings, p. 1148.

31. *Exemption of Postal Field Service from the Whitten Amendment*, Hearings before House Subcommittee on Postal Operations of the Committee on Post Office and Civil Service, 89 Cong. 1 sess. (GPO, March 23, 1965), p. 3-4.

32. *Legislative History of Temporary Employees–Career Status*, P.L. 90-105, H. Rept. 372, House Committee on Post Office and Civil Service (GPO, June 20, 1967), p. 1722.

33. Letter from John W. Macy, Jr., Civil Service Commission chairman, to the Hon. John W. McCormack, Speaker of the House, March 16, 1967, in House Report No. 372.

34. Postal Assaults and Personnel Ceiling, United States House of Representatives, Rept. 1822 (GPO, July 30, 1968), p. 5.

35. *Civil Service Reform Act of 1978*, S. Rpt. 95-969, P.L. 95-454, *Congressional Record*, vol. 124 (GPO, 1978), p. 131.

36. Grace Commission, *War on Waste*, President's Private Sector Survey on Cost Control (MacMillan, 1984), pp. 235, 250–51.

37. General Accounting Office, *Classification of Federal White-Collar Jobs Should Be Better Controlled*, FPCD-75-173 (December 29, 1975), p. 8.

38. General Accounting Office, *Employment Trends and Grade Controls in the DOD General Schedule Work Force*, FPCD-81-52 (July 28, 1981), pp. ii–iii.

39. It is useful to note that there are no specific data on Health and Human Services. With almost no one paying attention to the bulge indices after the Reagan administration, OPM only maintained the indices as they existed in 1987, meaning that HHS's 1997 data did not include the Social Security Administration and that the Social Security Administration was not included in the bulge indices. An OPM official noted that the bulge indices would probably be dropped for the lack of interest.

40. General Accounting Office, *Federal Downsizing: Better Workforce*, pp. 36–37.

41. *Presidential Memorandum for Heads of Departments and Agencies, Subject: Streamlining the Bureaucracy*, September 11, 1993.

42. *Contracting Out of Services by Federal Agencies*, Hearing before the House Subcommittee on the Civil Service of the Committee on Post Office and Civil Service, 103 Cong. 2 sess (GPO, October 5, 1994), pp. 10–11.

43. *Contracting Out of Services by Federal Agencies*, Hearing, pp. 36–39.

44. *Manpower Utilization by the Federal Government through the Use of Private Contract Labor*, S. Doc. 83-32, (GPO, March 20, 1953), pp. 3–5.

45. *Manpower Utilization by the Federal Government*, S. Doc. 83-32, p. 14.

46. *Manpower Utilization by the Federal Government*, S. Doc. 83-32, p. 16.

47. *Congressional Record*, August 11, 1978, H8470.

48. *Congressional Record,* August 11, 1978, H9405.

49. *Congressional Record,* August 11, 1978, H9405.

50. *Contracting Out,* Hearing before the House Subcommittee on Human Resources of the Committee on Post Office and Civil Service, 96 Cong. 1 sess. (GPO, September 7, 1979), p. 1.

51. The witness was Bun Bray, executive director of the National Association of Supervisors, *Contracting Out,* Hearings, p. 33.

52. *Oversight Hearing on Governmentwide Buyouts and H.R. 4488,* Hearing before the House Subcommittee on Compensation and Employee Benefits of the Committee on Post Office and Civil Service, 103 Cong. 2 sess. (GPO, September 22, 1994), p. 2.

53. *Oversight Hearing on Government Buyouts and H.R. 4488,* Hearing, p. 12.

54. *Contracting Out of Services by Federal Agencies,* Hearing, pp. 28–29.

Chapter Five

1. I am particularly appreciative to Rosalyn Kleeman for helping me understand how OMB allocates personnel slots, as well as for her more general and long-lasting encouragement of my work.

2. OMB argues that it is no longer managing to head count, as the practice is phrased. Because government as a whole is well below the targets embedded in the Workforce Restructuring Act, OMB is not paying much attention to the head count ceilings. This is a bit of semantic excess, however. As long as head count is going down, OMB is free to ignore head count. But imagine for a moment the effect of head count going up. Would OMB feel so loose if the government were starting to add jobs? Would the Clinton administration suddenly embrace increasing full-time-equivalent employment? Obviously not. As long as head count is going down, OMB can argue it is not managing to head count. But if it were to start creeping up, one can be sure that OMB and the White House would put even greater pressure on agency totals.

3. For the story of OMB's decline, see Ronald C. Moe, "Traditional Organization Principles and the Managerial Presidency: From Phoenix to Ashes," *Public Administration Review,* vol. 50 (March/April 1990), pp. 129–40.

4. For a history of this latest reorganization see the General Accounting Office, *Office of Management and Budget: Changes Resulting from the OMB 2000 Reorganization,* GAO/GGD/AIMD-96-50 (December 1995).

5. Office of Management and Budget, *Making OMB More Effective in Serving the Presidency,* Memorandum for All OMB Staff, Office Memorandum no. 94-16 (March 1, 1994), pp. 2–3.

6. The new job description can be found in General Accounting Office, *Office of Management and Budget,* p. 41.

7. Executive Office of the President, Office of Management and Budget, *Preparation and Submission of Budget Estimates,* Circular no. A-11, revised (Government Printing Office, July 11, 1998).

8. OMB Circular no. A-11, p. 18.

9. OMB Circular no. A-11, p. 31.

10. General Accounting Office, *Office of Management and Budget*, pp. 24–25.

11. I am particularly grateful here for the efforts by Carole Neves, a friend and colleague, to educate me on the appropriate balance between in-house and out-of-house capacity. Although I am hardly an expert, Carole helped me understand enough about contracting out to write this chapter. I am, of course, solely responsible for the mistakes that follow.

12. *Report to the President on Government Contracting for Research and Development*, S. Doc. 94, (GPO, May, 1962); reprinted in William R. Nelson, ed., *The Politics of Science: Readings in Science, Technology and Government* (New York: Oxford University Press, 1968), p. 196.

13. Nelson, *The Politics of Science*, p. 201.

14. Nelson, *The Politics of Science*, p. 203.

15. Nelson, *The Politics of Science*, p. 198.

16. Nelson, *The Politics of Science*, p. 198.

17. Bureau of the Budget, Bulletin 55-4 (1955), cited in Donald F. Kettl, *Sharing Power: Public Governance and Private Markets* (Brookings, 1993), p. 41.

18. Executive Office of the President, Office of Management and Budget, Circular No. A-76, Revised (GPO, August 4, 1983), p. 1; see also Kettl, *Sharing Power*, for a discussion of the general history of the circular.

19. Executive Office of the President, Office of Management and Budget, *Circular No. A-76 Revised Supplemental Handbook: Performance of Commercial Activities* (GPO, March 1996), p. iii.

20. These figures come from General Accounting Office, OMB Circular A-76: *Oversight and Implementation Issues*, GAO/T-GGD-98-146, (June 4, 1998), p. 4. The testimony before the Subcommittee on Oversight of Government Management, Restructuring and the District of Colombia was given by J. Christopher Mihm, associate director, Federal Management and Workforce Issues, General Government Division, who provided one of the most concise statements on why the A-76 process has not worked as effectively as possible in the past and how it might be improved in the future.

21. Office of Federal Procurement Policy, "Inherently Government Functions," Policy Letter-92-1 to the Heads of Executive Agencies and Departments (1992), p. 1.

22. "Inherently Government Functions," p. 7.

23. "Inherently Government Functions," p. 6.

24. See Michael D. Serlin, "In the Ring," *Government Executive*, vol. 29 (September 1997), pp. 14-22.

25. For a discussion of the legislative intent of the act, see *Federal Activities Inventory Reform Act of 1998*, S. Rept. 105-269, 105 Cong. 2 sess. (GPO, July 28, 1998).

26. These and other quotes from the debate can be found in the *Congressional Record*, October 5, 1998, pp. H9448–52.

27. Legislative Hearings on H.R. 716, the "Freedom from Government Competition Act," U.S. House of Representatives, Committee on Government Reform and Over-

sight, Subcommittee on Government Management, Information, and Technology, (GPO, March 24, 1998).

28. *Contracting Out of Services by Federal Agencies*, Hearing before the Subcommittee on the Civil Service of the House Committee on Post Office and Civil Service, 103 Cong. 2 sess. (GPO, October 5, 1994), pp. 29–30.

29. *Oversight Hearing on Governmentwide Buyouts and H.R. 4488*, Hearing before the Subcommittee on Compensation and Employee Benefits of the House Committee on Post Office and Civil Service, 103 Cong. 2 sess. (GPO, September 22, 1994) p. 43.

30. This quote and others cited in this section of the book come from a focus group conducted by the National Academy of Public Administration's Center for Human Resources Administration on April 17, 1998, on behalf of the author. My appreciation to Frank Cipolla, the center's director, and Sally Marshall, a former senior official at the Office of Personnel Management, for their help in facilitating the conversation.

31. National Academy of Public Administration, *Revitalizing Federal Management: Managers and Their Overburdened Systems* (Washington, D.C.: National Academy of Public Administration, November 1983), p. vii.

32. Office of Management and Budget, *Preparation and Submission of Budget Estimates*, Circular No. A-11, part 2, revised (GPO, July 11,1998), pp. 289–90.

33. Hearings on the "Inspector General Act of 1978: Twenty Years after Passage, Are the Inspectors General Fulfilling Their Mission?" Testimony before the House Government Reform and Oversight Committee, Subcommittee on Management, Information, and Technology, April 21, 1998, p. 2.

34. Presidential Commission on the Space Shuttle Challenger Accident, *Report to the President*, (June 6, 1986), p. 82.

35. Brian Friel, "Outsourcing Bills Debated," *GovExec.Com Daily Briefing* (March 25, 1998), p. 3.

36. Arnold S. Levine, *Managing NASA in the Apollo Era* (National Aeronautics and Space Administration, 1982), pp. 92–93.

37. Kettl, *Sharing Power*, pp. 64–65.

38. General Accounting Office, *Federal Grants: Design Improvements Could Help Federal Resources Go Further*, GAO/AIMD-97-7 (December 1996), p. 28.

39. Kettl, *Sharing Power*, p. 64.

40. Leslie Wayne, "The Shrinking Military Complex," *New York Times*, February 27, 1998, p. D1.

41. Dwight D. Eisenhower, (*Farewell Radio and Television Address to the American People*), January 17, 1961, *Public Papers of the Presidents of the United States, 1960-1961* (GPO, 1961), pp. 1038-39.

42. See National Academy of Public Administration, Center for Human Resources Management, *A Competency Model for Human Resources Professionals* (Washington, D.C., June, 1996), for an example of how the core competency model might be used to build an effective human resource unit.

43. Department of Transportation, *A Visionary and Vigilant Department of Transportation Leading the Way to Transportation Excellence in the 21st Century*, DOT Strategic Plan, 1997–2002 (Washington, D.C., 1997), pp. 62–63.

Chapter Six

1. For an excellent discussion of various theories of how government employment might change, see Christopher Hood, Desmond King, and B. Guy Peters, "Working for Government: Rival Interpretations of Employment Change in the Public Sector," paper prepared for delivery at the annual meeting of the American Political Science Association, Boston, Mass., September 3–6, 1998.

2. See Donald F. Kettl, *Reinventing Government: A Fifth Year Report Card* (Brookings, 1998), for the grades, which include an A+ for effort, an A for procurement reform, and a B for downsizing.

3. Paul C. Light, *The Tides of Reform: Making Government Work, 1945-1995* (Yale University Press, 1997), p. 95.

4. Al Gore, *From Red Tape to Results: Creating a Government that Works Better & Costs Less* (Government Printing Office, 1993), p. 21.

5. Office of the Assistant Secretary of Defense, Memorandum for Distribution, "Title 10 Civilian Personnel Legislative Authority," p. 4.

6. Paul C. Light, "A Virtual Department of Defense," *Government Executive,* (September 1997), p. 67.

7. Elke Löffler, "The 'Contract and Agency State' As a Multiple Principal-Agent Problem," in Arie Halachmi and Peter B. Boorsma, eds., *Inter and Intra Government Arrangements for Productivity: An Agency Approach* (Boston: Kluwer Academic Publishers, 1998).

8. Donald F. Kettl, *Sharing Power: Public Governance and Private Markets* (Brookings, 1993), p. 176.

9. I am again grateful to Carole Neves for her help in updating these data and cautioning me on their appropriate use.

10. National Academy of Public Administration, *Getting the Job Done: The Use of Intramural and Extramural Resources at the U.S. Environmental Protection Agency* (Washington, D.C., November 1994), p. 31.

11. See, for example, H. Brinton Milward, Keith G. Provan, and Barbara A. Else, "What Does the 'Hollow State' Look Like?" in Barry Bozeman, ed., *Public Management: The State of the Art* (San Francisco: Jossey-Bass, 1993).

12. Nina Bernstein, "Guiliani's Foster Care Plan Faces a Political Minefield," *New York Times,* June 7, 1998, p. A25.

13. Kettl, *Sharing Power,* p. 172, his emphasis; the point is made particularly nicely by John D. Donahue, *The Privatization Decision: Public Ends, Private Means* (Basic Books, 1989), chapter 4.

14. H. George Frederickson, *The Spirit of Public Administration* (San Francisco: Jossey-Bass, 1997), p. 179.

15. National Academy of Public Administration, *Getting the Job Done,* pp. 31–32.

16. National Academy of Public Administration, *Maintaining the Program Balance: A Report by an Academy Panel Examining the Distribution of NASA Science and Engineering Work between NASA and Contractors and the Effect on NASA's In-House Technical Capability,* vol. 1 (Washington, D.C., January 1991), pp. 55–56.

17. National Academy of Public Administration, *Getting the Job Done*, p. 3.

18. These quotes are from the National Academy of Public Administration's Center for Human Resources Management April 17, 1998, focus group cited in chapter five.

19. See Bernard Adelsberger, "Graying Government," *Government Executive*, vol. 30 (January, 1998).

20. National Academy of Public Administration, Center for Human Resources Management, *New Times, New Competencies, New Professionals: A Guide for Implementing a Competency Model for HR Professionals* (Washington, D.C., 1997).

Index

56–57; downsizers, 53–54; on parties' abilities to manage or reform government, 84; performance rating, 51; priorities, 51–52, 53; realigners, 53–54; on reform, 52, 53–58; reinventors, 53–58; services wanted, 48–50, 55; support for government activism, 53; trust in, 49, 52, 60; as wasteful, 48, 50–51, 53, 54, 57–58

Public service: blended work force, 165–66, 173; boundaries with private sector, 184; careers, 3–4, 191–93; changes in past fifty years, 190–91; contract work force, 4, 5; illusion of unity, 190–93; three-tiered system proposed in Defense Department, 182–83. *See also* Civil service; Shadow of government

Quayle, J. Danforth, 131

Raytheon, 168

Reagan, Ronald, 63; criticism of government waste, 87–88, 116; hiring freeze order, 117; political appointments, 67–68; presidential campaign (*1980*), 85, 87–88, 160

Reagan administration: A-76 position studies, 148; efforts to reduce middle level of bureaucracy, 124–25; hiring freezes, 106, 116, 117; increase in senior civil service positions, 69; privatization policies, 102, 152–53; prohibition on government involvement in commercial activities, 146; war on waste, 49, 102, 116

Recruiting difficulties in civil service, 103, 166; low pay compared to private sector, 159, 160, 164

Reductions in force (RIF), 108, 123; disadvantages, 111; efforts to avoid, 158; in private sector, 111. *See also* Downsizing

Reforms. *See* Management reforms; Reinventing government

Reinventing government campaign: annual reports, 59; anticipated cuts in

middle management, 96, 125–28; attitudes toward reform, 59–60; concerns of civil servants, 93; control functions as target of downsizing, 109–11, 158; downsizing achieved, 2, 41; Gore's leadership, 58–59, 65–66, 126–27; human resources policies, 181; procurement reform, 179; reform proposals, 65, 66–67, 68; study of contract jobs, 18–19, 25; themes, 54. *See also* Downsizing

Republicans: antigovernment stance, 85; political incentives to keep civil service small, 6, 9, 84–92; presidential campaigns, 85–92; public confidence in government management, 84

Research and development: federal contracts, 26, 30, 144, 167; Federally Funded Research and Development Centers (FFRDCs), 26; state and local government contracts, 26

Resource Management Offices (RMOs), 140–42

Revenue and Expenditure Control Act of *1968*, 121–22

RIF. *See* Reductions in force

Rivlin, Alice, 16, 141

RMOs. *See* Resource Management Offices

Roosevelt, Franklin D., 67, 114–16

Schroeder, Patricia, 97–98, 132, 133

Scientific management, 61, 63, 64

Seamans, Robert, 103

Senate: Armed Services Committee, 122; Civil Service Committee, 115; criticism of Clinton administration vacancies, 68; Environment and Public Works Committee, 34, 35; Federal Manpower Policies Subcommittee, 100–01, 130–31; Governmental Affairs Committee, 9, 13–14, 113; pork barrel projects in highway bills, 78; Postal Affairs Subcommittee, 120, 121; Post Office and Civil Service Committee, 100–01, 130–31